HIDDEN POWERS: How to Transcend Suffering

HIDDEN POWERS: How to Transcend Suffering

Glen Allison

HIDDEN POWERS: *How to Transcend Suffering*

Published by Ten World Press
Los Angeles, CA 90034 USA
https://www.GlenAllison.com

Developmental Editors: Tina Rubin and Giannis Angelou

Copyright © 2025 Glen Allison

All rights reserved.

No part of this book may be reproduced, distributed, or transmitted in any form or by any means, including photocopying, recording, decompiling, reverse-engineering or other electronic or mechanical methods or introduced into any information storage and retrieval system, without the prior written permission of the publisher, except in the case of brief quotations embodied in critical reviews and certain other noncommercial uses permitted by copyright law.

First Edition: 2025

ISBN: 979-8-218-66524-1

Library of Congress Control Number: 2025908663

Front cover photography © 2025 Glen Allison
Back cover photography © 2023 Mark Harmel
Back cover photography © 2024 Glen Allison

Table of Contents

Essential Introduction	1
PART ONE - LESSONS LEARNED	9
Chapter 1 - From Victim to Victor	11
Chapter 2 - From Self-Sabotage to Inner Power	17
Chapter 3 - Breaking Suffering's Code	31
Chapter 4 - The Flower Seller's Wisdom	45
Chapter 5 - To Dream the Impossible Dream	50
Chapter 6 - The Science of Dreaming Big	61
Chapter 7 - Hope and Optimism	75
Chapter 8 - Transforming Adversity into Benefit	91
Chapter 9 - Diamonds in the Making	108
Chapter 10 - The Prison of Pride	125
Chapter 11 - Breaking Free	139
Chapter 12 - The Price of Success	149
Chapter 13 - Rising from the Ashes	155
Chapter 14 - The Silent Ascent	173
Chapter 15 - Fortune's Adversary	185
Chapter 16 - Lessons in Flow and Fearlessness.	198
Chapter 17 - The Infinite Power of Resilience	212
Chapter 18 - The Sacred Ascent	222
Chapter 19 - Lessons from the Roof of the World.	235
Chapter 20 - Paradise Lost and Found	248
Chapter 21 - The Power of Unwavering Spirit	256
Chapter 22 - Endurance and Perseverance	264
Chapter 23 - When Wounds Become Wings	277
Chapter 24 - Wisdom Beyond the Horizon	283
PART TWO - THE REVELATION	301
Chapter 25 - Absolute vs. Relative Happiness	303
Chapter 26 - 3000 Realms of Existence	307
Chapter 27 - The Nine Levels of Consciousness	321
Chapter 28 - The Compassionate Revolution	327
Chapter 29 - Awakening	333
Chapter 30 - The Mystic Law	342
Acknowledgements	349
About the Author	353
Bibliography	355

Essential Introduction

Your Pain Is Not Your Destiny

Pain is real. But your inner strength is far greater.

While suffering marks a starting point, it will not author your entire story unless you acquiesce to its torture.

On October 9, 2012, a masked Taliban gunman boarded a school bus in Pakistan's Swat Valley. He asked, "Who is Malala?" Then he fired three bullets at the fifteen-year-old education activist who had been secretly blogging for the BBC about the Taliban's cruelty. One bullet tore through her head and neck.

The world held its breath.

Would this be another story of silenced courage? But Malala Yousafzai refused to let hatred and bullets write her final chapter. Two years later, at age 17, she became the youngest Nobel Peace Prize laureate in history for her unwavering activism.

"I don't want to be remembered as the girl who was shot," she proclaimed from her hospital bed in Birmingham, England. "I want to be remembered as the girl who stood up."[1]

In that moment of staggering clarity, Malala transformed what could have been her end into a powerful beginning. "The terrorists thought they would change my aims and stop my ambitions," she later reflected, "but nothing changed in my life except this: weakness, fear and hopelessness died. Strength, power and courage were born."[2]

This isn't just inspiration—it's a blueprint for human transformation.

Within you lies an ancient, untapped reservoir of boundless power—a deeper knowing that awaits your choice to kindle it. Like Malala, you can forge a direct path from suffering to purpose—one that will enable a timeless, sacred melody to echo outward.

The Alchemy of Adversity

Michelle Obama asserts: "You should never view your challenges as a disadvantage. Instead, understand that your experience facing and overcoming adversity is actually one of your biggest advantages."[3]

Standing before the world on December 10, 2014, at her Nobel Peace Prize acceptance ceremony in Oslo, Norway, Malala declared: "Education is neither Eastern nor Western. Education is education and it's the right of every human being."[4] Her wisdom comes not from theory but from lived experience—from reshaping an assassination attempt into a platform that has helped millions of girls access education. Despite near death, Malala's relentless resolve opened these doors.

Stand braced. We are about to uncode your limitations.

This book illuminates a dynamic practical approach to build within yourself the same steadfast life state that Malala possesses. Instead of attempting to circumvent difficulties or pursue elusive nirvana, we can harness adversity itself. Our goal is to create a life where happiness flows freely and where obstacles become catalysts for profound growth—a vibrant existence that flourishes amid life's ruthless storms.

Are you ready?

I did not discover the principles expressed here; I uncovered their impact. They flow from contemporary psychology, behavioral science, and timeless Buddhist teachings—insights I've studied and lived for over five decades. I've distilled this universal understanding into clear, actionable principles you can apply immediately.

Time Is Not Your Prison

Time isn't simply linear—our present actions reshape both past and future. Each moment mirrors our past choices while generating future reality. This convergence allows us to navigate toward better outcomes, dissolving suffering rooted in past choices.

The Roman philosopher Seneca remarked, "It is not that we have a short time to live, but that we waste a lot of it."[5]

Our present actions can remold not just our current circumstances, but our entire life trajectory. We can surpass what seemed like fixed limitations and create new possibilities where none appeared to exist. Even the residue of past choices need not determine our future.

Mahatma Gandhi once stated, "The future depends on what we do in the present."[6]

When we feel stuck, unable to fulfill our deepest aspirations, it's frequently because we've overlooked the significance of Now. We often allow precious opportunities to slip away untapped, forever lost. Many who are submerged in suffering doubt their capacity to evolve when confronted by seemingly insurmountable situations.

To stimulate our vitality and well-being, we must remain open to new ideas and concepts. As George Bernard Shaw pointedly stated, "Those who cannot change their minds cannot change anything."[7]

The present is not a prison built by your past, but a portal to renewal. Through wiser choices, we can tilt the balance in our favor once we discover how to access our inherent wisdom.

Riding the Waves of Challenge

Like Malala, when we fully embrace life's tumultuous waves instead of fighting against them, we can ride atop our trials. Their very force becomes our momentum—propelling us beyond suffering toward a marvelous renewal.

The Lebanese-American poet, Kahlil Gibran, said, "Out of suffering have emerged the strongest souls."[8]

The potential for immense joy dwells not over distant horizons, but in this very instant. Deep happiness springs from a shift in mindset and life state, not circumstances. Like the lotus flower rising from murky depths, our potential for evolution exists even in life's muddiest waters.

When we fixate on perceived limitations, we feed anxiety, fear, and self-doubt. However, a new system of resolute belief awaits —revealed and fortified by steady conviction—one that opens the door to a life free from worry and stress. These pages offer wisdom that will unleash such possibilities. When we access our deeper understanding, suffering dramatically recedes, allowing us to flourish even amid difficulties.

My own journey has been illuminated by timeless Buddhist wisdom. While you may find light in other spiritual traditions or walk without formal beliefs, the insights in this book will enable you to transcend your limits and seize control of your unique journey toward happiness.

The Awakening of Inner Power

When we channel our inner resources, we forge conditions that kindle our innate wisdom. This awakening revolutionizes our perspective, cultivating deep gratitude for every barrier conquered.

In this elevated state, adversity becomes opportunity, allowing us to conquer daunting tasks with the same exhilaration a climber feels near Everest's peak. Such moments reveal the limitless possibilities that emerge from unyielding strength and crystal clarity.

Greatness dwells within each of us, but few discover the keys to unlock it. From a loftier vantage point, we see that suffering is not our natural state—it's a temporary aberration. While our mental landscapes may fluctuate like seasons, we can develop the might to stand firm in any weather.

In her book *Risk*, the French-born American author, Anaïs Nin, proclaimed: "And the day came when the risk to remain tight in a bud was more painful than the risk it took to blossom."[9]

Envision yourself attaining an impregnable life state where even life's harshest trials cannot induce distress. When caught in despair, such freedom may seem impossible—yet this limited view stems from the same mental framework that created your problems. As Einstein noted in 1946, "a new type of thinking is essential if mankind is to survive and move toward higher levels."[10] A revolutionary shift in perspective is required to transcend our current limitations.

A deep sense of expansion and discovery keeps us vibrant and youthful. George Bernard Shaw observed, "We don't stop playing because we grow old; we grow old because we stop playing."[11] This insight reminds us that an open, exploratory approach to life's challenges preserves our vitality and expands our capacity for renewal.

This awakening process cultivates a depth of unshakable happiness that remains steadfast in any circumstance. Such an ideal life state dissolves suffering at its source. Imagine you can live with indomitable conviction and stand firm against life's trials, free from despair's grip and misery's negative undertow.

The discoveries in these pages will empower you to rise above personal pain and to channel your struggles toward a noble purpose. As we awaken to our hidden capacities, this change will ripple outward to touch countless lives, inspiring humanity and fostering waves of positive influence. This is how we change the world—one awakened person at a time.

Come with me on an extraordinary journey to ever-expanding enlightenment ... and let's change everything.

Glen Allison

PART ONE - LESSONS LEARNED

Glen Allison

Chapter 1 - From Victor to Victor

The impulse to blame others for our suffering is deeply human.

Here's how my awakening began...

My own journey through family discord illustrates this universal propensity to shift responsibility for our suffering to others. Early in my life, family torment seemed the direct source of my anguish, making it easy to point fingers. These experiences left lasting impressions that fundamentally shaped my inner landscape.

My father's mistreatment of my mother filled me with desperate fear. One night, I seized a kitchen knife, driven to protect her. I was nine years old. My father wrenched the knife away, pushed me aside, and continued his assault. The powerlessness of that moment left indelible mental scars that would echo through my life for years to come.

This childhood terror planted seeds of self-destruction deep in my psyche. The most dangerous manifestation was an inexplicable compulsion that intensified over time. Despite every rational instinct, I frequently found myself surrendering to sleep behind the wheel, drawn by some twisted, thrill-seeking sense of release. This unconscious death wish obliterated two vehicles in devastating crashes, harrowing episodes I'll detail in the next chapter.

Glen Allison

As I grew, disturbing childhood events shaped my view of life's worth, though I didn't recognize it then. These formative moments fed a propensity to blame others and existing circumstances for my suffering. Such trauma often leads us to justify our hurts, creating a hopelessness that can breed even more anguish.

Each memory left an eternal mark—my father's aggression toward my mother, his repeated abandonment, the dire straits in which we were left. These experiences ignited a desperate need to break free, yet escape seemed impossible, especially through a child's eyes.

I never forgave my father's unforgivable acts. Yet our relationship eventually evolved into something far deeper than forgiveness. By his passing in the mid-90s, after my first twenty-five years of Buddhist practice, I was able to not only embrace full responsibility for my circumstances but to manifest the inner might to do so, allowing past hurts to evolve.

Buddhism reveals that our karma is a living tapestry, where each thought, word, and action weaves new threads into its design. As understanding grows, we become master weavers consciously crafting the pattern of our existence.

In perhaps a shocking revelation, this concept suggests that our past choices—even from previous lifetimes—determine our birth circumstances: our parents, homeland, cultural context, sexual identity, and our innate propensities. From this lofty perspective, we bear complete responsibility for our current reality. This insight is liberating—the ability to shape our lives rests solely within us.

Initially, this conceptual teaching felt impossible to accept. But as this principle took root in my life, it completely revolutionized not only my understanding, but it enabled me to completely reshape my relationship with my father, which evolved into something far beyond conventional forgiveness.

When I claimed full responsibility for having chosen my parents and all the circumstances within which I was born, I finally broke free from the prison of blame. The overwhelming distress I had attributed solely to my father dissolved, and with it, my suffering. At last, I could release the frustration and hurt that had poisoned my spirit for so long.

The American memoirist, poet, and civil rights activist Maya Angelou declared: "Bitterness is like cancer. It eats upon the host."[1]

In the 90s, I plunged into a ten-year odyssey as I circumnavigated the globe nonstop numerous times during my travel photography pursuits—a journey born from devastating loss I'll share later.

During these wandering years, Los Angeles became merely a way station for brief family reunions once a year, typically of only a week's duration. My father's health failed during those years, yet my relentless travel schedule kept me in motion, even as time grew precious for him.

During one fleeting week in L.A., I discovered him the day he passed. An all-encompassing tranquility enveloped me—no tears, no sorrow—only absolute serenity. His death marked the completion of our journey from fear to understanding and revealed how far we'd both traveled from those darker days.

Yes, I'm convinced my relationship with my father changed over time as a direct reflection of the dynamic shifts in my own life state, which evoked a reciprocal change in him. Our environment always mirrors us—an immutable law that stands unchangeable, unbreakable, and undeniable. Clearly to me, my inner awakening allowed my father's past actions to ultimately not define his life's worth. The change within me helped foster a change in him.

While my past struggles once felt overwhelming, they pale when measured against the harrowing realities in war-torn regions, where each day brings unthinkable loss and where survival itself requires extraordinary courage. In a world scarred by tragedy, witnessing others' unfathomable hardships and struggles for recovery reveals humanity's remarkable capacity to not only endure but to surpass even the most devastating misery.

So how do we move beyond suffering and reimagine our view of adversity? When we liberate our truest self, hardship becomes an impetus that propels us forward and manifests change. When we awaken our inner potential, we expand beyond all limitations.

Absolutely nothing occurs randomly in the universal scheme of life. Every effect must originate from a cause. Science validates this reality. Every action has an equal and opposite reaction—Newton's Third Law of Motion, a fundamental principle in physics that explains the relationship between forces.[2] When we stand, the floor pushes back in equal resistance to our weight. Otherwise, we'd crash below. The eternal law of cause and effect remains ruthlessly strict and utterly consistent.

We alone bear complete responsibility for our current reality. This crucial insight stands monumental—it places the instruments of transformation entirely in our own hands.

Imagine a world where entire societies embrace this mindset to not blame others while at the same time its people manifest the strength of life state to live up to the task: wars would cease, revenge would vanish, and the "eye for an eye" mentality propagated by so many cultures would become a relic of the past.

Though initially quite skeptical, I wondered what I had to lose if I incorporated this empowering perspective into my worldview. The answer struck like lightning: I would lose nothing ... and perhaps I would gain everything.

When I finally claimed complete responsibility for my circumstances in life, I broke completely free from the prison and poison of blame. I was astounded. Personal agency now rested solely within my grasp. I alone commanded my destiny.

But I must admit, it took me time to root this life-altering insight deeply within and to make it an automatic response. Nevertheless, the process of my advancement awakened a deeper strength within me. Each step forward kindled a new flame of possibility and illuminated paths I never knew existed.

Though positive thinking alone has its limits, through my Buddhist practice, this enlightened perspective ultimately was

Glen Allison

embedded deeply within as a tangible state of life, not just a superficial, fickle, and transient state of mind. This fundamental change at the core radically reshaped past hurts into a far loftier, deeply ingrained realization about the original causes of my suffering that I had willfully initiated in the infinite past. It was this expansive, fundamental shift in perspective that led to a more value-creative way to approach my life.

Chapter 2 - From Self-Sabotage to Inner Power

I began to discover the regenerative capacity we all possess not in moments of triumph, but in my darkest hours as a teenager when I fought a shadow war against my own self-destructive nature. This wasn't merely a struggle for growth; it was a fierce battle for survival that would ultimately reveal a path to complete liberation from suffering's torment—the ability to forge an indestructible life state.

Your story likely echoes through these pages. Though you may not have drifted asleep at the wheel as I repeatedly did, perhaps you've felt self-sabotage's gravitational pull in other forms—walking away from a flourishing relationship, undermining opportunities with doubt, or "inexplicably" self-destructing after initial success. While our specific trials differ, what binds us is that deep yearning to break free from suffering's grip. I share these intimate battles not to showcase my journey, but to illuminate possibilities for yours.

Departure from Texas

"Falling Asleep at the Wheel"

Texas, June 1964

At nineteen, I drove with my father on an endless thirty-hour nonstop marathon from Texas to California. Each mile of asphalt stretched beneath us like a black ribbon of harsh memories while the crushing weight of a painful past filled my thoughts—a silent companion on our long journey west.

Los Angeles awaited us—a sprawling promise of reinvention. My father had secured a job there, and UC Berkeley had accepted me to study architecture. This move marked the starting point in my own uncertain path. Perhaps California would offer what Texas never could: distance from our history, different skies under which we might become different people. Yet as the Mojave's vast emptiness surrounded us, my hopes felt as barren as the landscape.

Across the endless stretches of the desert night, exhaustion crept over me as a seductive, dangerous whisper emerged from my subconscious: What if I yielded to sleep? What if I just ... let go?

Just close your eyes. Let the darkness take you.... No—I can't. My father... But isn't that perfect? One final act of rebellion that in one stroke would end my past misery and his existence. So peaceful ... just drift away ... Wake up! WAKE UP!

But the darkness had already won.

Seconds later, I jolted awake as my head slammed against the side window. The impact shocked me conscious as our car careened across lanes.

My father's knuckles bleached white on the dashboard; his breath caught in a sharp hiss as he jerked upright in his seat. "What the hell is wrong with you?" he roared, his voice taut with barely contained terror. "Are you trying to get us both killed?"

His face contorted with the same rage I'd seen directed at my mother countless times. "Pull over. NOW!" he commanded, slamming his fist against the glove compartment.

For the remainder of our journey, he banished me to the passenger seat, where I sat in hollow silence, a tormented witness to my own inexplicable recklessness.

This incident marked only the beginning—the opening chapter in a darker narrative—the first in a series of dangerous episodes where I fell asleep at the wheel.

In the years that followed, two vehicles would end their existence as twisted monuments to my apparent carelessness, death-escaping episodes I will share in the next section of this chapter. Yet each time, I emerged without a scratch, as if shielded by some mysterious force that protected me even as I courted destruction.

A year later, after the drive from Texas, the treacherous Siskiyou Mountains loomed before me as I drove alone from San Francisco to Oregon to visit my college girlfriend. Dense clouds pressed against my windshield and shrouded the world beyond in ghostly white that limited visibility to mere feet ahead.

Wouldn't it be beautiful to float away into the clouds? This is insane—I need to pull over. Just a few more seconds of peace...

Yet even here, suspended between cliff and sky, that familiar, perverse thrill emerged. I yielded to its seduction and let my eyelids drift shut as the mountain road twisted through the murkiness ahead.

Let go ... merge with the white void.... Something's wrong with me. This isn't normal. But it feels so right...

Consciousness snapped back to a world of white nothingness. My car had plunged deep into a dense cloud bank.

Fright seized me as I imagined a massive truck materializing from the void behind my car as it hurtled toward my annihilation. I quickly slowed down. With trembling hands, I inched toward the roadside until the crunch of gravel beneath my tires anchored me back to reality. As the clouds thinned, I saw how close I'd come to the edge. Mere feet had separated me from plunging into the gorge below.

This harrowing encounter was the first crack in my denial: perhaps my courtship with death went beyond random chance.

I began to sense something darker behind these moments of surrender, though I couldn't yet understand its depths. The weight of past inner turmoil, financial struggle, and gnawing self-doubt had taken root subconsciously in ways I couldn't yet fully comprehend.

The pattern continued over the next few years. My conscious mind would submit to sleep at the wheel. My car would drift from its lane as if drawn by some fierce dark gravity—a malevolent force over which I had no control.

Each time, I would snap awake at the crucial moment, saved by what seemed like chance but felt more like cruel fate. How could this go on? It could not. It should not...

Whispers in the Dark: A Stranger's Light

Los Angeles, California, February 1973

At twenty-seven, my UC Berkeley architecture degree offered no shelter from the harsh financial reality of my struggling career. I had married that college girlfriend but it was a union not destined to last. My focus in life had been centered on myself, one that didn't allow efforts to build harmony. The distortions in my life manifested dire circumstances. Now, home had become my van parked on Los Angeles streets while I pursued my architectural photography aspirations.

My lack of clients triggered deep depression that seemed to emanate from me like a visible, ominous aura. This repelled potential clients and fed a relentless cycle of rejection amid ongoing financial struggle. Success seemed a mirage that forever receded into the distance.

In February 1973, after months of struggling with very little work, a lifeline seemed to arrive in the form of a $1,000 commission to photograph bank interiors, a grueling project I worked on throughout the night.

After the shoot, I dropped the film off for processing that morning only to learn a few hours later that disaster had struck: a lab technician had switched on the lights in the darkroom, destroying every frame of my work in an instant.

Glen Allison

The timing couldn't have been worse. There would be no reshoot; the project had been completed under strict deadlines for an architectural awards submission. The photo lab would make no compensation.

This devastating blow shattered what little remained of my fragile hopes. What should have been a breakthrough job became another weight that dragged me further into despair.

It was the "ordeal," the darkest hour, as mentioned in Joseph Campbell's "The Hero's Journey."[1]

Deep within, I knew human beings surely must possess the power to transcend their own ordeals and rise above their suffering—yet this potential remained locked away inside me, unreachable. Even the simplest strokes of luck seemed to evade me.

Financial struggles drove me to new lows. Many nights, I would sneak through supermarket aisles and pilfer crackers from boxes I'd secretly opened—each bite an assault on my dignity.

And then one night it all changed in a dimly lit parking lot, as I slumped in my van drowning in self-disgust after another such transgression. I stared at my hands. They were an artist's hands—trained to capture beauty, now reduced to petty theft.

"What have I become?" I whispered as my voice cracked. The words hung in the stale air of the van, a harsh indictment of how far I'd fallen and the depth of humiliation I felt. I pressed my forehead against the steering wheel as I fought back tears of self-hatred.

Hidden Powers

How do I find a way out of this hell? This thought raced through my mind before I could stop it, raw and desperate in the gathering darkness.

A soft tap on my window startled me. A young woman stood there, her face etched with genuine concern—a rarity in Los Angeles, where people considered it practically a civic duty to avert their eyes from the suffering of others.

"Are you alright?" she asked, her voice cut through my isolation. Something in her gaze held me, really saw me, in a way I hadn't felt seen in a long while. When I failed to respond, she asked again, softer this time, "Are you okay?"

The genuine compassion in her voice suddenly broke dense walls open inside me. Words failed, but my eyes must have spoken volumes, because she stayed. Softly, she began to share her thoughts with me.

She introduced me to something unexpected that would alter my life's trajectory: the Mystic Law,[2] which promised activation of inner powers that would enable me to transform suffering into strength.

That night, in my desperation and eagerness to try anything, I let this stranger's words guide me toward an ancient Buddhist chant—its utterance alone would have seemed absurd to my former self, that narrow-minded kid from Texas.

As the first syllables of this mantra left my lips, a deep resonance stirred within me—a subtle shift that would soon avalanche into revolution, though I couldn't have known it then.

Glen Allison

Racing Against Darkness

What dreams have you set aside because the voice of impossibility spoke louder than your hope? You may be carrying burdens you've stopped believing you could put down—financial pressures that seem insurmountable, health challenges that appear permanent, or relationships that feel irreparably damaged. That space between your despair and possibility is where transformation begins. My darkest moments became doorways to discovery, and yours can too. The same principles that pulled me from the edge can reshape your reality, regardless of how deeply entrenched your struggles may seem.

Los Angeles, California, April 1973

In the months that followed, even as financial hardship maintained its stranglehold, the dynamics of my life shifted as a new inner force began to take root. Each day of Buddhist practice lit a fresh spark of awareness that awakened a long dormant determination to reshape my reality rather than merely endure it. This realization inspired me to reimagine my circumstances rather than succumb to them. Inner power began to emerge, a steady process that soon stopped my negative spiral.

As I embraced the Buddhist principle of life's inherent sacredness, a different kind of strength emerged—one that compelled me to turn my struggles into stepping stones rather than stumbling blocks. I discovered an invigorating way to face each day with enthusiasm as I fought to turn each obstacle into an opportunity for growth.

This radical shift didn't come easily for me; doubt still wrestled with hope daily, and dark days still clouded my path. But my Buddhist friends spurred me onward. Their inspiring encouragement motivated me to nurture what began as a mere spark of hope into a robust flame—one that would light my way from darkness.

Yet the negative forces within me refused to surrender quietly. My newfound faith faced a deadly test against my deep-rooted self-destructive impulses.

Will I ever truly break free? Or am I just pretending to change while death still beckons?

One evening on the Santa Monica Freeway, as I hurtled along at seventy miles per hour, sleep seduced me once more.

Not again. Please, not again. I thought I was stronger now...

When I jolted awake, I discovered my van had cut a path of devastation. It had plowed through seventeen posts of the center divider's chain link fence, and now balanced precariously on the thin steel central cable—all that separated me from the crush of oncoming traffic in an era before concrete barriers.

How many times will fate spare me before it collects its due? Why was I burning through my life so fast?

Glen Allison

Though my van was demolished, I emerged mysteriously unharmed, as if caught between two forces: one bent on destruction while the other refused to let me succumb.

What force keeps saving me when part of me still yearns for oblivion?

I had slipped through fate's fingers, as if protected by an unseen hand—a perilous game of Russian roulette where the chamber had, so far, always come up empty.

The message stood clear: my inner demons hadn't finished their dance of death, a stark reminder of the dark struggle that still raged subconsciously deep within me.

My final battle with this demonic force erupted during an all-night drive in early October 1974 from Los Angeles to the Albuquerque International Balloon Fiesta. I refused to waste money on a motel and chose to drive straight through—a decision that would prove nearly fatal.

I had grossly underestimated the journey time. Eager to photograph the dawn launch of 500 hot air balloons that I had dreamed about for years, I pushed myself and my car beyond reason; the speedometer repeatedly surged past 100 miles per hour.

Just a little faster. Just a little longer. I can't miss this chance. I won't.

But this time differed; the old whisper of self-destructive thrill had been replaced by genuine terror.

Stay awake! This isn't like before. I want to live. I NEED to live.

The familiar subliminal death wish had vanished, replaced by a primal fear of mortality. Desperate to stay awake, I thrust my head out the window into the blast of cold air. I pressed ice cubes from my cooler against my face and slapped my cheeks with such brutal force that I surely bruised myself. For the first time, I fought desperately to stay conscious, alternating between the fervent utterance of my new mantra and raw screams into the darkness: "I DON'T WANT TO DIE!"

No no no—not now. Not when I've finally found something worth living for...

The world suddenly went black.

Glen Allison

The Final Wake-Up Call

Albuquerque, New Mexico, October 1974

The collision was catastrophic.

My car crumpled against a concrete guardrail; metal twisted around me like a demented sculpture—a grotesque monument to folly. The passenger-side front tire had crushed so far inward it pierced the dashboard and lay thrust grotesquely against the seat beside me. Yet somehow, impossibly, I remained untouched —as if a final miracle, some higher universal force, had guided me toward what would be my very last chance to tempt death. Survival was now up to me alone.

This wreck dwarfed all my previous brushes with self-annihilation. In the aftermath, as I sat amid the twisted wreckage of both car and former self, a bone-deep certainty seized me. This had been my absolute final warning; another episode would mean certain death. Deep within my soul, I knew this with crystal clarity. At that very instant, I forged an unbreakable, iron-clad vow to never again let these self-destructive impulses pilot my destiny.

A new imperative ignited at my core—to discover my life's true purpose and to pursue it with ferocious intensity.

In the five decades since that day, I've driven countless nighttime journeys, but never again submitted to lethal temptation.

Accessing the Depths of Consciousness

Though professional counseling might have offered some insights, Buddhism gave me the tangible tools to battle and finally vanquish these inner demons.

While psychological therapy explores our subconscious motivations, Buddhist teachings reveal this realm as merely the seventh in a spectrum of nine levels of consciousness humans possess,.

To truly alter our subconscious drives, we must dig deeper—into the eighth level, where psychology can't reach and where karmic effects of past causes reside and need to be altered.

Yet even tapping into this core level isn't deep enough to initiate fundamental change in our life trajectory; our true innate power dwells in the ninth level, and only by accessing this deepest realm of strength and enlightenment can we effectively change our subconscious patterns that exist in the seventh level of consciousness.

We will explore "The Nine Levels of Consciousness" more thoroughly in a later chapter, but in those early days, my daily Buddhist practice enabled me to access this fundamental ninth level even without fully comprehending the mechanics involved. Through these daily efforts, I unleashed newly found reservoirs of strength and wisdom that had lain dormant within me all along.

This inner human revolution allowed me to activate the inherent power to not only cherish, but to permanently inscribe into every fiber of my being what I had once carelessly risked—the precious sanctity of life itself.

What began as a desperate fight for survival evolved into something far more significant: a path toward complete liberation from the anguish of suffering, an existence I could create through my own will.

The visionary philosopher Daisaku Ikeda proclaimed: "As long as you keep challenging yourself, there is hope. But if you give up and become self-destructive, you are extinguishing the light of hope through your own actions."[3]

What would your life look like if suffering no longer defined your boundaries? The concepts, tools, and principles I'll share in coming chapters aren't philosophical abstractions but practical instruments of change that worked when nothing else did. Our capacity for renewal doesn't depend on circumstances aligning perfectly or pain disappearing miraculously.

It emerges from the need for us to access the deeper levels of consciousness and wisdom where our true power resides—the same power that exists within you right now, waiting to be awakened. The journey ahead isn't about escaping life's challenges but about transforming your relationship with them, discovering that what once appeared as your greatest obstacle can become your most profound teacher.

Chapter 3 - Breaking Suffering's Code

So why do we suffer? And is suffering really necessary?

The seeds of unhappiness take root when life's trials appear insurmountable—as they once towered before me during my darkest hours. Yet beneath this seeming helplessness lies an extraordinary truth: within each of us burns an untapped power to transmute our pain into profound wisdom and vibrant strength. By awakening this dormant force, we forge not walls of stone to hide behind, but an unshakeable core of resilience rising from our deepest essence—rendering suffering powerless in the face of our awakened might.

Viktor Frankl, Holocaust survivor and psychiatrist, cogently observed: "When we are no longer able to change a situation, we are challenged to change ourselves."[1]

Those caught in suffering's grip radiate an almost palpable darkness. Have you ever noticed how suffering exerts its own gravitational pull? The moment its weight settles upon you, a downward spiral begins—your thoughts grow leaden, your energy drains away, and even your physical stance betrays suffering's presence. This internal void soon casts a negative imprint on your external reality, which functions as an invisible corrosive force that saps vitality from your surroundings.

Others instinctively avoid this field of negativity, leading to a self-perpetuating cycle of isolation. Each day weighs heavier than the last, opportunities fade like desert mirages—visible but forever out of reach—leaving only intensified suffering in their wake.

When trapped in this lethal web, many people search frantically for avenues of escape yet lack the tools to subdue, prevent, or banish their misery—as I discovered in my own battle with the malevolent forces that despair had stirred to life.

This reveals the insidious nature of all-consuming distress—it doesn't just wound; it rewrites how we perceive everything. The promotion at work loses its value. The sunset fails to register. The hand of friendship extended toward us appears suspicious or empty. In these moments, suffering evolves beyond mere feeling; it transforms into the very lens through which we view our entire world.

In our depleted life state, pain refuses confinement—it expands in widening circles.

What begins as a private storm soon touches every shore of our life, initiating a negative domino effect. Inner turmoil clouds thoughts and weighs our body with invisible burdens. This darkness then seeps outward to dim our closest bonds and stain daily work. Eventually, it can cast a pall across our broadest aims and deepest contributions.

Though waves of suffering may extend wide, its true purpose might be more redemptive than we initially perceive. Our greatest challenge sometimes can serve as unexpected beacons, illuminating aspects of life we previously overlooked.

Hidden Powers

> "You'll have bad times, but it'll always wake you up to the good stuff you weren't paying attention to."—Robin Williams as Sean Maguire in the movie, *Good Will Hunting*[2]

This poignant wisdom illuminates an essential insight about suffering's hidden purpose: our darkest moments of deep challenge often act as igniters that redirect us toward previously invisible opportunities and possibilities. What seems like misfortune can actually function as the universe's method of shifting our attention to what truly matters.

What if your current suffering stands not as an indictment of your life but as an invitation to uncover capabilities within yourself that would otherwise lie dormant? Which perception about your present struggle could you challenge today, not through positive thinking alone, but through a fundamental shift in how you face your life's challenges?

To extract the hidden value from our difficulties requires more than fleeting inspiration—it demands a consistent practice of reexamination. The following exercise offers a structured method to discover the concealed gifts within your challenges and to witness your evolution over time:

The Hidden Bounty

Beneath every ordeal lies a field of insight that yearns to be harvested.

Our difficulties conceal treasures invisible to the casual eye. What appears as misfortune holds the seeds of our

> most vital evolution. These seeds beckon us forward—not for mere recognition, but for deep cultivation.
>
> Select one challenge you have today and confront it directly. See beyond its harsh exterior to what it asks of you. Examine its four dimensions: the surface problem that everyone sees, the hidden invitation that calls to your deeper self, the exact quality you must now develop, and the future gift your growth will offer others.
>
> Each evening for a week, sit with this challenge. Watch how it shifts under your close examination. Notice how wisdom emerges not from escape but from engagement. Document each revelation, however modest.
>
> This four-dimensional framework differs markedly from conventional gratitude exercises, though appreciation remains both beneficial and crucial. My outlined introspective approach doesn't ask you to merely appreciate hardship, but to systematically extract its hidden value through each of the four lenses described above. What once crushed minds under suffering's weight now offers an alternative path—one where difficulties become doorways to unimagined strength.
>
> What once appeared as your greatest burden now stands revealed as your most essential teacher and becomes proof of what you extracted from adversity's pain.
>
> What awaits in your field of difficulties? The yield depends on your willingness to look beyond the obvious.

As powerful as these reflective practices can be, some suffering stems from deeper issues that require specialized support. In an article published by the Mayo Clinic, their staff clinicians warn that extreme suffering can lead to mental illness disorders affecting mood, thinking, and behavior—much like my subliminal death wish propensity.

Their research identifies symptoms such as deep sadness, disorganized thinking, heightened anxieties, mood fluctuations, social withdrawal, fatigue, delusional thoughts, impaired coping mechanisms, substance abuse tendencies, and self-destructive thoughts. They conclude, "A mental health concern becomes a mental illness when ongoing signs and symptoms cause frequent stress and affect your ability to function."[3] Though these findings perfectly described my early experiences, this reality remained completely hidden from me then, preventing me from recognizing the severity of my condition.

The Dalai Lama asserts that liberation from suffering demands a radical shift in our perception of adversity. In his book, *The Art of Happiness*, he states: "When we meet real tragedy in life, we can react in two ways—either by losing hope and falling into self-destructive habits, or by using the challenge to find our inner strength."[4] This proactive stance builds the mental agility necessary to spot opportunities within apparent misfortune.

He advocates for a deliberate adjustment in our approach to difficulties—a renewal process that yields staunch optimism enabling us to access the potential for growth within hardship. To convert challenges into opportunities, we need to draw upon our deepest reserves of inner strength and wisdom, particularly when confronting our most daunting circumstances.

The Dalai Lama's insight offers a theoretical framework for shifting our perception of life's challenges. When viewed through a constricted lens, our obstacles can often appear insurmountable. Yet, when we embrace an audacious mindset that allows new conceptual understanding, we can ignite remarkable change—a future illuminated by hope becomes a seedbed of wisdom and energy.

Daisaku Ikeda elaborates on this distinction: "Suffering is an inescapable part of being alive. Unhappiness is a result of being overcome by that suffering, losing hope and succumbing to despair. The only way to avoid that is to build a strong, expansive spirit that cannot be defeated by any hardship."[5]

Frida Kahlo's extraordinary journey through suffering to artistic liberation embodies this deep renewal. At age six, Kahlo contracted polio, which left her right leg thinner than her left. This physical disparity earned her cruel taunts from other children. Then at eighteen, a catastrophic bus accident shattered her spine, collarbone, ribs, and pelvis. A steel handrail impaled her body; it entered through her hip and exited through her vagina. Doctors doubted she would survive.

This accident condemned Kahlo to a lifetime of pain and more than thirty operations. She spent months immobilized in plaster body casts and endured excruciating treatments that often proved futile. "I am not sick," she would later write, "I am broken. But I am happy to be alive as long as I can paint."[6]

It was during her initial convalescence, confined to bed for months, that Kahlo began to paint. Her mother installed a mirror on the ceiling above her bed and provided watercolors.

With a makeshift easel that allowed her to paint lying down, Kahlo began to create self-portraits—the mirror reflected back the only subject available to her. "I paint myself because I am often alone," she explained, "and I am the subject I know best." [7]

Kahlo's story captivates us not merely through her endurance of suffering but through her complete reimagination of it. Rather than allow her physical pain to diminish her, she directed it into art of searing honesty and emotional depth. Her 143 paintings—55 of them self-portraits—don't shy away from her broken body, her miscarriages, or her emotional torment.

Through her art, she didn't escape her suffering; she reshaped it into something meaningful and enduring.

In "The Broken Column" (1944), her painting portrays her body split open, her spine replaced by a crumbling column, her body pierced by nails, tears stream down her face—yet her gaze remains steady and dignified. This artwork embodies both excruciating pain and unswayable spirit. Her work became not just a reflection of her suffering, but a complete elevation of it.

"At the end of the day," Kahlo wrote, "we can endure much more than we think we can."[8] This wasn't empty optimism from someone who had been spared life's hardships—it was hard-won wisdom from a woman who had been "bent and broken," as the 19th-century English novelist Charles Dickens opined: "Suffering has been stronger than all other teachings and has taught me to understand what your heart used to be. I have been bent and broken, but—I hope—into a better shape."[9]

Both Kahlo and Dickens discovered what lies at the heart of suffering's paradox—the same force that brings us to our knees can lift us to unprecedented heights. Their experiences illuminate a universal truth about our relationship with adversity: suffering has power only to the extent we perceive it as our master rather than as our teacher. Yet this very quality that makes suffering so pervasive also exposes its vulnerability: If suffering draws its strength from the distortion of our perception, then a shift in that perception—not just at an intellectual level, but at the core of our being—can unlock the path to its unraveling.

This initial mental shift merely opens the door compared to the profound renewal that will occur through the more substantial principles and practices we will explore later. But if you begin this process now, you can lay the foundation for a more expansive outlook, which will nurture your capacity for development.

This expansion beyond self-focused viewpoints echoes what Daisaku Ikeda observed about our tendency toward isolation during difficult times: "When we suffer some misfortune, we tend to imagine that no one could possibly be as unhappy or as unfortunate. It's easy to drown in self-pity and turn a blind eye to everyone and everything else. But dwelling on our own pain or discontent and hopelessness only causes our life force to wane even further."[10]

Through the courageous pursuit of new solutions, we create the conditions for flourishing circumstances to emerge. When we learn how to release our authentic selves, we discover the capacity to reshape our flaws, setbacks, and past wounds into foundations for a vibrant new existence—one that rises far above suffering.

The following exercise provides a practical method to apply this wisdom in your daily life:

> **The Liberation Lens**
>
> Our minds craft both our cage and our wings.
>
> When darkness sweeps in, pause to notice how suffering warps your view—how it curves reality, twists meaning, and bleaches vibrancy from your world. This deliberate halt creates crucial space between you and your pain.
>
> Step beyond your limited perspective. The voice that narrates your suffering cannot guide you past it.
>
> Pose illuminating questions to your loftier self: What would this wiser perspective see in your situation that you cannot? What essential lesson hides within this challenge? Which qualities must you now cultivate that comfort could never nurture?
>
> Then execute one definitive action—not to resolve your entire situation, but to disrupt the downward force. A single step toward light can fracture despair's stronghold and redirect your journey.
>
> Our difficulties mirror not our boundaries but our concealed capacities. From this elevated vantage point, what seemed insurmountable becomes merely one chapter in your unfolding story. Pain that once

> dominated your viewpoint becomes instead a signpost directing you toward unexplored strengths within.
>
> Your liberation begins the moment when you realize the narrator of your pain cannot be the author of your freedom.

While these perspective-shifting practices offer powerful starting points, they represent just the beginning of a deeper journey. The initial insights they provide, though valuable, serve as entry points toward more profound change. Most people discover that momentary shifts in viewpoint, though illuminating, aren't enough to fully activate their dormant capabilities or to establish lasting resilience against suffering.

In the sections that follow, I'll share specific concepts that will allow you to intensify your inner life force and maintain this elevated mindset, which will forge it into a robust life state—one able not just to endure life's trials, but to reconfigure them at their core.

Life spares no one from challenges and hardships. Even those who enjoy seemingly ideal circumstances can find themselves caught in suffering's misery—consider the countless celebrities whose fame and fortune turn into poisoned chalices that drive them toward substance abuse and self-destruction.

The Art of Inner Revolution

During those early years in Texas, suffering had seemed as vast and inescapable as the state itself, its challenges particularly daunting to my young mind. Yet even before I could fully articulate it, a deep hunger within me reached for what I couldn't yet name—an absolute, sovereign happiness capable of weathering life's fiercest storms.

At the time, I didn't realize my encounter with Buddhism had sparked more than spiritual revelation—it eventually ignited a quest to uncover my life's true purpose. At the core burned one essential question: "How could I break free from past chains and forge a new reality?"

This journey taught me that triumph over adversity demands nothing less than absolute ownership of our lives. Each present action contributes to shaping our future destiny, which makes courage in the face of challenges non-negotiable.

When we shirk this responsibility, we don't just avoid difficulties —we erode the very foundation of our self-belief. Indeed, it's rarely life's obstacles that defeat us, but rather the faltering of our own resolve. Yet through resolute commitment to elevate suffering toward a loftier purpose, this very same agony can become the source of our agency and liberation.

When we rely solely on our fluctuating emotions and inconsistent resolve, life's steepest challenges can easily overwhelm us. In recognition of this human paradox, Ikeda observed, "There is nothing more vulnerable, nothing more corruptible than the human mind; nor is there anything as powerful, steadfast and ennobling"[11]

This battle wages not in the external world, but within ourselves—between our aspiring and yielding natures.

When we succumb to weakness, we invite defeat; when we pursue our nobler aspirations, we trigger the momentum to chart our desired course. Through this internal revolution, we attain not just victory but the capacity to reshape adversity into good fortune, which can redefine our lives in exciting and unexpected ways.

This principle resonates throughout history. In the mid-13th century, Nichiren Daishonin, a Japanese Buddhist visionary, stated: "Put into flames, a rock simply turns to ashes, but gold becomes pure gold."[12]

Before I could truly begin my journey of personal development, I needed to unlock the awesome capacities Buddhism promised—innate abilities that would enable me to conquer my self-destructive tendencies.

This passage from despair to awakening sparked within me a deep reverence for life itself that empowered me to embrace challenges with steadily growing resolve and an increasingly fearless fortitude.

You can begin your own journey toward renewal with this insightful approach to address life's challenges:

The Trinocular Perspective

Not only what we see, but more importantly, what we perceive dictates what we become.

Most people view their hardships through a single lens—the immediate pain, the obvious loss, the direct obstacle. This narrow vision traps them in cycles of reaction and regret. Their difficulties become dead ends rather than doorways.

A wiser eye sees beyond the surface. It discerns three distinct dimensions in every challenge we face: what hurts now, what builds within us, and what awaits beyond the horizon.

First, acknowledge your present reality and the suffering it causes. Face the raw facts of your situation without embellishment or denial. This honest assessment grounds you in what IS rather than what you wish might be.

Next, direct your attention to the inner qualities this challenge demands you develop. Every obstacle calls forth specific capacities—patience, courage, resilience, focus, humility. These qualities form the invisible foundation of our character.

Finally, extend your vision to future benefits that remain invisible to others. While most see only current limitations, we need to perceive the eventual advantages that will emerge from this difficulty once mastered.

This triple vision lifts us from victim to orchestrator of our life experience. Like the master sculptor who sees the

> finished figure within raw marble, we can learn to recognize the ultimate good concealed within apparent misfortune.
>
> When applied consistently, this perspective will reshape your entire relationship with difficulty. What once appeared as life's cruelest blow reveals itself as the chisel that carves your finest qualities into being.

Though valuable, intellectual comprehension alone cannot fully release the unlimited capabilities buried at our core—a reality we'll explore more deeply in coming chapters.

As you progress through this book, you'll discover how accessing the vitality and wisdom that awakens when we connect with the Mystic Law—the fundamental universal force that pulses through all life—will magnify and deepen your journey of renewal. This will activate a pivotal shift that extends far beyond the capabilities of these suggested initial practices. Your path might begin with these introspective methods but ultimately must culminate in something far more significant—a complete rebirth that reaches the very essence of your being and radiates outward to redefine your entire existence.

When suffering no longer dictates our story, our true narrative bursts forth with magnificent possibility.

Chapter 4 - The Flower Seller's Wisdom

Jaisalmer, Rajasthan, India, October 2015

Life's most consequential lessons often arrive in unexpected moments, through unexpected teachers.

When was the last time wisdom found you when you least expected it? Perhaps it appeared in the quiet compassion of someone who owed you nothing, yet offered everything, or in that moment of perfect clarity that emerged from chaos. You may have searched for answers in books and teachings, yet wisdom has whispered to you through the ordinary—a child's innocent question, a chance remark from someone who crossed your path only once, or nature's silent rhythms. What unexpected teacher has most profoundly touched your life?

While my earlier years of Buddhist study taught me the fundamental principles of changing suffering, my subsequent countless encounters across decades and continents deepened these truths into ever-expanding wisdom.

Perhaps you've experienced this yourself—that electric moment when a stranger's gaze meets yours and something magnetic passes between you, a silent acknowledgment that transcends the superficial. These fleeting connections often reveal more truth than hours of conversation.

One such moment remains eternally etched in my memory. It came not during my desperate search for answers in those early

Texas days, but much later, after years of practicing these principles had yielded unexpected fruit. By then, I had learned to recognize wisdom in its many disguises, to see teachers in unlikely places. Yet sometimes the most potent lessons still catch us by surprise.

After decades of global travel in my career that taught me through both unpleasant missteps and battle-tested insights, I returned to the familiar dusty alleyways of Jaisalmer in Rajasthan, India—a fortress town I had explored countless times before. This remote desert outpost could have emerged from scenes in the 1962 epic film, *Lawrence of Arabia*.[1]

There I met an ancient soul—a flower vendor whose weathered face mapped countless seasons. His earthly possessions consisted of a modest collection of desert blossoms and clothes that had long since yielded to time. Yet his smile, as radiant as dawn over the desert, revealed wealth beyond measure. Each flower under his care seemed to bloom more vibrantly through his tender attention, as if it celebrated some sacred understanding between keeper and kept.

When our eyes met, I saw deep wisdom in the old man's gaze—a knowledge that bridged languages and cultures to touch unexplored depths within me. His eyes sparkled with an inner light, a luminous quality that struck me as both rare and precious.

During my travels across countless countries, I had grown accustomed to hollow stares—the vacant expressions of those who merely existed rather than truly lived. This emptiness marked the glazed eyes of Tokyo executives who trudged through underground stations at dawn, their spirits dimmed by decades of fluorescent-lit cubicles and meaningless meetings and reports. I recall a particular investment banker in Manhattan whose expensive suit couldn't mask the death behind his gaze—a man who confessed over drinks that he couldn't remember why he'd chosen his career path or what he truly wanted from life.

Even among friends back in the States, this spiritual vacancy spread like a modern plague. My college roommate Robert, once aflame with literary ambition and creative purpose, now stared at spreadsheets ten hours daily in a windowless office, his once-passionate eyes dulled when we met for lunch the previous year in Austin, Texas. He spoke of his upcoming retirement as salvation, having sacrificed forty precious years to work that now held little meaning beyond a paycheck.

But this flower seller's eyes held galaxies of experience—suffering changed into wisdom, hardship recast into compassion. His face showed neither resignation nor desperation despite his humble circumstances. Instead, it radiated a heartfelt aliveness—an awakened presence that made those with material wealth but spiritual poverty appear as mere hollow vessels.

His eyes reflected something I'd witnessed only a handful of times: in a Tibetan monk who had endured decades of imprisonment yet radiated boundless compassion; in an aging jazz musician in New Orleans whose arthritic fingers could barely bend yet whose eyes danced with creative fire; in a Brazilian grandmother who had raised eleven children in dire poverty in a favela yet who walked through life with the grace of someone who understood its deepest purpose.

As I shared my moment of silence with the old man in Jaisalmer, a young boy of no more than six or seven approached. His hollow eyes and tattered clothes spoke of an empty stomach rather than appreciation for the delicate petals before him.

Each colorful blossom expressed unique qualities. Wildflowers don't compete with each other. They bloom gloriously according to their individual potential.[2]

The old man, who owned nothing but his flowers and his compassion, lifted a single blossom to the child's face. Words in Hindi, soft as prayer, flowed between them. In that pure moment, hunger yielded to beauty—the boy's face lit up as he breathed the flower's fragrance, though sustenance, not beauty, had drawn him near.

The child accepted this gift with natural grace; then he dissolved into the crowd like a drop of water into dry sand. Soon he emerged again to offer his botanical treasure to passing strangers until someone recognized its worth in rupees.

I watched as coins passed into tiny hands. Then my eyes followed the boy's swift steps to a nearby vendor whose fresh chapatis scented the air—simple bread that meant survival for one more sun's arc across the sky.

When I turned back to the flower seller, his smile had deepened far beyond joy—a knowing radiance that spoke of life's inherent perfection and limitless potential for endurance, even amid want and struggle—a basic truth I wouldn't have grasped so deeply years earlier.

Without hesitation, I opened my wallet and extracted all the banknotes. I folded the money without counting and placed it gently into his wrinkled hands. My smile matched the breadth of his own as I purchased his entire remaining stock of flowers.

Our exchange concluded without a single word between us, yet this wordless communion spoke volumes—a conversation more meaningful than any I might have conducted with words. Then, I moved through the crowd to find other hungry children. To each, I offered not just a flower, but a path to dignity—a chance to earn rather than beg, to stand tall rather than stoop.

The old man's lesson unfolded again with each exchange: sometimes the most precious gifts arrive wrapped in petals rather than prosperity.

Chapter 5 - To Dream the Impossible Dream

Los Angeles, California, 1977

My encounter with the flower seller's wisdom came decades after my first tentative steps toward inner growth. But looking back now, I see how each stage of my journey revealed its own precious insights—though I wasn't always ready to accept them back then.

In those early career days, as the oppressive fog of my struggles lifted, I began to recognize wisdom in unexpected places. A new clarity emerged to reveal possibilities I had previously dismissed as unattainable. Yet this insight didn't arrive as a sudden burst of enlightenment—it came through a series of often painfully-earned victories over my own doubts.

The lotus blossom became my mental talisman. This unique flower rises from muddy depths to bloom most beautifully from the darkness below. My daily mantra, which contains the word "renge" (pronounced "ren-gay"), that translates to "lotus flower," carved this symbolism deep into my psyche. *How can a flower so pure, so exquisite, emerge from the foulest waters?* This question both challenged and inspired me.

While Buddhism activated boundless hope, during some nights of often reoccurring weakness, I still questioned if I had just exchanged one form of magical thinking for another. I frequently teetered on the edge of despondency, unsure if I, too, could rise from the mire and muck of my circumstances. The specter of my early career setbacks haunted me, poised to pull me back into despair with each step forward.

Yet, as time passed, an inner change began to blossom. The restless drive that had always propelled me—that had fixed my eyes on distant horizons even in my Texas childhood—began to surge with renewed intensity. The very air seemed to crackle with possibility. Happiness, once elusive, now gleamed almost within reach.

Buddhism became my North Star. As its teachings cleared my mind's haze, my vision of possibility expanded. Aspirations that once tormented me and highlighted my limitations no longer loomed as distant, unreachable peaks

When my inner world shifted, my outer circumstances followed. New clients appeared, ones who seemed to trust me with assignments despite my inexperience—perhaps a reflection of my burgeoning inner change.

Even as new opportunities arose, failure's ghost lurked at the edges of my consciousness and whispered that I didn't deserve success. But each new assignment became a battle won, proof of my strengthened will. Yet for every client who took a chance on me, three others rejected me. Each dismissal reopened old wounds.

Still, I pressed forward.

The Los Angeles Times Home Magazine became my proving ground, though I fought for that first assignment tooth and nail back in the early 1970s. The magazine soon offered more opportunities, each one a chance to sharpen my skills and build my reputation. The editor must have spotted a spark of potential in me—one I had just begun to recognize. It wasn't enough, not yet, but it marked a beginning. Within a year after that pivotal supermarket parking lot encounter, I secured a small photo studio.

No longer adrift in my van, I now had a base of operations, meager as it was—a place to survey the vast landscape of possibilities. Financial struggles persisted and most days dawned with uncertainty because a strong life force, I discovered, emerges only through difficult challenges. So, I fought harder. The remnants of my career struggles now showed how far I'd come and how far I had yet to climb—a vital battle I learned to embrace willingly though not at first.

In that tiny studio, a greater force stirred within. My yearning, once a constant source of frustration, evolved into a driving energy that compelled me to envision grander vistas and dream bigger dreams.

Wrestling with Shadows

"A Photographer's Quixotic Quest"

Spain, July 1977

My newly awakened reservoir of inner strength powered me to confront whatever challenges lay ahead. *But who was I to dream of photographing world-class architecture?* The voice of my past self ridiculed such presumption. Yet as my aspirations rose higher, more energy surged within to pursue my dreams. Though I didn't recognize it at first, I had begun to tap into my innate hidden powers.

But my Buddhist practice hadn't magically filled my bank account. Each month demanded a careful dance with debt. My growing confidence battled daily with years of ingrained negativity. But over a relatively short time, I had evolved from a desperate photographer fighting finances amid frequent hopelessness. Now, visions beckoned of an intrepid explorer of life's potential, perhaps poised at the brink of a grand adventure —if only I could summon enough courage.

A wild adventure lurked just ahead....

With passion, I devoured Miguel de Cervantes' masterpiece, *Don Quixote*.[1] The tale of La Mancha's ingenious gentleman struck a deep chord. Here stood a man who saw the world not as it was, but as it could be. His indomitable commitment to ideals, however outlandish they seemed to others, mirrored my rising desire for adventure.

The new rhythm in my life unleashed good fortune. An assignment from *The Los Angeles Times* Sunday magazine connected me with a Spanish architect in L.A., Rafael Franco, who enchanted me with tales of Ricardo Bofill's architectural marvels in Spain.

Bofill's firm enlisted not just draftsmen, engineers, designers, and architects, but also economists, historians, philosophers, and poets. Their innovative approach? First, they explored the wildest ideas through the lens of history, poetry, and philosophy. Only after this quest would they adapt the extraordinary artistic visions to fit budgets and site constraints. This bold creative strategy birthed radical designs that launched Bofill to international fame.

As Rafael spoke, a grand quest crystallized in my mind. His words crafted vivid imagery that transported me to a realm of architectural wonders. He described Bofill's masterpiece, La Fábrica—reimagined architecture that ascended from the ruins of an abandoned cement factory.

In my vision, Bofill emerged as a modern-day wizard, who recast cold, industrial structures into magical edifices. He had stripped away the superfluous to unveil hidden forms dormant for years. Towering silos, once filled with cement, now harbored bustling offices and living spaces. His designs eclipsed renovation—they proclaimed rebirth, a potent declaration of potential that slumbered in the discarded and overlooked.

Hidden Powers

But when my new friend described Bofill's La Muralla Roja, my pulse raced. This structure soared beyond innovative architecture; it stood as a fortress of dreams that commanded Alicante's cliffs. Its name, "The Red Wall," belied its riot of color that swept across the rocky cliffs.

I envisioned myself threading through its labyrinthine corridors, where each turn revealed a new vista. Bridges spanned impossible gaps, staircases zigzagged skyward, and walkways crossed spaces like red rivers rushing toward the sea. The interconnected shapes defied the eye—a masterful blend that fused modularity with artistic vision.

Bofill's design absorbed echoes of distant lands and ancient times. He distilled and reimagined North African casbahs and Arab Mediterranean architecture into this cliffside marvel. He appeared to extract inspiration from *One Thousand and One Nights*,[2] the classic collection of Middle Eastern folktales, and cast these influences in concrete modernist form.

With each enticing detail, my photographer's imagination ignited with anticipation. These weren't just glorious architectural edifices—they were stories that awaited discovery, adventures ready to unfold. Deep within my heart, I knew I must see these wonders firsthand, to capture their essence through my lens.

My mind blazed with excitement as I cast myself as a knight-errant of photography embarking on a quixotic quest to unveil these architectural rarities to the world. La Fábrica and La Muralla Roja stood not only as triumphs of design, but as my fortresses to storm, my impossible dreams made tangible.

Glen Allison

Tilting at Windmills

Don Quixote's fervor propelled me as I proposed an ambitious idea to my editor at *The L.A. Times Home Magazine*: a special issue on Spanish architecture. To my delight, she not only approved but arranged for Rafael to serve as my guide. We'd become Don Quixote and Sancho Panza, bound for our own adventure across Spain's sun-baked plains.

Our first stop: La Mancha's ancient white windmills that crowned the rolling hilltops. As we approached, excitement surged through me. I saw more than mere structures of plaster, wood, and canvas—they loomed as giants to conquer, their sweeping arms a challenge for my lens.

A sudden sandstorm forced me to shield my camera with my body; fine dust threatened to destroy my equipment. As visibility shrank to mere feet, our tight schedule haunted us like a specter. Each hour lost to weather meant another piece of the story might remain untold.

Finally, the skies brightened and I scaled the hillside, my camera my lance, determination my armor. The merciless Spanish sun blazed down, but I ignored it. My focus remained absolute, my quest clear. Each shot became a battle, each angle a skirmish in my campaign to capture the essence of this magical place.

But my eager rush caused me to lose my footing on the rocky slope. I tumbled, and my precious camera smashed against the unforgiving ground. As I lay there, dust in my mouth, self-doubt's laughter jeered at me. But then I recalled Don Quixote, who discovered enchantment where others saw defeat. I rose to my feet and declared to my concerned companion, who had hurried to help, "Our resolve faced only a mere test!"

The next day, my Nikon camera body, my essential piece of equipment, started to fail in the intense Spanish heat. The film advance lever caught repeatedly and threatened to tear the film or strip the gears with each forced advance. Each click of the shutter sparked anxiety—would this frame ruin the entire roll? With no camera repair shops in rural Spain, I persisted, resolved that equipment failure would not doom the assignment.

My dread intensified as my light meter failed in the stark Spanish sun. This failure forced me to bracket each shot's exposure extensively, which consumed precious film at triple the planned rate. With limited film and no budget for extras, each frame became a gamble. Would enough film remain to complete the assignment? Would any of these exposures seize the ethereal quality I pursued?

From La Mancha, we ventured to Alicante's coast, where Bofill's La Muralla Roja residential complex towered defiant on steep cliffs above endless ocean views. In my vision, the building's twisted corridors and dizzying crenelated staircases stood as an impregnable castle, its walls beckoned to be scaled.

We arrived at this magnificent structure to find our contact absent. Rafael's Castilian Spanish met vacant stares from locals who spoke only Valencian. We spent most of the morning in a seemingly futile attempt to access the building, as precious early light faded while security guards questioned our credentials.

Glen Allison

The weight of *The L.A. Times'* expectations pressed down on me as the sun rose higher; harsh midday shadows threatened to destroy the shots I'd traveled so far to capture. As I stood before La Muralla Roja, exhausted and sweaty, I questioned if I had challenged more than I could master. Deep within, I knew this Spanish quest would either forge or break my career.

Minutes stretched into two hours. I paced nervously as I calculated if distant exterior views could salvage the assignment. My mind raced through impossible contingencies—we couldn't return tomorrow since our evening flight loomed. No nearby structure could replace La Muralla Roja's iconic presence.

The security guard disappeared, then returned with a colleague. They conferred in rapid Valencian as they gestured toward us repeatedly. My stomach tightened as their animated conversation fell silent. The guard approached; keys jangled at his side. Would he wave us away or unlock the gate? In that suspended moment hung weeks of planning and my professional future.

At last, our persistence prevailed and we gained entry.

But La Muralla Roja's vertiginous staircases tested more than my artistic vision. As I carried heavy equipment up narrow steps in the summer heat, dizziness assaulted me. One misstep could shatter not only equipment but a dream. Each level unveiled new architectural vistas—and new anxieties to confront.

Our final challenge loomed at La Fábrica, Bofill's bizarre yet mesmerizing office and home that was born from abandoned factory ruins. Before the towering silos, fatigue and doubt invaded. The magnificent structure seemed to dwarf my novice attempts to capture its essence. *Who was I to presume I could translate Bofill's genius through my lens?* Past failures whispered that I remained that same struggling photographer, just on costlier ground.

Yet here, amid industrial decay and visionary design, I discovered the perfect metaphor for my own growth. Like Bofill with his factory ruins, I had now begun to reshape my life's raw materials into something beautiful and purposeful.

There, surrounded by our quest's achievements, I realized I had become the knight-errant of my own story. Though battle scars marked our journey, my will soared higher than ever.

When the magazine appeared on August 28, 1977—featuring La Muralla Roja on the cover and spreads of Bofill's office and Don Quixote's windmills—I experienced triumph beyond professional success. I had tilted at windmills and vanquished all doubt. I had pursued impossible dreams and manifested them into reality.

In that moment, I grasped my journey's true gift surpassed the stunning photographs. It revealed the unassailable reality that with perseverance, imagination, and a touch of madness, any dream could manifest. Like Don Quixote, I had discovered the potential of visionary insight—and thus blazed a path that defied conventional limits. My quest expanded beyond mere goal achievement—it illuminated the far-reaching impact of the pursuit.

The force that drove me to chase these impossible dreams in Spain now altered my perception of the world and my place in it. I had tapped a hidden reservoir of resilience that strengthened with each challenge.

Though these insights had not yet fully crystallized, they promised vast possibilities.

Chapter 6 - The Science of Dreaming Big

Dream magic ignites precisely at the intersection of imagination and our limiting realities.

Our dream waits not in some distant tomorrow but in our next deliberate move. The bridge from fantasy to fulfillment exists only in what we choose to do right now. By consciously connecting today's small actions with tomorrow's vision, we can build momentum that accumulates into significant progress.

Nice theory, but my own path twisted through messy terrain.

During those sleepless nights in my van-turned-home so long ago, positive thoughts alone failed to pay my bills. Only when I confronted my limitations while I held fast to my dreams did breakthrough begin.

Some mornings, my chanting echoed like shouts into a void. Yet gradually, I expanded my efforts to face reality as I refused to surrender hope. This new spirit gradually reshaped my world.

The journey—perhaps for all who travel this path—was arduous. To overcome my financial crisis seemed as impossible as walking on water. Each small assignment loomed as a desperate gamble rather than a stepping stone. Yet through my daily Buddhist practice and persistent action, "impossible" gradually lost its sway over me, even as doubt stalked my steps.

The courage to dream big, to envision a reality beyond our present circumstances and abilities, exceeds mere idle fantasy. It functions as an essential psychological tool that can reshape our mental landscape.[1]

> "Sometimes you wake up. Sometimes the fall kills you. And sometimes, when you fall, you fly."—Neil Gaiman's line spoken by Joseph Gordon-Levitt as Dream in the movie, *The Sandman*[2]

This evocative line captures the exquisite uncertainty that accompanies any worthwhile dream. When we step beyond our boundaries into uncharted territory, we cannot know the outcome in advance—this is precisely what makes the journey exciting. What appears as a potential fall might become the very moment we discover our capacity for flight, but only if we can summon the courage to leap beyond the familiar can we unleash regenerative capacity when we confront our challenges directly with courage.

This principle echoes in *The Diary of Anaïs Nin, Vol. 3*, where she declares: "Life shrinks or expands in proportion to one's courage."[3] Renewed determination changes everything.

My early Buddhist practice began to rewire my brain to detect new possibilities. Our greatest advances await just beyond "can't." The line between falling and flying exists only through perception.

In his book, *Never Play it Safe: A Practical Guide to Freedom, Creativity, and a Life You Love,* Chase Jarvis states, "Your limitations live only in your mind. But if you use your imagination, your possibilities become limitless."[4]

During my darkest periods, joy and happiness appeared as distant realms beyond reach. Even as Buddhism sparked inspiration, my thoughts frequently raced toward potential disasters rather than finding comfort in present achievements. As I learned to recognize victories amid ongoing struggles, this evolved into its own practice—one I vowed to master.

In *Learned Optimism: How to Change Your Mind and Your Life*, Dr. Martin Seligman, father of positive psychology, examines learned optimism and its impact on life. He explores the balance between optimistic thinking and pragmatic reality assessment, vital for sustained motivation while one confronts life's challenges. This approach enables dreamers to preserve their vision while they navigate reality's obstacles.[5]

Dr. Seligman's insights on learned optimism paralleled my own faltering journey from despair to hope.

While Buddhism provided tools for renewal, my entrenched thought patterns resisted change. Even after successful assignments, imposter syndrome would often strike—a voice that whispered each achievement stemmed from luck rather than growing expertise. Slowly, I began to understand a crucial factor: when I balanced optimism with practical action, I could acknowledge these doubts but not permit them to dictate my choices.

Unknown to me at the start, my Buddhist studies had aligned naturally with these psychological principles.

More crucially, it inspired my perseverance and offered concrete methods to summon inner strength and wisdom amid challenges. Faith alone can waver, but when we create undeniable actual proof, it revolutionizes everything. This reflects the Buddhist principle of "changing poison into medicine"—the concept that obstacles can become opportunities for renewal and evolution, but only when we access our inner wisdom, courage, and life force.[6]

The theory sounds compelling, but how do we apply this in daily life?

In their landmark article "Posttraumatic Growth" published in *Psychological Inquiry*, psychologists Richard Tedeschi and Lawrence Calhoun discovered that significant adversity often sparks positive psychological changes, including heightened life appreciation, deeper relationships, and a stronger sense of personal strength.[7]

When I first encountered research on post-traumatic growth, memories of my father's aggressive, sometimes violent nature, erupted with renewed force. *How could such darkness birth light?* Yet even as I questioned this possibility, I recognized how hardships had forged resilience I might never have discovered on an easier path. Still, some days the burden of past hurts and failures outweighed any wisdom they might have kindled.

When I examine my life's journey, I see that the pursuit of dreams itself remolded me, regardless of outcomes. Yes, I've had many failures along the way. But each setback forged grit, each small victory built confidence. The quest for the impossible dream, I discovered, shapes the seeker as profoundly as the quest itself.

Miguel de Cervantes, through Don Quixote, proclaimed: "Too much sanity may be madness — and maddest of all: to see life as it is, and not as it should be!"[8]

This insight aligns with psychologist Albert Bandura's "self-efficacy" concept. His influential 1997 book, *Self-efficacy: The Exercise of Control*, stands as a cornerstone in social cognitive theory that illuminates our understanding of human motivation and behavior. Bandura's research reveals that people with high self-efficacy view difficult tasks as challenges to master, not threats to avoid.[9]

Bandura's research validates my stumbling path decades ago toward self-belief. Though I didn't recognize it then, each small photography assignment served as my own test case for his theory.

In words attributed to Ralph Waldo Emerson: "What lies behind us and what lies before us are tiny matters compared to what lies within us."[10] This insight captures the essence of self-belief and inner power.

This mindset opens pathways to unlimited possibilities and can reshape not just our circumstances but our essential nature. Yet it demands more than mere positivity—we need to discover ways to activate our internal strength to propel change into value-creative momentum.

In his 1990 book, *Flow: The Psychology of Optimal Experience*, psychologist Mihaly Csikszentmihalyi reflects: "The best moments in our lives are not the passive, receptive, relaxing times.... The best moments emerge when a person's body or mind stretches to its limits in a voluntary effort to accomplish something difficult and worthwhile."[11]

Between Faith and Fear

Success in Spain illuminated a vital insight: achievement doesn't eliminate doubt—it teaches us to navigate uncertainty with greater skill.

Sara Blakely's path from door-to-door fax machine salesperson to billionaire founder of Spanx exemplifies how seemingly impossible dreams can become reality. After she failed the LSAT twice and abandoned her law school aspirations, Blakely spent seven years selling fax machines door-to-door in Florida, where she faced constant rejection and limited prospects.

Her entrepreneurial journey began with just $5,000 in savings and a simple frustration: she couldn't find the right undergarment to wear under white pants. She used scissors to cut the feet off her pantyhose and discovered her makeshift solution worked better than anything on the market. This moment of practical innovation sparked her vision.

With no business education, industry connections, or manufacturing experience, Blakely wrote her own patent application to save the $3,000 lawyer fee. When she approached hosiery manufacturers, she met universal rejection. The male-dominated industry dismissed her idea repeatedly until one manufacturer, moved by his daughters' belief in her concept, decided to help.

Without a budget for traditional advertising, Blakely demonstrated her product in person in department store aisles and sent sample products to Oprah Winfrey's wardrobe stylists.

When Oprah named Spanx one of her "Favorite Things" in 2000, sales exploded.

Blakely's remarkable achievement lies in her complete ownership retention without external investment. She claimed the title of youngest self-made female billionaire in history, with Forbes valuing Spanx at $1.2 billion in 2012—merely 12 years after its founding.

"Don't be intimidated by what you don't know," Blakely advises. "That can be your greatest strength and ensure that you do things differently from everyone else."[12]

Her journey demonstrates how innovation, persistence, and resilience can reshape everyday frustrations into extraordinary success, even without conventional resources or experience.

Persistence through repeated failure almost always precedes extraordinary achievement.

After my sojourn in Spain, I stood at the threshold of self-awakening and my next adventure. I had begun to grasp a principle that would later become central to my philosophy: the true value of dreaming the impossible dream dwelled not just in potential achievements, but in my reinvention through the pursuit. Courage, resilience, and determination aren't merely tools for success but the essential rewards themselves.

When we venture into unexplored territory, we can unlock doors to magical experiences forever closed to those who remain within familiar boundaries.

Hidden Powers

Throughout my extended travels during the decades after my adventure in Spain, I've witnessed the extraordinary effects of small brave actions manifest in the lives of others—ordinary people who faced extraordinary challenges as each wrote their own impossible dreams into reality.

I remember Elisa, a single mother I met during my time in Barcelona. She worked as a hotel cleaner by day and studied English by night. She often practiced her limited English speaking abilities with tourists during brief moments between rooms. Her dream to become a tour guide seemed distant—her accent thick, her grammar hesitant, her circumstances demanding.

Many of her co-workers advised her to "be realistic," and suggested that women her age, especially those from her background, rarely succeeded when they tried to change careers. When she told me about these warnings, I encouraged her to tap her innate capability and strength of will and to continue her charge forward toward her dream. Then I shared with her my own path when I discovered the Mystic Law.

Elisa rose to the challenge and refused to yield to the difficult realities of her life. Each day, when I returned to the hotel after my shoot of local iconic tourist sites, she would approach me with simple questions to practice her language skills. "How did your visit to La Sagrada Familia go today?" or "Have you seen Parc Güell?" Each interaction served as both classroom and affirmation.

Three years later, I returned to find Elisa leading tours through the Gothic Quarter. Her English remained imperfect though better, but it was her passion that ignited each historical detail. When tourists complimented her authentic delivery, they unknowingly validated her impossible dream.

Over the years, I've collected such personal journeys like treasured photographs—Javier in Spain, who reshaped an abandoned rural property into an eco-retreat after being laid off at fifty-seven; Lucia in Puerto Rico, who opened a neighborhood library in her living room when budget cuts closed the public one her children depended upon; Carlos in a coastal town in Mexico, who learned computer programming through free online courses after his fishing industry collapsed.

None achieved overnight success. All encountered skepticism, setbacks, and self-doubt. Their paths forward rarely resembled straight lines. Instead, their journeys took the shape of spirals. They sometimes circled back through familiar struggles before they advanced to new territory. What united them wasn't extraordinary talent or luck, but extraordinary persistence—the ability to hold both their dreams and their current reality in sharp focus simultaneously.

Howard Schultz's journey from housing project to business visionary exemplifies this delicate balance between impossible dreams and stark reality. Born in 1953 in Brooklyn's Bayview Housing Projects, Schultz grew up as he watched his father struggle through a series of low-paying jobs. When Schultz was seven years old, his father, working as a delivery driver, broke an ankle. With no health insurance or worker's compensation, the family faced financial devastation. "I saw the fracturing of the American dream and my father's dignity,"[13] Schultz later recalled. But this childhood trauma became both wound and driving force.

After Schultz became the first person in his family to attend college (on a football scholarship), he worked his way up through sales jobs and into a management position that sent him on a fateful 1981 business trip to Milan, Italy. During a client visit—a small coffee bean company called Starbucks—he experienced an epiphany in Milan's coffee bars. He envisioned the creation of a "third place" in America between work and home, centered around coffee culture and community.

When Schultz pitched his vision to the Starbucks owners, they rejected it. Undeterred, he left his secure executive position at a housewares company to pursue what colleagues considered a quixotic dream. It took a year of rejections—250 potential investors declined to fund him—before he raised enough capital to open his first coffee shop.

Even after he acquired full ownership of Starbucks in 1987, Schultz faced near-bankruptcy in the early 1990s when rapid expansion strained the company's resources. During this period, he maintained what he called "the fragile balance between dreams and reality."[14] While he never abandoned his vision of building a national coffee culture in a country dominated by fast food and instant coffee, he confronted his harsh financial realities with pragmatic determination and often worked through sleepless nights to solve immediate problems.

"I never dreamed more than five years ahead," Schultz revealed in his memoir; "but I always dreamed five years ahead."[15] This approach—he dreamed audaciously while he confronted current challenges—elevated a local coffee bean retailer into a global phenomenon with over 33,000 stores in 80 countries.

Schultz's story gains particular relevance through his navigation between faith and fear, between vision and vulnerability. "Very few people, whether you've been in that job before or not, get into the seat and believe today that they can make a difference," he once reflected. "They believe that the problems are too big, the bureaucracy is too complex, the systems can't be fixed."[16]

While my journey led to international photography and authorship, the people in these examples arrived at different destinations—some modest by conventional measures, others extraordinary in scope. Yet each represents the essential victory: an unwillingness to surrender agency over one's life, regardless of circumstance. This refusal to relinquish control demands a dynamic balance between bold vision and present reality, an orientation toward life that honors both possibility and present limitations simultaneously.

Both Blakely with her makeshift solution and Schultz with his coffee revelation reshaped their reality. These visionaries never muted their practical voice but instead invited it into dialogue with their aspirations. They acknowledged every barrier and refused to bow before any. They viewed rejection not as final verdict but as temporary resistance that tested their resolve.

Within us resides two vital voices in constant conversation. The first calculates odds, measures resources, and assesses boundaries. The second envisions futures that no map has charted and possibilities that defy precedent. Most people turn up the volume on one while silencing the other, which creates either hollow fantasy or stunted resignation. Our true potential ignites when we refuse this false trade-off.

World-changers like Blakely and Schultz never muted their practical voice for comfort. They invited it to challenge their vision while never allowing it to become a jailer. They acknowledged every obstacle precisely, then found the narrow crack where light broke through. They faced rejection not as defeat but as intelligence gathering that strengthened their approach.

This delicate balance between immediate reality and future vision often creates inner tension. Yet, this internal dialogue forms not a battlefield but a workshop where today's limits and tomorrow's breakthroughs collide to create innovation. The realistic voice asks "What exists?" while the visionary voice declares "What must exist!"

Your finest achievements wait not in silencing either voice, but in their electric connection. From this creative friction springs exactly the insight needed to advance your boldest aspiration one tangible step forward today.

The American poet Robert Frost captured this essence in his words: "Two roads diverged in a wood, and I - I took the one less traveled by, And that has made all the difference."[17]

As I advanced in my early career days from limitation to possibility, Buddhist practice strengthened my resolve, yet some days the old despair still overwhelmed me. Back then, an abyss separated intellectual understanding from emotional reality. Even as my portfolio expanded, the dark clouds of past failures sometimes paralyzed me before important shoots. But each challenge I faced with quixotic courage reinforced not just a burgeoning belief in my ability to overcome obstacles but unleashed more capacity to do so.

This oscillation between resolve and hopelessness occurs naturally on any meaningful journey. Our greatest visions die not from lack of capability but from this momentary paralysis where thinking displaces doing.

In the first century BC, Seneca, the Stoic philosopher of Ancient Rome, observed: "It is not because things are difficult that we do not dare; it is because we do not dare that they are difficult."[18]

Our future hinges on these moments when we step forward despite uncertainty. Those who wait for confidence rarely begin. Those who move amid their questions reach heights others only imagine.

During my photographic journey, I gradually discovered that meaningful achievement isn't separate from struggle—it emerges through it.

The impossible surrenders not to idle dreams, but to resolute determination backed by relentless action that refuses to accept defeat.

Chapter 7 - Hope and Optimism

Hope transforms pessimism into optimism. Hope is invincible. Hope changes everything. It changes winter into summer, darkness into dawn, descent into ascent, barrenness into creativity, agony into joy," declared Daisaku Ikeda. "Hope is the sun. It is light. It is passion. It is the fundamental force for life's blossoming."[1]

This radiant power of hope to pierce life's deepest trials echoes through the ages. Desmond Tutu once reflected, "Hope is being able to see that there is light despite all of the darkness."[2]

In the early 2000s, I met Desmond Tutu in Bali, Indonesia, at a conference dedicated to happiness, hope, and possibility. Before he ended his keynote address, Tutu shared a story that would resonate in my mind for years.

He spoke of a gangly, misshapen bird whose awkward appearance drew mockery from his peers. Shunned and isolated, the young bird carried the burden of otherness, yet something extraordinary stirred within him—an inexplicable dignity that exceeded his outer form.

While others saw only imperfection, the wise farmer who tended the flock perceived a hidden majesty in the bird's bearing. Day by day, the farmer nurtured this unique creature, focused not on appearances but on the promising essence within. As seasons passed, the ugly duckling's true nature emerged—not a common bird at all, but a magnificent eagle.

On the revelation day, the farmer lifted this renewed creature toward the endless sky and commanded with quiet authority, and in ever-increasing intensity: "Fly. Fly. Fly."

Without another word, Tutu suddenly dropped his microphone to the floor. The resultant crash thundered through the auditorium, leaving a silence heavy with meaning. Then, with characteristic grace and confident ease, he donned his floppy hat, descended from the stage, and vanished into the crowd. His dramatic exit left us to contemplate the profound simplicity of his message.

His exit embodied a potent metaphor for hope's elevating effect: sometimes we must release who we think we are to become who we're meant to be.

Tutu's vivid portrayal of the eagle taking flight carries a crucial lesson beyond mere inspiration—it emphasizes that hope without action remains unfulfilled potential. Hope, by itself, is not a plan. The farmer didn't simply believe in the bird's capabilities; he actively nurtured it day by day, acts that created conditions for remarkable change.

Similarly, our hopes must pair with deliberate steps toward change. Hope provides vision, but our consistent actions—often small and unglamorous—forge the path from vision to reality.

Your journey to establish concrete progress can begin with a practical exercise like this:

Shadows Illuminated

The capacity to see beyond current circumstances distinguishes those who merely survive from those who ultimately thrive.

Our most dire situations contain hidden seeds of renewal. Like the farmer who saw an eagle in what others dismissed as a misshapen duck, we should strive to perceive the spectacular potential that exists within our present limitations.

This perception demands honesty about where we stand without judgment that freezes our position. Journal your current reality with clarity—not to resign yourself to it but to establish the exact point from which you must launch. Then envision what might emerge from this precise challenge, not despite it but because of it.

Between these two points—what exists now and what could be—lies a small action that honors both. This action becomes the first plank in your bridge from present to future. Not a grand leap but a deliberate step that accepts current constraints, one that allows us to advance toward greater possibilities.

As you repeat this pattern—seeing clearly, envisioning honestly, acting deliberately—your mind develops new capacities. It begins to automatically detect opportunity within difficulty, purpose within pain, and direction amid disorientation.

The eagle flies not when someone simply tells it to soar but when it discovers its own wings. Your ascent can follow the same principle—hope paired with action

> creates the updraft that lifts you beyond current limitations into the vast sky of your fullest capacity.

The effectiveness lies in consistently linking honest assessment with forward movement—not the denial of struggles, but the actions to reshape your relationship with them. Over time, this mental habit reinforces thought patterns that sustain hope even during difficult periods.

When hope illuminates our path, we can shape our environment with intention and build foundations for success. A hopeful mindset radiates purpose and creates an invisible shield against the corrosive currents that surge with negativity around us. With a hopeful outlook, we can stand firm in the present moment, free from past regrets and future anxieties. Instead, hope will enable us to direct our energy toward the possibilities that arise.

I experienced this principle firsthand in an unexpected encounter that forever changed my perspective about how hope can steer action. Later in the evening, after Tutu's address and through a friend's gracious invitation—she was the event coordinator—I joined an intimate gathering for his farewell party.

While dignitaries filled the room, the two dozen young students—present at Tutu's specific request—claimed his attention. Here stood a man who saw beyond titles and status to recognize the seeds of future change. As music filled the air, Tutu launched into dance with an infectious joy and energy that defied his years; his movements expressed a vitality that humbled guests a quarter his age. His presence radiated the hope he so often championed.

Hidden Powers

When did you last surprise yourself? Perhaps you spoke up when you typically stay silent, extended kindness when resentment felt easier, or persisted through a challenge after your mind shouted "enough." These unexpected moments—when you acted beyond your usual limits—offer glimpses of your hidden capacity. What if these weren't anomalies but previews of who you could develop into? I ask because our conversation about hope isn't theoretical—it lives in these brief, remarkable instances when we exceed our own expectations and discover strengths we didn't know we possessed.

When our paths finally crossed that evening, Tutu's first words cut through all pretense. "What is your mission in life?" he asked, his penetrating gaze locked with mine.

The question, though unexpected, evoked my immediate response: "To expand, to encourage." His hand seized mine with the fervent surety of someone who had moved mountains with faith alone.

"Please inspire countless others," he said, his words bearing the weight of a vital mission to fulfill. Through that handshake, I sensed the pulse of his indomitable will—the same force that had helped reshape his nation from apartheid to democracy as he forged history hand-in-hand with Nelson Mandela.

You can begin to harness the same motivational energy that propelled Tutu by studying those whose journeys mirror the path you wish to walk:

Hero Echo

Our life shifts permanently when we move beyond casual admiration of great figures to deep absorption of their essential qualities. The difference exists between a tourist who takes photos of monuments and an apprentice who studies under a master—one collects souvenirs while the other acquires skills.

Select individuals whose journeys resonate with your own path. Study how they faced their early challenges, the specific ways they responded to major setbacks, and the daily habits they maintained during their darkest hours.

Examine how their influence expanded beyond themselves to affect others. These details contain the actual formula of greatness, not just its final appearance.

Notice the gap between your automatic responses and theirs. When you confront similar obstacles, what distinguishes your reaction from theirs? This honest comparison reveals exactly what you must develop within yourself.

Then hold an imaginary council with this figure. Ask what advice they would offer for your specific situation. This mental dialogue accesses a deeper wisdom than intellectual analysis alone. Their imagined voice often cuts through confusion with unexpected clarity.

What matters most is not the prestige of your chosen mentor but how thoroughly you absorb their essence. When Tutu asked about my mission and commanded, "Please inspire countless others," he passed a torch. Such moments of connection—whether direct or through

> intensive study—plant seeds that grow into mighty capacities.
>
> Your heroes achieved greatness not through superhuman abilities but through ordinary qualities applied with extraordinary consistency. These same qualities await your cultivation.

The morning after my encounter with Tutu, dawn revealed one final synchronicity.

As I drove into town, my car halted at the head of a line of vehicles, stopped by an approaching motorcade. Sirens pierced the morning calm, red lights sliced through the early haze, and diplomat flags snapped in the wind atop the lead vehicle. Inside sat Desmond Tutu, bound for his flight back to South Africa. This perfect alignment—my car first in line to witness his departure—surpassed mere coincidence. The universe itself appeared to arrange this final moment of our connection, a reminder that when we flow with hope's current, even brief encounters can carry extraordinary meaning.

Glen Allison

The Dual Voices Within

In words attributed to Martin Luther King, Jr.: "Let your hopes, not your hurts, shape your future."[3] This message resonate in my mind as I contemplate my own battle with hopelessness and pessimism in my youth.

Decades before my pivotal encounter with Desmond Tutu, I battled an internal dialogue that threatened to extinguish the light of possibility. Some mornings during my early struggles, I'd wake to find my thoughts already full with worst-case scenarios—a habit that had served as a protective mechanism for so long it felt like an old companion.

What's the point of hoping? That cynical voice whispered throughout my youth. *Better to expect the worst and be pleasantly surprised.* How often had I retreated to this defensive pessimism with the belief it would shield me from disappointment? I built walls against potential hurt, blind to how these same barriers blocked the very force that could elevate my existence.

"Some people, when they experience a series of sad events, conclude that they are unfortunate and weak, and extinguish the light of hope with their own hands. But such an attitude itself is what makes one unhappy,"[4] Daisaku Ikeda observed.

As I continue to delve deeper into understanding human potential, I recognize why hope exerts such an important influence over our lives. It surpasses mere positive thinking—it's a vital energy source that revolutionizes our approach to challenges. Those who nurture abundant hope move through life with unmistakable passion and zest. Their energy radiates differently, more vibrantly, more sustainably.

Hope requires us to remain open to possibility, to stand vulnerable before life's uncertainties. This openness—this willingness to risk disappointment—ignites the magnificent energy that drives extraordinary lives forward.

In Desmond Tutu's ugly duckling story, I see my earlier self in that awkward bird. How often had I cut my own wings, too afraid to test their strength? The farmer in Tutu's tale perceived beyond surface limitations to the majestic potential within. But to serve as your own witness, your own witness to possibility, often proves to be a far greater challenge.

Through my study of human consciousness, I've explored the internal dialogue that shapes our perception of everything we encounter. Within each of us exists a fundamental duality—two distinct voices vie to interpret our experiences: one lifts us up, the other knocks us down.

Nelson Mandela, the anti-apartheid activist, became the first black president of South Africa in 1994. His evolution during his 27 years of imprisonment offers a remarkable example of hope's extraordinary ability to exceed even the most crushing circumstances. Confined to a tiny cell on Robben Island—just eight feet by seven feet—Mandela faced conditions designed to break not just the body but the mind. For 18 of those years, he slept on a straw mat on the floor, performed hard labor in a limestone quarry that permanently damaged his eyesight, and was permitted only one visitor and one letter every six months.

Despite these hardships, when he came to power, he didn't seek vengeance against those who had imprisoned him. Instead, he created enduring value by establishing the Truth and Reconciliation Commission, fostering national healing through dialogue rather than retribution. Surely this is an exemplary quality for any leader—a reflection of deep character and uncompromising integrity.

Mandela's story resonates with extraordinary meaning beyond mere endurance through his remarkable internal growth. Rather than allowing bitterness to consume him, he used his imprisonment as what he later called "the university of life." This process of turning confinement into education offers a compelling metaphor for our own challenges.

> **The Hidden University**
>
> Your current limitations contain lessons available nowhere else.
>
> Each restriction, each barrier, each painful constraint serves not as a prison but as a specialized institution designed to teach wisdom impossible to acquire in comfort.
>
> Name your challenge—financial hardship, health crisis, relationship breakdown—and grant it the dignity of a formal title: "The University of Financial Constraint," "The Institute of Health Challenges," "The Academy of Relationship Reconstruction." This simple act of renaming shifts your relationship from victim to student, from passive recipient to active learner.

Hidden Powers

> Within this personal academy, specific courses await your attendance. The curriculum includes lessons in patience you cannot learn through ease, resilience impossible to develop in security, and insights available only through difficulty.
>
> Identify what this unique environment offers that no other circumstance could provide.
>
> Take inventory of what you've already acquired in this classroom of challenge. What skills have you developed? What lessons now live in your bones? What wisdom ripens even now as you face this difficulty?
>
> Seek guidance from those who excelled in similar circumstances—whether through their presence, their writings, or their example. These "professors" earned their credentials through their own suffering and emergence.
>
> Schedule regular hours for extraction and application of this wisdom. Just as Mandela turned twenty-seven years of imprisonment into a university that prepared him to lead a nation, your limitations offer preparation for purposes you cannot yet imagine.

Mandela learned Afrikaans—the language of his captors—not just to understand their conversations but to connect with them as human beings. "If you talk to a man in a language he understands, that goes to his head," Mandela later explained. "If you talk to him in HIS language, that goes to his heart."[5]

In his autobiography *The Long Walk to Freedom*, Mandela reveals the conscious choice he made about his internal dialogue: "I knew that people expected me to harbor anger toward whites. But I had none. In prison, my anger toward whites decreased, but my hatred for the system grew. I wanted South Africa to see that I loved even my enemies while I hated the system that turned us against one another."[6]

This deliberate cultivation of hope and compassion rather than hatred enabled Mandela to emerge from decades of imprisonment not as a broken man who sought revenge, but as a visionary leader able to unite a deeply divided nation.

When he finally was freed and left prison on February 11, 1990, he said: "As I walked out the door toward the gate that would lead to my freedom, I knew if I didn't leave my bitterness and hatred behind, I would still be in prison.... There were many dark moments when my faith in humanity was sorely tested, but I would not and could not give myself up to despair. That way lays defeat."[7]

The aftermath unfolded as nothing short of miraculous—Mandela negotiated a peaceful end to apartheid and became the president of South Africa. Rather than seek retribution, he championed a vision of a unified "Rainbow Nation" that overcame racial divisions. At his presidential inauguration, he invited his former jailers to sit in the front row as honored guests, a gesture that embodied his understanding that hope must exceed even the deepest personal wounds to create meaningful change and unprecedented value.

Nelson Mandela set an extraordinary example. Though he was only one voice, he understood that each of us can unleash boundless possibility even when harsh circumstances constrain us.

When we heed this aspect of ourselves, the world blossoms into a landscape of potential opportunities that await discovery. Challenges become invitations for growth; setbacks become redirection toward greater outcomes. This is our soaring eagle that rides thermal currents of possibility and surveys the vast panorama of what might be.

The other voice stays fixed on what could go wrong. It scans for threats, calculates potential failures, and urges caution at every turn. This earthbound critic keeps us tethered to "reality"—or at least perhaps a limited interpretation of it. This voice believes its vigilance ensures our safety, unaware that it simultaneously constrains us.

> "Hope is a good thing, maybe the best of things, and no good thing ever dies."—Andy Dufresne in the movie, *The Shawshank Redemption*[8]

This simple yet striking line speaks to hope's extraordinary resilience. Throughout the film, Andy faces seemingly insurmountable obstacles—wrongful imprisonment, corruption, violence, and decades of confinement—yet he maintains an inner light that ultimately guides him to freedom. His hope isn't naive optimism; it's a deliberate choice to see beyond his current reality to what *could* be.

This same choice faces us daily: will we listen to the voice that sees only walls, or the one that imagines tunnels through them? The strength of Andy's story lies not just in his eventual escape, but in how hope sustained his humanity during those long years in darkness.

> ACTION: If you want to seize control in an effort to rise above these two battling voices, identify which one dominates your thinking by keeping a simple tally for one day. Make a mark each time you catch yourself as you focus on threats versus possibilities. This awareness alone often shifts the balance without complex techniques.

I've learned to identify both perspectives within myself. Neither voice lacks truth—the eagle needs occasional ground contact, and the critic sometimes prevents costly mistakes. But I've discovered that the quality of my life hinges on which voice dominates my internal narrative. The choice between how I perceive a world of opportunity or a landscape of danger shapes not just my experience, but the outcomes I create.

When Tutu's microphone crashed to the stage floor in Bali, the harsh reverberant sound shook us from complacency, much like life's challenges can jolt us from limiting beliefs. "Fly. Fly. Fly." The command reaches beyond that liberated bird—it beckons to all who restrain themselves from their full potential.

Ikeda reflected, "When people become pessimistic, it is as if they hide themselves behind dark clouds that prevent joy and hope from entering their hearts."[9] I've sheltered behind those clouds and believed they offered protection. But true sanctuary emerges not when we hide from life's storms but when we develop the strength to soar above them.

Hidden Powers

Our minds often remain trapped in the cage of immediate circumstance until we rise above it. When troubles surround us like thick forest, each tree appears as an insurmountable barrier. Our vision extends only to the next obstacle, each problem magnified by proximity until it fills our entire field of view. When your face is pressed hard against the bark of a single tree, your eyes can't see very far.

We need to lift ourselves above this dense undergrowth. Imagine elevation to a height where your current situation appears not as an all-consuming crisis but as a small segment in the vast landscape of your life. From this altitude, patterns emerge that remain invisible at ground level. Past obstacles that once loomed large now appear as mere dots on your journey map.

The eagle sees what the earthbound creature cannot—not because its eyes function differently but because its position affords greater vision. Our minds work the same way. Rise above your circumstances, not to escape them but to see them truly for the first time.

Hope requires courage. It embodies the determination to take flight despite uncertain winds. Each time I choose hope over habitual pessimism, I honor that brief but meaningful connection I shared with Tutu. Years after asked, his penetrating question—"What is your mission in life?"—still urges me to rise beyond my self-imposed limitations—to soar above mere concern for my own happiness.

A 2020 study in the journal *Global Epidemiology* reveals hope's tangible impact. "A greater sense of hope was associated with better physical health and health behavior outcomes: fewer chronic conditions, lower risk of cancer, and fewer sleep problems, higher psychological well-being, and better social well-being."[10] Science confirms what my journey demonstrates—hope elevates emotion to become a life-giving force.

We cannot simply hope away obstacles; we need to actively dismantle them. Even when we face seemingly insurmountable challenges, when we identify one actionable step forward, we prevent hope's deterioration into fantasy.

History's most effective change-makers—like Mandela and Tutu—altered circumstances precisely because they refused to separate hope from action. Hope rises above denial of life's challenges—it enables us to envision the opportunities within them. In its purest essence, hope aligns with the universe's fundamental rhythm—The Mystic Law—as it heralds a future that pulses with possibility and victory.

A life infused with hope flows unstoppably.

The optimism the Dalai Lama advocates isn't blind positivity that ignores problems, but a practical orientation that recognizes challenges while it maintains confidence in our capacity to address them. With characteristic simplicity, he concludes: "Choose to be optimistic; it feels better."[11]

In that choice, united with our efforts to engage the natural energy, wisdom, and rhythms of the universe, lies our ability to excel—to soar—to thrive.

Darkness does not define light.

Chapter 8 - Transforming Adversity into Benefit

Though my understanding of hope and optimism matured over decades, my early attempts to elevate my life condition were fraught with doubt and obstacles—challenges I now recognize were essential to build my inner strength, determination, and tenacity. These experiences unveiled wisdom about converting hardship into advantage, even when the way forward remained shrouded. Looking back at those pivotal years illuminates how our most harrowing struggles can blossom into unexpected evolution and inner awakening.

Chasing Light

"A Photographer's Leap of Faith"

Holland, April 1978

In early 1978, magazine assignments surged with increasing frequency as my photography business gained momentum. This career upturn aligned with another momentous event—my marriage to a talented writer, Tina Rubin, whom I'd met at a Buddhist gathering. Our partnership clicked like two puzzle pieces finding their match and the instant recognition of an eternal connection. Three months later, we married. Far beyond our creative synergy, we shared an ineffable bond that eclipsed even love—a sacred spiritual dynamic that imbued everyday moments with the radiance of intertwined souls. Our creative aspirations merged with this union in perfect synchronicity.

Over morning coffee at our tiny kitchen table, we dared to dream beyond the confines of our modest Los Angeles existence. The world stretched before us, ready for exploration, capture, and chronicle through our combined talents.

One January morning, an impromptu decision accelerated our career opportunities. During what should have been a routine visit to the *LA Times* magazine office, my pulse quickened as an audacious idea seized hold.

With our latest assignment photos and story in hand, and little to lose, I heard myself casually mention our "upcoming trip" to France—a pure invention born of equal parts eagerness and determination.

The words suspended in the air like a high-wire act without a safety net. Tina masked her surprise at my comment and played along astutely. I hoped this bold fiction might propel our careers —at least I wanted to plant a seed.

To our astonishment and quite coincidentally, the editor revealed her plans already underway for an upcoming special issue on France. She had chosen another photographer for food and garden features. But since we would "already be there" and considering my background in architecture, she could justify assigning us the residential pieces since the magazine wouldn't need to cover our international flight expenses.

Hidden Powers

The timing surpassed mere chance—our synchronistic rhythm had positioned us precisely where opportunity would discover us. When I reflect now, I marvel at how the universe aligns to help us achieve our dreams, if our determination burns strong enough, even when they begin as desperate hopes, or spark from an audacious move as in this instance. Yet the outcome surpassed mere luck—it demonstrated how bold action, even from a place of uncertainty, can launch extraordinary opportunities. Our road ahead would prove challenging, but in that moment, a spark of possibility had ignited into tangible momentum.

Our euphoria when we left that office collapsed abruptly as we began to face our brutal financial reality. Our credit cards stood maxed out, our bank account barely maintained a pulse, and this golden opportunity—perhaps our best shot at breaking into international photography assignments as a team—threatened to dissolve before our eyes.

We had no way to fund the flight costs to Europe.

Each passing day felt like watching sand pour through an hourglass we couldn't turn over. The following weeks loomed as a gauntlet of closed doors and depleted resources, but defeat wasn't an option.

And then, the unexpected happened ...

A possibility materialized when I stumbled upon a magazine feature about Holland's Keukenhof gardens. The photographs of tulip fields with geometric patterns stretching to the horizon sparked an idea. Perhaps we could extend our French assignment to include Holland. If successful, we might convince the Dutch tourist office to provide complimentary press access. The next morning, we pitched a tulip story to the *LA Times* editor. To our relief, she agreed to cover our train fare from Paris to Amsterdam if we delivered compelling photos.

At last, we secured the foothold we needed.

Within hours, driven by our next bold move, we presented our credentials at the Dutch tourist office in Los Angeles and framed them strategically to emphasize our strongest accomplishments. The response exceeded our wildest hopes: they offered us a press junket including round-trip KLM flights, hotel accommodations, a free rental car, and a guide.

The Los Angeles sunshine intensified as we emerged victorious. That evening, we celebrated with champagne we couldn't afford —each sip infused with possibility.

Our cramped apartment turned into a war room of creative ambition. Dog-eared maps claimed every surface like exotic wallpaper. Research books from the public library teetered in precarious stacks that threatened to avalanche at any moment, and handwritten notes multiplied like scattered puzzle pieces. The air crackled with promise and caffeine-fueled determination.

Far beyond the garden shoot, we unearthed stories demanding to be told: centuries-old cheese markets still operated in traditional fashion, resourceful women who had converted historic windmills into homes, innovative warehouse loft conversions, and the vibrant world of canal houseboats. Though we kept it secret, our ambition soared—we would capture enough material for an entire magazine issue on Holland, created on speculation, of course.

The morning of departure dawned with surreal clarity. At our first-class seats, a bottle of champagne with a white bow materialized. We felt like interlopers in someone else's fairy tale.

Through the window, the setting sun painted defiant streaks of crimson and mauve across a boundless sky, as if nature herself celebrated our audacity. Below us, the vast Atlantic dissolved into darkness, much like the reality of the daily life we'd left behind.

We soared not just toward Amsterdam but toward a future we would forge ourselves—one filled with bold dreams. In that moment, suspended between two continents and an ever-expanding horizon of hope, we felt the quiet thrill of unlimited possibility.

Glen Allison

Winter's Awakening

Reality struck harshly as we descended toward Schiphol Airport. My stomach lurched at the sight below.

"Oh my god," Tina gasped as she pressed her face to the window. "It's all white."

An endless expanse of snow stretched beyond view; in an instant, the hope in our hearts became frozen. In our meticulous planning, we had neglected the most basic element—weather. Holland lay imprisoned by a merciless late winter. Our dreams, our careers, everything hinged on those dormant tulips breaking through the snow before our time and limited funds evaporated.

I suppressed the wave of panic that rose in my throat. *We can't have come this far just to fail.*

The magic of Europe, however, prevailed over our fears. After hotel check-in, we explored Amsterdam's icy rain-washed streets, where a slight hint of reprieve lingered in the air— freezing rain was better than falling snow. As the frozen streets began to thaw, rekindled tentative hope began to rise. Along the Prinsengracht canal, the steady patter of raindrops against our shared umbrella blended with the city's ancient pulse.

"Look at those reflections," Tina murmured as she pointed to canal house lights shimmering on the dark water. "Even in the rain, it's perfect."

Despite our uncertainty, each step felt right—we had forged an impossible dream into reality through sheer determination and creative impulse. Now we just had to trust we could summon the same force that had propelled us this far. Those tulips must bloom. They *had* to.

Amsterdam embraced us in its centuries-old charms. We found temporary sanctuary from our anxieties in dimly lit cafes where animated conversations and clinking glasses created a lively, unorchestrated collage of Dutch social life. The evening lights fractured on the dark canal waters, rippling reflections of the city's night. At the Rembrandt Haus, surrounded by echoes of artistic genius, I wondered: *Would our own work ever achieve even a fragment of such lasting impact?*

Beyond Amsterdam's borders, we uncovered a story that embodied the essence of human resilience. Near Volendam, our earlier research guided us to a widow living in a windmill. As I photographed her extraordinary home, Tina, with gentle patience, extracted the woman's heart-rending story.

"I haven't touched the windmill blades since that day," the widow confided, her weathered hands quivering slightly as she clutched her teacup. "Sometimes I hear them crying in the wind."

Her husband had perished in a tragic accident the previous year, struck by the massive, whirling blades. Their shared dream home had become the vessel of her deepest loss. Since that day, the blades had stood motionless, frozen like her grief.

For our visit, however, something awakened. She rose suddenly from her chair, keys jingling in her hand. "Perhaps," she said softly, "it's time."

As she unlocked those giant blades for the first time since her husband's death, neighbors appeared spontaneously, drawn by the revival of the ancient mechanism as it creaked back to life. We had come seeking picturesque dwelling photos but found ourselves witnessing a moment of life-altering healing—a reminder that rebirth often arrives bearing unexpected gifts.

With rapidly dwindling funds, we pressed on to France for our assignments there, though we harbored desperate hopes for blooming tulips upon our return. By our final day in Paris, we hit rock bottom—our resources completely exhausted, our stomachs as empty as our wallets.

"We still have each other," Tina reassured me that night. She attempted a smile as we huddled in our tiny hotel room. "And our determination." I nodded, but internally, doubt gnawed at my conviction.

The City of Light revealed an indifferent face as we trudged one last time back to our hotel, where tomorrow's complimentary breakfast loomed as potentially our last meal before our flight home. After breakfast, survival instinct conquered propriety as we tucked extra bread and fruit into our daypacks. Shame crept across my face.

At checkout, necessity spawned invention—and guilt. Each word of my fabricated story about a stolen wallet in Place Pigalle felt like I had swallowed broken glass. The kind-hearted desk clerk's acceptance of my U.S. check became both salvation and burden. *Never again,* I silently vowed. *Whatever it takes, I'll make this right.*

Four hours on a train delivered us back to Amsterdam, where bitter cold assaulted us like a slap in the face. Night approached with stark reality: we would spend our final hours on the train station's cold floor, sustained only by thoughts of the next night's airline meal. Our cash had vanished completely.

"We need a miracle," I whispered to myself as I stared out at the darkening city. *How can we traverse Holland for our remaining two shoots?*

Yet surrender remained unthinkable. Our Buddhist practice had taught us that our darkest moments often precede breakthroughs. We needed transportation to reach both the northern cheese market the next morning and the western tulip gardens in the afternoon, before we had to race back to Schiphol for our evening flight to L.A.

In a final gambit, I braced myself for one last push against seemingly impossible odds. With nervous fingers, I dialed the Amsterdam tourist office director. "You see," I explained. The words tasted like ash in my mouth. "My wallet was stolen…" The lie felt like a betrayal of everything we stood for, yet survival demanded it. Her offer of one more day's free car rental flooded me with relief—until she mentioned the catch.

The vehicle awaited at Schiphol Airport, an hour away by train, and we lacked even the fare.

Glen Allison

From Darkness to Bloom

The Amsterdam streets bit with newfound coldness.

Each step along the rain-slicked cobblestones echoed with memories of my desperate supermarket thefts years ago. The following minutes challenged my pride as I begged on Amsterdam's indifferent streets. The words clotted in my mouth with each request for spare change—a lesson in humility. Most people hurried past, averting their eyes. Each rejection stung, yet somehow fortified my resolve. We had crossed an ocean on audacity alone—we couldn't surrender now.

"This isn't how I pictured our European adventure," I confessed to Tina, who stood in the shelter of a doorway. Her eyes reflected both concern and resolute faith.

"We'll succeed," she promised. "We always do."

After what seemed like hours, a dignified businessman in a charcoal suit paused and studied me with piercing blue eyes. The depth in his gaze conveyed understanding rather than pity.

"I'll repay you," I vowed as he pressed ten guilders and his business card into my palm. "I promise."

He smiled faintly. "I know." Just two words, but they restored my dignity that empty pockets had threatened to shatter.

Those ten guilders became our pathway to possibility. Within the hour, we raced toward Schiphol and our waiting car, the gleaming precious coins now converted into train tickets clutched tightly in our hands.

Dawn painted the sky in watercolor grays as we reached the Alkmaar cheese market. Our night had passed in the car. We took turns watching for police patrols, our breaths creating ghost-like patterns on the windows. Throughout the ordeal, Tina's passionate embrace renewed my will and resolve.

The morning air carried the sharp bite of winter, but something else too—possibility.

"Look at that color." Tina pointed to the rows of golden Gouda wheels arranged by merchants in traditional dress. My stomach growled audibly at the sight, but I channeled that hunger into fierce concentration. Through my viewfinder, each cheese wheel glowed like a beacon, each merchant's movement a dance to capture and preserve.

"Sometimes our greatest difficulties forge our finest work," Tina observed, noticing my intensity. She was right—desperation had honed my vision to a razor's edge.

Throughout it all, one certainty blazed brighter than hunger: we must fight with every fiber of our being to manifest our wildest dreams. Self-doubt existed as a luxury we couldn't afford.

Keukenhof gardens in Lisse awaited as our final assignment destination of the day—and our last chance to claim full victory. But each barren tulip field we passed delivered a body blow to our hopes. Yet the crowded parking lot ahead kindled tentative optimism.

"Ready?" Tina squeezed my hand as we approached the entrance.

I only nodded; I couldn't trust my voice. Everything—our reputation, our future, our dreams—hinged on what lay beyond those gates.

The first glimpse stopped our forward motion entirely. Color erupted everywhere—rivers of red tulips flowed into lakes of purple, oceans of yellow stretched to the horizon. The garden's secret unveiled itself: carefully tended nearby hothouses had nurtured blooms that workers transplanted daily into outdoor displays. Nature might delay, but human ingenuity had prevailed.

Time dissolved as I worked; my camera evolved from a tool to an extension of my soul. Each frame captured not just flowers but resilience—every vibrant petal testifying to persistence, each intricate pattern declaring victory over circumstance. The memories of my colorless Texas childhood vanished in this tsunami of life and possibility.

Yet fate imposed one final test. At Schiphol's security checkpoint that evening, a guard reached for my undeveloped film as X-ray machinery hummed ominously nearby.

"No." The word erupted harder than intended. "These cannot go through X-ray."

His eyes narrowed. "Then no flight."

Minutes stretched like hours as more guards gathered, their patience visibly evaporating. Everything we'd fought for dangled by a thread. Through the tension, I caught Tina's eye—her slight nod conveyed all the strength I needed.

"I cannot allow you to destroy these images," I declared firmly as I drew myself up straighter. "There must be another way."

Only the last-minute intervention of a KLM representative, who confirmed our airline guest status, finally resolved the impasse. As we walked toward our gate, exhausted but triumphant, Tina slipped her hand into mine.

"We succeeded," she whispered.

"No," I corrected her softly. "We're just beginning."

Glen Allison

Light Chasers

Back in Los Angeles, reality cast troubling consequences over our victory.

Hundreds of spectacular photos lay undeveloped in their canisters—precious cargo for which we had no money to process. The irony struck me each morning as I gazed at them: priceless images imprisoned in darkness by our empty bank account.

"We'll find a way." Tina's confidence stood unshakable as she stirred our meager breakfast of boiled beans. The decorative kitchen jars that had once artistically displayed pasta and beans now served as our actual pantry. I had sold our car and most of my professional lighting equipment to finance our European gamble, which left us with bare walls and emptier cupboards.

"At least we're masters at creative problem-solving," I attempted to joke, but my voice cracked. The weight of our situation—the bounced check to the hotel in Paris, our mounting debts—sat heavy on my shoulders.

As the French issue deadline approached, desperation spawned further recklessness. My hand wavered as I wrote a check to the photo lab; I knew it, too, would bounce. The guilt crashed over me, immediate and crushing.

"We've come too far to falter now," I muttered to Tina that night. She nodded; she understood both the necessity and the cost to our principles.

A day later, we sat in the magazine editor's office, our hearts pounding in unison. The editor's distracted manner as she progressed through the French images made my stomach tighten. Just cursory nods, occasional murmurs—nothing like the reaction we'd risked everything to achieve. She lifted her notebook and prepared to leave the room.

"Wait," I implored as she began to rise. "Please ... there's more." Faster than lightning I loaded the carousel with our Holland slides. Everything hinged on these precious moments.

The projector hummed to life. Images blazed across the screen—tulips painted the earth in sweeping brushstrokes of color, windmills cut dramatic silhouettes against pearl-gray skies, houseboats reflected in mirror-still canals, golden wheels of cheese glowed like captured suns—Dutch life distilled into crystalline moments.

The editor's reaction sparked instant and electric. Her spine straightened, her eyes sharpened with sudden interest. "Show me those again," she commanded, leaning forward as if pulled by an invisible force. The air in the room shifted, charged with the energy of dreams.

Three months later, as we held the *Los Angeles Times* Sunday magazine in our hands, it felt surreal. Our Dutch photos graced the cover; our stories and photos filled an entire issue—something unprecedented in the magazine's fifty-year history for freelance work submitted on speculation. We had accomplished the impossible armed with nothing but determination, creative dreams, and each other.

That evening, I carefully composed a letter to the Amsterdam businessman who had trusted a stranger with ten guilders. As I enclosed his money and a copy of the magazine, my hand lingered on the envelope as I pondered our accomplishment. His response arrived two weeks later; his words brought unexpected emotion: "Your repayment has restored my faith in humanity." Like ripples in still water, our desperate gamble had created waves of positive change we never could have foreseen.

"We achieved more than just success," Tina reflected one morning, as sunrise painted our slightly upgraded kitchen in shades of new beginnings. "We proved we could handle anything life threw at us."

Like my earlier Spanish journey, this triumph surpassed mere career advancement. We had demonstrated that steadfast determination and stalwart life force, when paired with creative thinking, could convert impossible dreams to achievable reality. Our relationship had strengthened in adversity's fire, our spirits tempered by challenges that might have broken us individually but had fortified us as a team.

Most crucially, we had learned the vital importance of a solid financial foundation—a base for future dreams. The price we paid when we operated without a safety net had risen too high, both practically and ethically. We resolved to never again stretch ourselves so thin, no matter how tempting the opportunity.

The light we had chased through France and Holland had dwelled within us all along. Now, tempered by adversity and illuminated by triumph, it would guide us toward whatever challenges awaited. Our quest, we knew with quiet certainty, had truly just begun.

In the darkest moments of our journey, we discovered that the most precious light wasn't captured through our camera's lens but had been kindled within us—a flame that once ignited, no circumstance could extinguish.

Chapter 9 - Diamonds in the Making

dversity's harshest blows conceal the most precious gifts.

This paradox echoes through our struggles on Amsterdam's cold streets and the indifferent boulevards of Paris, where each obstacle unveiled an unexpected benefit.

Think of a moment when circumstances demanded more than you thought possible—that impossible deadline you somehow met, the loss you survived when collapse seemed inevitable, or the conflict you navigated when every instinct urged retreat. What did that experience teach you that no book ever could? Your lived experience contains insights no theoretical knowledge can match.

When we elevate our life condition to its highest potential, we access a magnificent regenerative energy that turns every ordeal into opportunity.

Have you ever noticed how the obstacles that seemed most devastating in your life often revealed the potential to become unexpected accelerants for personal turning points? The promotion you didn't receive that led to a better opportunity. The relationship that ended painfully but freed you for something more fulfilling. The health scare that altered how you prioritize what truly matters.

Almost everyone resists their difficulties because they cause discomfort. Whether you face an overwhelming project, a difficult colleague, or financial constraints that keep you awake at night—these aren't merely obstacles but classrooms for developing capabilities you didn't know you needed. Those who approach obstacles with curiosity rather than resentment discover unexpected treasures: an executive sees a market downturn as a chance to innovate; a parent views a child's rebellion as an opportunity to deepen bonds; an artist uses limitation as a constraint that unleashes meaningful art.

Rather than seek an idyllic problem-free paradise, it's better to cultivate a magnified life state that redefines our relationship with adversity itself, even as we battle our doubts at every step.

The traditional vision of nirvana often portrays it as an escape from suffering—a state of perfect bliss beyond life's burdens. But modern Buddhist perspectives offer a more dynamic vision: rather than view hardships as burdens to escape, we can forge a new relationship with them.

What separates those who break from those who evolve? The answer doesn't lie in the magnitude of our challenges, but in how we choose to meet adversity. For the widow in her windmill, her greatest loss became the entrance to her healing.

This uplifting perspective found vivid expression in 13th-century Japan through the Buddhist teacher Nichiren Daishonin. "One should regard meeting obstacles as true peace and comfort,"[1] he taught. His insight challenged conventional wisdom about the nature of happiness. His teachings exceeded mere philosophical speculation; they emerged directly from his own experiences of persecution.

This principle materialized during our Holland journey: each setback—the winter weather, depleted funds, hunger, no transport for the final day—initially appeared to block our path. Yet these very hurdles compelled us to develop creative solutions and forge deeper determination. The apparent barriers became necessary ingredients of change.

Nichiren poetically illuminated this principle in a letter to a follower: "Neither the pure land nor hell exists outside ourselves; both lie only within one's own heart. Realize that hell is itself the Land of Tranquil Light."[2]

Regarding this conundrum, Immaculée Ilibagiza, a Rwandan survivor of the 1994 genocide where nearly one million people were slaughtered, had this to say about experiences representing either heaven or hell: "Each day, with each thought, you choose which one you inhabit."[3]

As I stood in that Amsterdam train station, stomach growling and pride wounded, I uncovered this realization firsthand. Our relationship with any situation—whether hellish or heavenly—stems from our inner life condition rather than external circumstances.

Buddhist philosopher Daisaku Ikeda illuminates this paradox with striking precision: "You may wonder how encountering obstacles could be a source of peace and comfort. But the truth of the matter is that through struggling against and overcoming difficulties, we can transform our destiny and attain enlightenment. Confronting adversity, therefore, represents peace and comfort."[4]

Forging Strength Through Resistance

Yet this understanding must evolve beyond mere intellectual grasp to become lived reality. Simple positive thinking crumbles in the face of genuine hardship like dried leaves swept by wind. What's needed is a fundamental reorientation of our life condition itself, a rebirth as momentous as the windmill widow's healing.

When we face moments of genuine suffering—whether physical deprivation, crushing defeat, or acute uncertainty—mere willpower proves insufficient. What sustains us must be something far deeper: a fundamental life state tempered through difficult trials. This journey will lead us to discover our authentic purpose and to unleash our loftier, unrestricted self.

We develop our capabilities through persistent engagement with resistance. Our avoidance patterns often reveal precisely which capabilities remain underdeveloped in our lives. The person who sidesteps difficult conversations might notice their communication abilities plateau, while someone who procrastinates on complex challenges might find their strategic thinking remains elementary.

When we gently confront even one area of habitual avoidance, our capacity for handling discomfort naturally expands, which can open doorways to development that previously seemed inaccessible. This awareness alone often initiates subtle but meaningful shifts in how we approach life's necessary challenges.

Just as the practice of an instrument reshapes mental patterns and turns hesitant fingers into skilled conduits of expression, when we confront and overcome challenges, we elevate our fundamental capacity to handle obstacles. A teacher who faces a difficult classroom, a parent who guides a child through illness, a student who conquers a challenging subject—all demonstrate this principle. I see this in my own evolution from that frightened child with the kitchen knife to someone who can reshape desperate circumstances into triumph.

Like a garden that needs care or a craft that requires mastery, our inner development follows natural laws: we need to venture beyond comfort, maintain steady practice, and allow time for reflection and integration. The cook who once struggled with basic recipes eventually creates magnificent meals through persistence.

As civil rights icon Rosa Parks observed, "What really matters is not whether we have problems but how we go through them."[5] Her words reveal a crucial insight: our relationship with difficulty matters more than the challenge itself.

I had the great fortune to photograph Rosa Parks during a dialogue she had with Daisaku Ikeda on January 30, 1993.[6] That day, her gentle warmth and presence of staunch character belied a core of steel. At 80, life's hardships had carved wisdom into her face, yet could not dim the quiet smile that never left her lips.

Here was humility fused to unwavering conviction—a combination that would alter the course of history when she defiantly held her ground on that bus in Montgomery, Alabama, and refused to sit at the back. Her solitary act of courage sparked the civil rights movement in the United States that would reshape history. Her actions created change that revolutionized a nation's conscience and proved that one person's indomitable stand for justice can ignite the hearts of thousands—millions.

Oprah Winfrey's journey further exemplifies this remarkable reconstitution of adversity. Born into rural poverty in Mississippi to a single teenage mother, her early years were marked by hardship most would find insurmountable. She endured sexual abuse beginning at age nine, became pregnant at fourteen (losing her baby shortly after birth), and was sent to live with her strict father in Nashville.

These circumstances could have defined and limited her if they had become justifications for a life of bitterness or resignation. Instead, Winfrey changed these painful experiences into the foundation of her extraordinary empathy and compassion for others. "Turn your wounds into wisdom,"[7] she often says, a philosophy she embodied when she channeled her understanding of suffering into compassionate communication.

She began her career in local radio at seventeen, and eventually she revolutionized daytime television when she created a space where authentic conversation about difficult subjects became possible.

Winfrey's story is particularly insightful because she consistently refused to be defined by her circumstances. "You become what you believe," she maintains. "You are where you are today in your life based on everything you have believed."[8] This internal evolution—from seeing herself as a victim of her circumstances to recognizing herself as the author of her own story—exemplifies the transformative power of reframing our relationship with adversity.

In 2003, Winfrey became the first African American female billionaire, but her true impact surpasses wealth. Through her book club, philanthropic work, leadership academy for girls in South Africa, and her ability to create meaningful conversation, she has demonstrated how personal pain, when reshaped through wisdom and compassion, can become a force for global good. Her life provides compelling evidence of the principle that your greatest challenges often contain the seeds of your most effective contributions.

This stand-alone quality appears in words commonly attributed to Indira Gandhi, stateswoman and former Indian prime minister: "Difficulties are not necessarily unfortunate. It depends on your attitude. You can either let difficulties crush you, or you can use them to build your strength."[9] This type of awakening reflects a fundamental choice we face in every challenge: to retreat or to advance.

Ikeda expanded on this principle: "Whether we regard difficulties in life as misfortunes or whether we view them as good fortune depends entirely on how much we have forged our inner determination. With a dauntless spirit, we can develop a *self* of such fortitude that we are able to look forward to life's trials and tribulations with a sense of joy."[10]

This isn't mere philosophical musing—it's a practical approach to living. Our life force diminishes when we choose to avoid hardship. An unused piano gradually loses its tune; friendships fade without regular contact; languages slip away without practice. Each time we shrink from our difficulties, we reinforce patterns of hesitation. Each time we advance, we build our capacity for courage.

Those who navigate challenges successfully describe a decisive shift—from fighting against uncomfortable feelings to an ability that functions alongside tension with curiosity. When we actively engage with struggles rather than avoid them, they evolve from imposing barriers into familiar companions on our journey toward meaningful achievement.

While obstacles can appear intimidating, through consistent effort, we can develop the fortitude Mahatma Gandhi described: "Strength does not come from physical capacity. It comes from an indomitable will."[11]

Nature itself demonstrates this principle magnificently. I once watched a wildlife documentary which captured a scene that has stayed with me: a massive crocodile emerged from the water as it targeted a lion drinking at the lake's edge. Instead of retreat, the lion roared to life and charged with such immediate ferocity that the larger predator backed away in fear. Far more than mere physical prowess—the lion's immediate charge toward the crocodile embodied the impact of absolute confidence in one's own strength and its immediate, unhesitating response to danger.

This natural example illustrates a crucial point about human potential: if we can develop absolute confidence, our response to difficulty becomes immediate and potent. We don't need time to gather courage or steel ourselves for action—we meet each challenge with spontaneous strength, just as a lion king does.

> "Why do we fall, sir? So that we can learn to pick ourselves up."—Michael Caine as Alfred Pennyworth to Bruce Wayne in the film, *Batman Begins*[12]

This quote is from a scene where Alfred is helping a young Bruce Wayne after he falls into a well. The quote appears again later in the movie when Bruce is an adult, making it one of the more memorable lines from the film that encapsulates Alfred's mentorship role and the movies's theme of overcoming difficulty.

This basic wisdom cuts to the heart of adversity's purpose in our lives. Throughout the film, Bruce Wayne's journey from traumatized child to vigilant protector isn't a straight line but a series of devastating falls and remarkable recoveries. Alfred's insight reminds us that falling isn't failure—it's an essential part of our development.

Each time we stumble, we gain the opportunity to discover strength we didn't know we possessed. The wisdom doesn't lie in avoidance of falls altogether, which is impossible, but in recognition that each recovery builds capacity that remains with us long after the bruises have healed.

"Let me embrace thee, sour adversity," Shakespeare wrote, "for wise men say it is the wisest course."[13] This poetic revelation unveils a timeless wisdom—if we learn to embrace challenges rather than flee from them, we discover untapped reservoirs of strength within ourselves.

During our Dutch adventure, each obstacle we faced became a gift in disguise, though we couldn't perceive it in the moment.

Modern research at Duke University confirms what ancient wisdom has long taught: your mental stance toward your challenges—whether you view them as threats or opportunities—directly impacts your psychological wellbeing. Professor of Psychology and Neuroscience Ahmad Hariri's studies reveal that our perception of challenges significantly shapes our neurological responses.[14]

This finding bridges modern science with timeless wisdom about human potential. You can create a virtuous cycle that not only enables you to advance but reduces your suffering along the way.

Like tulips that break through winter's grip, with each new challenge you face boldly, you too can reshape adversity into opportunity.

The Hidden Masterpiece

Even with this insight, we all will encounter moments when our peace feels disturbed, when comfort seems distant. These disquieting experiences often signal not failure, but the need for greater inner stability—much like an athlete's muscle soreness indicates areas that need additional training. The critical difference emerges in how we perceive these moments: as opportunities to fortify our life condition rather than as setbacks.

Shift your perspective about obstacles with this effective approach that will help you to recalibrate your mindset:

> **Mind Pivot**
>
> Behind every wall stands a door.
>
> Your problems aren't problems. They're unopened gifts.
>
> When life delivers challenges, most people shrink. Their vision narrows to focus only on escape. But what if these moments aren't traps but turning points? What if difficulty isn't your enemy but your most devoted teacher?
>
> Try this: When faced with any obstacle, give yourself two minutes. Write every possible advantage that hides within your challenge—even wildly unlikely ones. Instead of asking "Why is this happening to me?" ask "What might this prepare me for?" or "How can this help me turn things around?" This simple act redirects your brain

> from fear circuits to possibility pathways. The obstacle hasn't changed, but your relationship to it fundamentally shifts.
>
> A mind hunting for opportunity grows sharp and adaptable. A mind fixated on barriers becomes dull and brittle. Both confront identical circumstances yet inhabit entirely different realities.
>
> This mental reorientation requires no dramatic gestures—just consistent, slight adjustments in focus. One degree of change in trajectory, maintained over distance, delivers us to an entirely different destination.
>
> Begin now. Select one obstacle in your path and identify three potential benefits it holds. This small practice installs new mental habits that automatically extract value from every obstacle you encounter.
>
> Your challenges exist to build exactly what you need for what awaits you. The question isn't whether your difficulties contain gifts, but whether you possess the vision to find them.

As the Roman poet Horace proclaimed in the first century BC, "Adversity reveals genius."[15]

Helen Keller's extraordinary life represents perhaps the most striking example of human perseverance in modern history. At just 19 months old, illness left her deaf and blind, cutting her off from the world in ways few can comprehend. For years, she existed in total darkness and deafening silence, unable to communicate effectively. The barriers she confronted weren't merely external but tied fundamentally to how humans process and understand the world.

When Anne Sullivan arrived as her teacher in 1887, Keller was nearly seven years old and lived in isolation that would crush most spirits. Their breakthrough—when Keller finally understood that Sullivan's finger movements in her palm symbolized "water"—came only after countless repetitions and unwavering persistence from both teacher and student.

Keller's achievements reveal extraordinary human potential. She learned to read and write in braille, then graduated cum laude from Radcliffe College in 1904—history's first deafblind person to earn a Bachelor of Arts degree.

Throughout her 87 years, she wrote 14 books, became a renowned speaker, and advocated passionately for people with disabilities. In her book, *The Story of my Life*, she wrote: "The best and most beautiful things in the world cannot be seen or even touched," she wrote. "They must be felt with the heart." Keller's journey proves our greatest limitations exist not in our circumstances but in our willingness to persist beyond them. In the same book, she also declared: "Only through the experience of trial and suffering can the soul be strengthened, ambition inspired, and success achieved."[16]

In "Effects of Stress on Immune Function," Firdaus Dhabhar, PhD, Professor of Psychiatry at the University of Miami Miller School of Medicine, details how acute stress can actually enhance immune function.[17] Our nervous system, our psychology, even our cellular biology—all are designed to grow stronger through appropriate resistance. Just as our immune system requires exposure to pathogens to develop resistance, our character requires exposure to adversity to develop strength and integrity.

This biological imperative for growth through pressure takes fascinating forms. Research on emotional brain patterns suggests that when we venture beyond comfortable limits—whether we learn a new skill, face a fear, or pursue an ambitious goal—we activate brain circuits that enhance our adaptability and resilience.[18] Our tolerance level, rather than a fixed boundary, proves remarkably elastic. Each time we stretch its limits, it expands, which allows us to handle greater challenges with increasing confidence, a neurological adaptation process that reflects our brain's remarkable capacity for emotional growth.

Albert Schweitzer, who earned the 1952 Nobel Peace Prize for his humanitarian work, captured this wisdom perfectly: "One who gains strength by overcoming obstacles possesses the only strength which can overcome adversity."[19] This realization points to a crucial distinction—true strength isn't inherited or granted, but earned through direct engagement with life's difficulties.

Each trial we overcome can forge an unshakable resilience within us. This earned strength then becomes a steadfast foundation precisely because we know its source—we've tested it, proved it, and can trust it completely.

I felt different when we returned from Holland compared to when we first departed. Unlike theoretical knowledge or borrowed confidence, this personally-built capability becomes part of our essential nature. It reshapes not just our abilities but our fundamental identity.

The 19th-century American poet Ella Wheeler Wilcox captured this revolutionary process in vivid terms: "Difficulties are but dares of fate, obstacles but hurdles to test skill, troubles but bitter tonics to give strength; and he rises higher and looms greater after each encounter with adversity."[20]

New challenges can be scary. They push us outside our comfort zone. Yet this very discomfort serves an essential purpose—it signals the beginning of our expansion.

Just as physical exercise creates microscopic tears in muscle tissue that ultimately lead to greater strength, mental and spiritual challenges create temporary discomfort that leads to expanded capacity.

The process to overcome hardship can fundamentally reshape our character. Like a sword tempered in fire, we can emerge from our struggles not just tested but reborn. This isn't merely psychological—it represents a fundamental shift in our life perspective, our life's essence, and our very way to exist in the world.

As Ikeda observed: "Nothing can match the strength of those whose lives have been shaped and forged through challenging and overcoming hardships. Such people fear nothing. To cultivate such an invincible core is, in itself, a victory."[21] His wisdom illuminates a fundamental reality: the ultimate value of each challenge extends far beyond the conquest of specific obstacles to the fundamental reconfiguration of our life that results from the process.

Our circumstances may shape our experiences, but they need not determine our destiny.

This fundamental shift in identity—from product of circumstance to creator of possibility—can radically reconstruct our approach to life. When we choose to become stronger rather than merely endure, we unlock access to reserves of energy from deep within—fuel that emboldens an indomitable will.

We can see this in nature: when winter grips the earth, tulip bulbs don't admit defeat. Instead, they draw upon internal resources and gather strength beneath the frozen ground. The same restrictive force that compresses their internal energy ultimately empowers them to explode in a burst of glorious life and magnificent color. The very harshness of winter compresses an inner strength the magnitude of which empowers cherry blossoms to emerge forth in grand celebration.

Your own moments of compression—whether career transitions, educational struggles, or geographic displacement—can serve the same purpose. When devastating circumstances crop up unexpectedly, your personal efforts to manifest an indefatigable resolve, even small steps to do so, can ultimately enable you to manifest results that might at first glance appear hopeless.

In such pivotal moments, our determination must radiate with such ferocity that the Universe itself seems compelled to align in our favor. This isn't mystical thinking—it's a focus and commitment so unfaltering that we naturally detect and seize opportunities others might miss. Even the direst circumstances hold the potential to birth triumphs, like metals strengthened through fire. We all possess the internal resources to change restrictive forces into rocket fuel.

This is where the profound principle of the Mystic Law reveals its life-changing value. Like a cosmic symphony, it embodies the perfect vibration that pulses through every particle of the universe. That night in the windmill, as I watched its blades turn for the first time since tragedy, I felt this resonance. When you engage this ultimate law of life, you awaken this same magnificent force that lies dormant in the depths of your own life. We will later delve more deeply into how to activate the Mystic Law within our daily lives.

Far beyond the reach of mere willpower, life's potential implores us to attune ourselves with the energy of this universal rhythm, which unleashes an inexhaustible wellspring of courage and innate hidden might.

The moment you achieve this perfect resonance with life's fundamental vibration, change ignites. You strip away your perceived limitations and unveil the magnificent potential that has always existed within.

Chapter 10 - The Prison of Pride

"Burgeoning Success Crushed in Utter Defeat"

Los Angeles, California, 1980

Success, when it finally arrived, felt like vindication. My photography business expanded dramatically. Magazine assignments cascaded in, each more prestigious than the last. *The Los Angeles Times* Sunday magazine, impressed by our Holland issue, soon dispatched us to capture England's most contemporary architecture and Mexico's vibrant colors.

When they sent me solo to Australia and New Zealand on two separate journeys, I thought, *This is it. I've made it.* My work also graced the pages of *House Beautiful* and *House & Garden*, and even adorned the cover of *Bauen & Wohnen*, the leading architectural magazine in Germany. Magazine features of my work in Tokyo and Moscow further boosted my ever-expanding ego as new worldwide publications kept arriving monthly.

Then reality began to set in....

I should have seen the warning signs. I should have heard the alarm bells that echoed through my increasingly shallow conversations with Tina. I should have felt the growing chasm between us as it widened with each passing day. But in the pursuit of professional success and personal indulgence, I remained oblivious to the impending collapse of what mattered most. Beneath the shimmer of professional triumph and the intoxication of selfish pursuits, dark clouds started to gather.

My mounting self-absorption cast a widening gloom, not just over my work, but over something far more precious—my marriage. Looking back now, I can trace the fault lines that eventually shattered everything.

My Buddhist practice had given me strength, yes—but over time I wielded it like a shield rather than a lens for self-examination. While it fortified my external courage, I mastered the art of evasion when faced with my core flaws: hubris and self-centeredness. Like a magician specializing in misdirection, I developed countless techniques to avoid the sight of my own reflection.

I'm doing this for us, I would tell myself as another evening vanished in the darkroom. *This success will give us everything we dreamed of.* But those were just pretty lies I wrapped around an ugly reality: my career had morphed into an addiction, and selfish indulgences clouded my judgment. Each new assignment, each accolade, fed a hunger that grew more voracious with every bite. I couldn't stop. Worse, I didn't want to.

The first years of our marriage had bloomed like a garden in spring. But as my professional progress mounted, I neglected that garden with increasing indifference. Every moment devoted to our relationship felt like time stolen from my personal desires and career ambitions. My ego expanded, while our bond withered like untended flowers.

Hidden Powers

When Tina filed for divorce, it shouldn't have surprised me. Yet somehow it did. Our once-beautiful bond had crumbled to dust, eroded by the acid rain of my self-absorption. Even then—even watching my second marriage dissolve for the exact same reasons as my first several years earlier—I couldn't see the pattern. Or rather, I refused to see it. Sometimes blindness is a choice.

The Ma Maison assignment should have been just another triumph—a magazine assignment to photograph Wolfgang Puck's exclusive West Hollywood restaurant, playground of the Hollywood elite. Instead, it became the flashpoint for my undoing. The restaurant's unlisted phone number captivated me. Their exclusivity, their carefully curated inaccessibility, resonated with something dark and hungry in my soul.

I now recognize it as hubris in its purest form—that ancient Greek concept of dangerous pride, the fatal flaw that brought even the mightiest heroes to their knees. The Greeks understood two thousand years ago what I failed to understand in the present: excessive self-confidence invites downfall and divine retribution. Not even the immortal gods of Olympus escaped the consequences of their arrogance when they overstepped humanity's sacred boundaries.[1]

Under the spell of this ancient folly, I made a decision that proved catastrophic: I rendered my business phone number unlisted. The logic, if you could call it that, was seductive. True success, I told myself, meant being accessible only to the most elite clients—those connected enough to get my number through magazine editors. I built walls; I didn't realize I had begun the construction of my own prison.

Glen Allison

Tina's departure triggered an avalanche. We often bury our deepest flaws beneath layers of denial until they erupt and demand to be faced. Financial collapse followed with brutal swiftness. My assignments didn't just decrease—they vanished. Yet even as my income evaporated, I clung to my delusions of grandeur with the desperation of a drowning man clutching at smoke. *They'll find me*, I told myself. *The truly worthy clients will find a way.*

The crushing despair that followed felt like karmic justice, though I still couldn't—wouldn't—admit it. Life has a way of shattering our ego with ruthless clarity, forcing us to confront realities we've spent years dodging. My career, which had soared with a measure of international acclaim, now lay in ruins. And still, I refused to confront my deeper demons.

I had faced my self-destructive tendencies before—the ones that had manifested in those terrifying car crashes. However, this was different. While self-destruction was dramatic and obvious, self-centeredness, ego, and arrogance were subtler poisons. They didn't crash and burn; they rotted you from the inside out. And I had let them fester, unchallenged and unchanged, beneath the glittering surface of my burgeoning success and self-serving choices.

In Buddhist tradition, it is said that the lion king faces no threat from external enemies; his only true foe is the parasite that lives within his bowels. Like the mighty lion, I had focused on mastering external challenges while the parasite of ego flourished within, which gradually consumed my life force from the inside.

How had I ascended so high, only to plummet further than ever from where I needed to be?

Days and months blurred into a time-lapse warp as I wallowed in my distorted perception. The true answers hovered just beyond my grasp—visible yet unreachable through the fractured prism of my inflated self-image and shallow indulgence.

Glen Allison

Rock Bottom's Revelation

Debts piled up, each unpaid bill another layer in winter's coming burial. My rent checks, my car payments—all lay dormant, withered like forgotten promises. *Just one more month*, I kept telling myself. *Something will turn around.* But nothing did.

The night everything changed for the worse began with a sound —the metallic rattle of chains—that sliced like a blade through my fog of self-pity. At first, I tried to ignore it, the way I'd ignored everything else. *It's nothing. It's not what you think.* But when I finally pulled myself to the window, reality struck a harsh blow. There, under the sickly glow of a street lamp, a tow truck hoisted my van—my mobile studio and lifeline to what remained of my career—onto its back like some giant mechanical predator claiming its prey.

The harsh night air bit my face as I bolted outside; panic rose in my throat. "Hey! What do you think you're doing?" My voice sounded thin, desperate—a far cry from the commanding tone I'd used with clients just months ago.

The driver turned; moonlight caught his massive frame. Built like a lumberjack, he seemed to embody all the immovable forces now aligned against me. "I'm repossessing this vehicle!" His fist clenched as it rose from the hydraulic lever, a resolute gesture that evoked both power and finality.

I felt myself shrink, physically retreat. *Is this what I've become?* "How can I work without my van?" The question escaped as a plea rather than a demand.

Hidden Powers

The man's shrug carried all the weight of heavy karmic retribution. "Pay your bills!" The cab door slammed like a judge's gavel as I watched my last connection to my former life disappear around the corner, red taillights burning like dying embers in the darkness.

How far I've fallen, I thought, as I stood alone on that sidewalk. *From international assignments to this.* The magnitude of my failure pressed down like granite on my shoulders, leaving both my body bent and my spirits crushed, Each breath was a struggle against the weight of accumulated consequences.

In the days that followed, I discovered what true imprisonment felt like. Los Angeles, a city built for cars, became my cage.

Shackled to bus routes and schedules, I watched my world contract. No more impromptu trips to the mountains where I once found solace in landscape photography. No more meditative drives up the Pacific Coast Highway, where the endless horizon once mirrored my limitless potential. No more midnight escapes to the desert, where the vast emptiness had always restored my sense of proportion. Now my horizons extended only as far as the next bus stop.

You did this to yourself, my thoughts would taunt as I waited at those stops. *Your ego built these bars.* Each passing car felt like a reminder of my hubris, each bus like a mobile cell in my prison of consequences.

Marooned in this concrete archipelago, I had even severed ties with my Buddhist community—my last potential lifeline. That decision, like so many others, sprang from pride. *I can't let them see me like this*, I'd thought. *I can't face them.* So instead, I chose solitude and allowed myself to plunge deeper into the abyss of my own creation.

When the eviction notice arrived after six months of unpaid rent, it felt less like a shock and more like the final seal on a fate I'd been writing for myself all along. Homelessness loomed not as some abstract threat but as an imminent reality that rendered me hopeless. Alone in my apartment—soon to be someone else's apartment—I finally confronted the wreckage of my life with clear eyes.

That taste of success I'd savored had been poison all along; its sweetness masked a toxin that corrupted everything: my judgment, my Buddhist faith, my marriage, my very sense of self.

Rock bottom arrived not with a crash but with a moment of crystal clarity. As I sat there staring at the official document demanding my departure, I realized that my only salvation lay in what I'd abandoned—my Buddhist practice. That night, surrounded by the ghosts of my former glory, I threw myself into hours of desperate prayer and contemplation. I chanted until my voice grew hoarse as I sought to reawaken the now dormant power of the Mystic Law within me.

Through tears that seemed to wash away years of accumulated pride, a revelation emerged, simple but electrifying: They could take my possessions, my career, my marriage, my home—but my fighting spirit? That remained mine to surrender or reclaim.

Hidden Powers

This awakening became my foundation stone, the bedrock beneath the rubble of my former life. Hunger gnawed—with no money in my pocket, I hadn't eaten in over twenty-four hours. Even so, I felt new light stirring in my soul. Or perhaps something ancient had reawakened. The absurdity of my unlisted phone number scheme, once a source of pride, now pierced me with brutal clarity: in my effort to make myself unreachable to clients, I had rendered myself unreachable to wisdom and life itself.

And then something happened—perhaps minuscule in scale yet magnificent in timing. After hours of chanting that had stilled my chaotic thoughts and unleashed fresh wisdom and energy, I stepped outside for air. The weight that had been crushing my chest seemed if not lifted, at least shifted. A fundamental change had occurred deep within me—a magnificent realignment, like the first imperceptible shifts of tectonic plates before they alter landscapes radically.

As I stood there, my gaze fell downward. There it was: a twenty-dollar bill lying on the sidewalk, illuminated by streetlight as if spotlighted for my discovery. I picked it up with an odd reverence; suddenly, I understood. Then, as if the universe wanted to underscore this lesson in humility, I realized this windfall had a meaning far beyond mere sustenance: the smallest crack in the walls of ego could allow wisdom and light to penetrate.

This time, I promised myself, *there will be nowhere to hide from the truth.*

Glen Allison

Nine Flat Tires

Dawn broke over Los Angeles with the kind of piercing insight that only follows a night of soul-shaking revelation.

Today will be different. Today I will be different, I told myself. My borrowed bicycle gleamed in the early morning light. The Buddhist gathering was miles away, but distance seemed trivial compared to the psychological barriers I'd already begun to dismantle. Little did I know that the universe had crafted an elaborate lesson in humility—a pivotal test of my newfound resolve. It used nothing more sophisticated than air and rubber.

The first flat tire struck one mile in. *Really?* I thought, as the tire deflated with almost comical timing. *This is how it's going to be?* In previous weeks, when my life condition scraped bottom, such a setback would have sent me skulking home in defeat. But something had shifted within me. The gas station that appeared around the corner felt less like coincidence and more like cosmic choreography.

By the fourth flat, I began to appreciate the absurdity. Each hiss of escaping air, I realized, echoed exactly like my deflating ego. The fifth and sixth flats brought sweat and aching muscles, but also a strange sense of peace. The seventh and eighth tested not just my resolve but my comprehension of what it meant to persist. Each time I found myself near a gas station in this vast urban sprawl—a statistical improbability that increasingly resembled divine intervention.

Hidden Powers

When the ninth and final flat occurred, I stood directly before an auto repair shop, as if the universe had finally decided to end its elaborate metaphor. The owner, a seasoned mechanic with knowing eyes, examined the tire and discovered a faulty valve stem. "Fifty cents for the part," he said. His modest charge felt like the final punctuation mark in a long sermon about humility.

Nine flats, I mused as he worked. *One for each year I've spent building walls around myself—like a cat's nine lives, each punctured and deflated in turn.*

When I finally reached the Buddhist gathering, sweat and effort had soaked through my clothes. But the physical depletion carried a strange sweetness—the satisfaction of a battle well fought, not against the world, but against my own resistance to change. The welcome I received from fellow members struck me with unexpected force. *This*, I realized, *is what I've walled myself off from all along.*

Their genuine warmth rekindled the fighting spirit and sense of hope I'd allowed to die during my descent into darkness—not just passion, but soul-deep connection itself. The very thing I'd avoided in my pursuit of exclusivity had remained the key to salvation all along.

This renewed spirit demanded action. Humility still felt foreign to me when I dialed an old client's number. His response shattered my carefully constructed illusions: he'd attempted to reach me for months, thwarted by the very barriers I'd erected to appear more valuable. *The irony would be funny*, I thought, *if it weren't so painful.* When he offered me immediate work, my first act after hanging up was to restore my listed phone

Glen Allison

number. The walls of my self-made prison didn't fall so much as dissolve, exposed as the illusions they'd always been.

The next test of my emerging humility arrived wrapped in exquisite karmic packaging: I needed to borrow a car from my first ex-wife—the same person who had endured the earliest storms of my self-centeredness. Her gracious agreement, despite our history, revealed the cost of pride in a way no abstract lesson could. *How much generosity have I ignored*, I wondered, *in my determination to need nothing from anyone?*

The payment from this new assignment sparked more than just financial recovery—it triggered an epiphany. A print shop window advertised promotional postcards. My old self would have sneered at such a pedestrian marketing approach. Instead, I asked my client if he'd ever received such promotional materials from architectural photographers. His "no, never" response felt like permission to embrace simplicity.

I selected my strongest portfolio image and addressed postcards to local architects and designers. Each card became a windowpane toward humility, each stamp an acknowledgment that I needed to rebuild not just my business, but my entire approach to the world. No more concealment behind artificial scarcity; it was time to make myself available to life itself.

As I stamped the last postcard, a subtle realization kindled within me. Perhaps the winds of fortune were changing—not in their nature, but in a direction I could finally perceive with clarity.. *Or was I the one changing?* The realization dawned on me with the force of ancient wisdom: the winds would always do what winds do—blow capricious and untamed across life's vast ocean. My catastrophe wasn't in encountering storms but in my stubborn refusal to adjust my sails.

The response overwhelmed me: $10,000 in new assignments the very next month. This wasn't just financial recovery—it validated a completely new approach to life and work.

The next five years saw my business generate its first million, built not on exclusivity but on its opposite: accessibility, humility, and genuine service. Yet even as success returned, I preserved the memory of those nine flat tires. Egoistic pride, I reminded myself daily, is a slow leak in the soul.

Glen Allison

From Pride to Odyssey: The Gift of Catastrophe

This vigilance proved crucial when, five years later, the California real estate market collapsed and sparked another financial crisis for the state and for me.

Bankruptcy arrived like summer lightning, sudden and devastating. But this time, instead of retreating into wounded pride, I recognized the opportunity for a deeper renewal.

What appeared as a nightmare propelled me into an extraordinary odyssey—a new career redefining my photographic skills that would span a decade during which I encircled the globe nonstop numerous times, traversing over a hundred countries. Each nation became a lesson in how vast the world expands when we cease positioning ourselves at its center.

My universe, once confined to an unlisted phone number, now stretched beyond anything I could have imagined. Through immersion in hundreds of diverse cultures, I uncovered a world far more expansive than my ego had ever allowed me to perceive. But that epic story—that miraculous transformation—deserves its own chapter.

Chapter 11 - Breaking Free

Think of an inflated ego as an autoimmune disease of the soul.

It turns our natural self-protection instincts against us, typically arriving quietly, often disguised as healthy confidence or legitimate self-worth. I remember the day I decided to make my phone number unlisted, how righteous that decision felt, how obviously correct when viewed with distorted vision.

I had rendered myself literally unreachable—a perfect embodiment of the psychological walls I constructed around my vulnerabilities. No one tears down their own fortress consciously. Yet in rare moments of brutal honesty, we often see how defenses that once sheltered now only isolate. Perhaps the most courageous act requires us to dismantle, stone by stone, what we built, thinking it would protect us, but now constrains us.

Confidence stems from genuine competence and self-awareness, lifting others as it rises. Arrogance feeds on illusions of superiority, growing hungrier with each false feast.

This distorted mirror warps everything it reflects—it magnifies our achievements while shrouding our flaws in shadow.

The Price of Pride: My Relationships in Ruins

My painful journey during the crash of my business and my marriage breakup with Tina illustrates what psychologists and philosophers have long observed: genuine happiness becomes impossible when self-centeredness and arrogance rule our lives. These traits don't just build walls; they forge barriers that blind us from criticism, growth, love, connection, and joy itself.

"People can overlook any shortcoming, but they will not tolerate arrogance,"[1] observed Sushma Swaraj, India's former Minister of External Affairs. Her words echo through the ruins of my own experience—a collapsed business, the repossession of my car, an eviction notice, two shattered marriages. *How many relationships must I sacrifice on the altar of my fabricated self-importance?*

Arrogance leaves scars that resist healing.

Linda and Charles Bloom, in their research for *Secrets of Great Marriages,* highlighted that partners often sense and recoil from underlying superiority long before the arrogant person recognizes it in themselves. Their conclusions were chilling: "This frustration," they wrote, "can deteriorate into resignation. If these feelings continue, the prospects for restoring well-being to the relationship are slim to none."[2] As I read their words now, it feels like a review of the autopsy reports of my two failed marriages.

The science confirms what my heart learned too late.

Hidden Powers

In retrospect, I see it so clearly—how my first wife's gentle suggestions hardened into frustrated silence, how my second wife's attempts to mend cracks in our relationship met my wall of indifference. Maya Angelou's wisdom cuts deep here: "People will forget what you said, people will forget what you did, but people will never forget how you made them feel."[3]

Arrogant behavior often triggers defensive responses in others creating a cascade of deteriorating relationships. Like ripples in a pond, except the ripples consist of acid—they eat away at every bond they touch.

In the early days of my career, each international magazine assignment became more than work well executed; it became irrefutable evidence of my self-constructed exceptionalism—the Uber-Glen. *Look how far I've risen,* I'd marvel, as each success cemented another brick into my wall of isolation.

To break this distortion requires a deliberate shift in focus. Our minds often construct invisible barriers that dictate what we'll see and what we'll miss.

Our defensive mechanisms operate with ruthless efficiency. They filter feedback, justify flaws, and maintain comfortable illusions. This selective perception can create a reality that validates existing beliefs while it rejects contradictory evidence.

When locked inside one perspective, we often see others as mere projections. Their motivations, fears, and hopes remain invisible, casualties of our restricted vision. This narrow sight can warp every interaction, stripping our connections of essential depth.

Our minds contain three distinct lenses; each reveals different facets of reality. One captures only our experience—our needs, desires, and assumptions. Another focuses on others—their wishes, anxieties, and intentions. The third hovers above, an impartial witness to the complete exchange.

When all three perspectives activate simultaneously, our awareness expands beyond the cramped frame of self into a panoramic view that encompasses everyone involved. This multi-dimensional sight reveals previously hidden options in conflicts, uncovers concealed solutions to problems, and opens passages formerly blocked by self-absorption.

These blind spots remain invisible to us by definition. The world changes not when others adjust to accommodate us, but when we expand our field of vision to include them.

Have you ever caught yourself defending a position long after you secretly began to doubt it? Think about a time when your certainty became a prison—perhaps in a heated argument where admitting uncertainty felt like defeat, or a decision you doubled down on despite growing evidence it wasn't working. We all construct these invisible cages. I've built mine brick by brick, each one cemented with the mortar of "I know best." The most significant growth often begins when we start whispering these difficult words: "I might be wrong." What conversation might transform today if you approached it with genuine curiosity instead of predetermined conclusions?

When we crown ourselves extraordinary, we tend to instinctively reject any feedback that might fracture our meticulously crafted facade.

Typically, others detect our superiority complex long before we recognize it ourselves. They feel the subtle current of dismissal in our tone, the near inconspicuous shifts in our attention when they speak, the slight narrowness in our eyes as if we don't respect their thoughts. This can cause the ideas and insights of others to wither and their input to diminish. Once formed, their impressions of us heal slowly—like tissue that scars without proper care.

When we inadvertently tarnish vital connections to our community, this separation becomes both the symptom and the cause of our disconnection. We often walk alone not from brilliance but from broken links of genuine exchange.

> ACTION: Ask one person today, "How did my words and actions affect you?" Then commit to listen without interruption or defense. This brief practice of attentive listening opens a window to our understanding impact over intention.

Without such awareness and correction, a destructive cycle becomes predictable: we dismiss our mistakes, scorn other viewpoints, and lose the ability to engage in real dialogue. Trust erodes. Resentment grows. Relationships wither and die.

Leo Tolstoy captured it exquisitely: "An arrogant person considers himself perfect. This is the chief harm of arrogance. It interferes with a person's main task in life—becoming a better person."[4]

Steve Jobs' journey offers a compelling modern example of this evolution from arrogance to wisdom. In 1985, at just 30 years old, Jobs was forced out of Apple, the company he had co-founded. His legendary stubbornness and what colleagues described as "unbearable arrogance" had made him increasingly difficult to work with, despite his visionary talents. Jobs himself later admitted, "I was a very public failure."[5]

This fall from grace initiated what Jobs called "one of the most creative periods of my life."[6] While few of us will experience such dramatic public humbling, we can invite smaller, constructive failures into our lives as teachers.

During Jobs' wilderness years, he founded NeXT Computer and reshaped Pixar from a struggling graphics division into an animation powerhouse. It was later purchased by the Walt Disney Company for approximately 7.4 billion dollars. Yet the true evolution didn't occur in the business accomplishments of Steve Jobs but in his evolving approach to leadership and relationships.

When he returned to Apple in 1997, colleagues noticed a remarkable shift. His biographer Walter Isaacson noted that Jobs had developed "a greater understanding of people's weaknesses, a more refined sense of loyalty to those who had stuck by him."[7] In his 2005 Stanford address, Jobs reflected, "Getting fired from Apple was the best thing that could have ever happened to me. The heaviness of being successful was replaced by the lightness of being a beginner again, less sure about everything."[8]

His story instructs us beyond his spectacular success after failure through the timing of his greatest innovations, which all came after his greatest humbling. The iPod, the iPad, and the

Hidden Powers

iPhone—products that would revolutionize multiple industries—emerged from the mind of a Steve Jobs who had learned, painfully, the limits of his own knowledge and the value of collaborative wisdom.

> "You must unlearn what you have learned."—Yoda to Luke Skywalker in the movie, *Star Wars: The Empire Strikes Back*[9]

This seemingly contradictory wisdom encapsulates the enlightening journey of true knowledge. In the film, Luke Skywalker arrives on Dagobah convinced he already understands what it means to be a Jedi, only to have his preconceptions systematically dismantled by a small green master.

As we acquire deeper understanding, we simultaneously awaken to the vast expanse of what remains unknown. This realization doesn't diminish our knowledge—it contextualizes it and places our limited understanding within the boundless landscape of potential discovery. True expertise isn't measured by how confidently we assert what we know, but by how comfortably we acknowledge what we don't.

Shedding the Expert's Illusion

The knowledge and expertise that earned our reputation can easily calcify into certainty that resists change. The very mastery we worked so hard to achieve can quietly become the boundary of our evolution.

Our mind collects beliefs, identities, and behaviors that chain us to former versions of ourselves. These elements often persist long after their usefulness ends, invisible to us yet glaringly obvious to others.

Choose one area where you consider yourself knowledgeable. Now, deliberately step back into curiosity about this topic. Ask genuine questions. Seek conflicting viewpoints that challenge your established thinking. Learn from unexpected teachers you would typically dismiss.

An honest inventory will illuminate what no longer fits: professional identities maintained from habit rather than passion; opinions defended without recent examination; relationship patterns that once protected but now isolate. This assessment doesn't require immediate action or harsh judgment—merely acknowledgment.

This voluntary demotion from expert to apprentice creates pathways for innovation. It shatters rigid assumptions and invites fresh discoveries. When we approach familiar territory with beginner's eyes, previously invisible details emerge from the background.

Our questions now hold more value than our declarations. Our willingness to reconsider demonstrates strength, not weakness. Our humility creates receptivity that arrogance forbids.

Before your next absolute declaration, pause to consider alternative viewpoints. This brief hesitation introduces flexibility where rigidity once ruled. The mental muscles that hold our certainties will resist this exercise—which precisely indicates its value.

> Humility flows not from self-deprecation but from accurate self-perception that acknowledges both capabilities and limitations. It permits acceptance of critique while it sustains grounded self-esteem.
>
> The most significant advances often come not through acquisition of something new, but through deliberate release of what no longer belongs. Each outdated belief, identity, or behavior you shed creates space for who you might evolve into next.
>
> A snake sheds its skin, guided by nature's silent wisdom. It intuitively knows when to release what no longer serves—an inner knowing I had yet to access back then. We often cling to our former selves out of insecurity or habit.
>
> Our most meaningful evolution awaits not in what we will gain, but in what we finally let go.

Modern psychology has revealed how self-importance actually atrophies our brain's capacity to learn and grow. When we believe ourselves beyond reproach, we often develop mental rigidity that automatically rejects challenging feedback.[10]

As I look back now, I recognize my lifelong odyssey from arrogance toward humility reflects a radical rebirth. Each setback, each failure, each marriage lost, each moment of painful self-recognition helped dissolve another layer of false pride—a process I know will continue for as long as I draw breath.

My journey continues. It requires constant vigilance. For the walls of arrogance, I've learned, rebuild themselves slowly and almost silently if we let them. But now, I remind myself daily, I know the sound of those bricks as they fall into place. I recognize the seductive whisper. I must choose, again and again, to remain open, changeable, human.

The keys to our cell rest in our own hesitant hands.

Chapter 12 - The Price of Success

Los Angeles, California, 1985-1990

T he Los Angeles sunset painted my hillside home in hues of gold and bronze and irony that evening in 1990, as shadows had already crept across my empire of success—bankruptcy loomed. Within months, that darkness would consume everything I'd built, teaching me lessons that no amount of prosperity could buy.

How strange, I thought, as I watched the fading light play across the sleek surfaces of my pristine Modern Museum of Art furniture, *how the same sun that once illuminated my achievements now seems to highlight their impermanence.*

As I stood in my stylish Silver Lake home, I could hardly believe that my architectural photography business—which had crossed the million-dollar threshold just months before—would crumble beneath my feet. The phone on my desk, once constantly alive with calls from eager clients, now sat silent like a relic of former glory. *When did the rhythm of ring tones shift into this deafening quiet?*

The real estate market's collapse hit like a Southern California earthquake. It sent aftershocks that ricocheted through the architectural community, which had once celebrated my work. As assignments evaporated, I watched my substantial savings drain away, month by month. I was immersed in a desperate attempt to maintain payroll and overhead. The weight of responsibility for my five team members—a secretary, three full-time photo assistants, and an in-house writer/researcher—pressed heavily on my conscience. I strived to somehow conjure solutions from the growing darkness.

My photographs had graced countless covers of renowned architectural magazines worldwide. Through my images, I had reimagined spaces into dreams captured in light and shade. *The Los Angeles Times Home Magazine* had become almost a second home for my work—over fifty covers, hundreds of features. I'd become the go-to photographer—the poster boy—for countless local architects who sought to showcase their vision, their artistry. Local publication in *The LA Times* brought both prestige and clients to them. And they knew my long-standing connection with and extensive publication in the magazine could facilitate their careers with local publication of their work in *Home Magazine*.

Now here I am, I thought, as I watched my own carefully constructed image lose its brightness like a photograph left too long under the harsh rays of sun and heat.

The echoes of past triumphs only amplified the present silence.

I remembered the heady days of jetting between continents as I captured architectural masterpieces in Australia, New Zealand, the Netherlands, France, England, Mexico, and Spain. *The Times* had commissioned entire magazine editions that featured my images. UCLA had sponsored my photography workshop in Tahiti. Architects would wait up to six months and pay fifty percent upfront just to secure a spot on my calendar.

Hidden Powers

My custom-made camera cases—those faithful companions that had accompanied me across the globe—now sat in the garage gathering dust. Their weight, once a comfortable reminder of purpose, felt like lead as I began to pack them away. *Each lens I wrap feels like sealing away a chapter of my life*, I reflected, as I carefully cushioned many thousands of dollars worth of equipment that would soon be surrendered to bankruptcy proceedings.

The previous year, many of the architectural projects I photographed had won all the top four honor categories at the annual competition hosted by the Los Angeles chapter of the American Institute of Architects. Now, those same award plaques were carefully enclosed in bubble wrap, destined for cardboard boxes that would never be unpacked. The sound of wrapping tape pulled across cardboard became a monotonous rhythm that scored the dismantling of my professional life.

The designer furniture that had once seemed a fitting backdrop for my success now stood as silent witnesses to this latest downturn in the economy. The rich smell of leather upholstery—once a source of pride—now seemed cloying, suffocating. Each piece inventoried for bankruptcy felt like a testimony to my misplaced priorities. *When did possessions become so entwined with my sense of self?*

Yet beneath the surface of this financial catastrophe, a deeper realization emerged. Though this collapse had been triggered by market forces beyond my control—unlike my previous financial crisis five years earlier—I recognized now that my mindset had rendered me vulnerable. Despite my progress to battle self-centeredness and arrogance through Buddhist practice, I had allowed my rebuilt success to seduce me into a delusion of invulnerability. I had prioritized lavish indulgences—expensive meals for my staff, unwise investments—over financial prudence.

The most mortifying moments came when I faced peers and esteemed clients in the industry. Each encounter felt like walking through fire, yet two decades of Buddhist practice had forged a resilience I previously had not possessed. *I will not let this setback define me*, became my second daily mantra. This wasn't an ending, but a chance for an astounding rebirth.

To survive this crisis, I took a job that would have seemed unthinkable at the height of my success—pizza delivery.

That first night as I stood in an ill-fitting uniform beneath the garish neon sign of "Mario's Authentic Italian," I felt the weight of my journey pressed down upon me. The previous year my work had commanded thousands. Now, I clutched a stack of pizza boxes while teenagers less than half my age explained the delivery zone boundaries.

But despite my circumstances, I had gradually come to understand that each moment contains everything.

I decided that if I now must be a pizza delivery boy, I would become extraordinary at the task. Not from ego, but from the fundamental understanding that how we do anything is how we do everything.

Each delivery became a spiritual practice.

Customers began to request me specifically. "Send the Buddhist pizza guy," they'd say, though I rarely spoke of my practice during work. Perhaps they sensed the intention with which I handled their order—as if each pizza were a mandala, a sacred offering.

One rainy Tuesday, I delivered to an elderly woman who lived alone. When she opened the door and looked inside the box, confusion clouded her eyes. "I didn't order this," she insisted, though the address matched. Rather than argue, I asked if she liked pizza. When she nodded hesitantly, I said, "Then perhaps this one is meant just for you." The smile that blossomed across her wrinkled face contained more value than any photographic commission I'd ever earned.

The peculiar chemistry of those weeks magnified my understanding of self-worth. True dignity isn't conferred by status or wealth—it emanates from how fully we inhabit each moment, how completely we offer ourselves to whatever task lies before us.

My manager soon noticed my dedication and promoted me to shift supervisor. When I later departed in pursuit of my ultimate quest to reinstate my wildest dreams—this time on a foundation of genuine service rather than ego—he seemed genuinely perplexed. "Why leave? You're the best delivery boy we've ever had." My weeks of pizza delivery had delivered me to myself.

There is a unique dignity that lies in never giving up: a radical dimension of peace not measured in magazine covers, accolades, or award plaques.

Glen Allison

Looking back now, I can see how my potentially devastating crisis carved away layers of artificial self to reveal a more genuine understanding: the bankruptcy proceedings that stripped away my material possessions also stripped away illusions about what truly matters.

Without an iota of doubt, I was absolutely certain I could rebuild from my ruins, but this time with wisdom that tempered ambition I had let run wild. I would exert more focus to acquire business acumen balanced with a new level of previously unleashed artistic vision like never before.

What I couldn't know then, as I surrendered my hillside home to the bankruptcy court and moved into my van for the second time in my life, was that this apparent ending actually marked a dynamic new beginning that would propel me beyond my wildest expectations.

A transformative odyssey awaited me—one that would launch me around the globe as a massively prolific travel photographer, an adventure that would open doors beyond my wildest imagination. But that journey, with all its turbulence and triumph, will be told in another chapter.

Sometimes, I realize now, we must lose our way temporarily to find a more meaningful path.

My journey taught me the essential: our dreams must not diminish in times of hardship—they must clarify, they must intensify, they must explode wide open wildly. It was not the dream that needed to change; it was the foundation underneath.

Chapter 13 - Rising from the Ashes

Resilience doesn't mean a life without scars, but the skill to allow them to mold us. What stands in the way becomes the Way, as Marcus Aurelius and the Stoics taught.[1]

My journey from a recognized photographer to pizza delivery boy wasn't just a story of financial setback—it was a dynamic lesson in the nature of adaptation and the true meaning of fulfillment. *Who would have thought,* I mused, *that the path to wisdom would smell like pepperoni, mozzarella, and garlic?*

The same hands that once carefully adjusted thousand-dollar lenses now counted out small change under streetlights as I found unexpected grace in those humble pizza transactions.

The van that once transported my expensive photography equipment across Los Angeles now served as both workplace and home. Its confines, though cramped, provided a peculiar kind of sanctuary. At night, parked in safe, quiet corners of the city, I observed the same stars that had witnessed my rise and fall; their eternal rhythm reminded me of life's continuous flow. The universe, I realized, doesn't distinguish between a hillside property and a van—it holds both with equal tenderness.

When everything else falls away, only then can we discover what remains.

Have you ever found yourself standing in the ruins of what you once built? Think about a moment when life stripped away your

Glen Allison

carefully constructed identity—perhaps a long-held belief system that suddenly rang hollow, a cherished role that vanished when children grew up, or physical abilities lost to illness or age. How did you make sense of that void? Most of us initially see such losses only as endings. We focus on what's been taken rather than what might be revealed.

I've spoken with countless people who describe these moments as feeling "naked" or "exposed"—as though the costume they'd been wearing suddenly vanished, leaving them wondering who they truly are without it. What did your moment of radical change teach you about yourself? The answer to this question contains the seed of your deepest rebirth.

Though my radical, overnight transition from accomplished photographer to food courier living in his van might seem distant from your experience, the emotional landscape of loss and renewal speaks a universal language. Your specific circumstances may differ, but that raw, vulnerable space between who we were and who we could be connects us all.

When life strips everything away, what truly matters becomes crystal clear. Our worth exists beyond our achievements, possessions, and public validation. When our external markers vanish, certain qualities remain intact despite radical shifts in situation—our ability to find beauty, our capacity for kindness, the quiet dignity that cannot be diminished by loss.

The compass needle always finds north. Similarly, our core qualities point toward who we truly are, regardless of the storms we must navigate. These constants form the bedrock upon which we must rebuild, not just to recover what was lost, but to discover what waits beyond previous limitations.

When we recognize what cannot be damaged by circumstance, we acquire an unassailable center from which all meaningful action can flow.

This perspective builds awareness of what educator Tsunesaburo Makiguchi called "unchanging value"[2]—the aspects of life that remain steady amid fluctuation.

Life in such close quarters in my van with only my thoughts for company proved both challenging and illuminating. The metal walls amplified every new internal revelation, every doubt, every realization. During sleepless nights, when the city's hum created a gentle backdrop to my meditation, I began to comprehend the astounding potential of resilience. It wasn't, as I had once believed, about how to maintain an exterior shield. Rather, it involved how to flow with life's currents while I kept my inner compass intact.

This understanding found scientific validation years later, when Columbia University professor Dr. George A. Bonanno published his landmark research on "Loss, Trauma, and Human Resilience" in 2004. His findings published in the *American Psychologist* journal revealed what I had discovered through personal, lived experience—that resilience isn't a rare superhuman quality, but a fundamental aspect of human nature, as common as breath itself.[3]

The streets of Los Angeles became my new classroom; each delivery route taught lessons in humility and perseverance. On one occasion, I found myself delivering pizzas to a building I had once photographed, its architectural beauty now viewed from a different angle. *How many times,* I wondered, *had I captured these structures in golden light, never imagining I'd one day approach them from the service entrance?*

These moments of stark contrast could have become bitter pills, but my Buddhist practice had taught me to perceive them differently. Each such encounter offered an opportunity to challenge my ego, to recognize the artificial nature of the barriers we create between different types of work, different measures of worth. The warm weight of a pizza bag against my shoulder carried its own dignity, no less valid than the weight of a camera.

Charles Darwin's insight that adaptability, not strength or intelligence, determines survival[4] resonates deeply with my experience. My photography skills, my industry connections, my past successes—none of these could help me navigate this new pizza delivery terrain. What mattered was my ability to adapt, to find meaning and purpose in changed circumstances, to remain open to life's lessons regardless of their packaging.

The van's small space also exemplified another core principle from my Buddhist practice and that almost everyone understands on the deepest level: material possessions don't foster true happiness. Each item I kept had to earn its place, had to justify the precious space it occupied within the confines of my van—a concrete manifestation of what my studies had always emphasized: not the elimination of possessions, but a clear-eyed understanding of their proper place in our lives. This practical application of Buddhist wisdom led to mental decluttering as well. *When did I start believing that success could only look one way?* I wondered, as I watched the city lights paint patterns on the van's ceiling. *How many other illusions am I still carrying? How many other misconceptions?*

You can map these hidden beliefs that shape your life with this simple exercise:

> **The Hidden Scripts of Your Life**
>
> Society hands us a script about success long before we recognize its voice. This invisible manuscript dictates the paths worth walking, the achievements worth celebrating, and the life worth living. Yet these judgments often crumble when tested against lived experience.
>
> Take a blank page now. Draw a simple line down its center. On the left, list everything you were taught to pursue as evidence of accomplishment—financial status, professional titles, possessions, accolades, relationships that match a particular template. Be exhaustive. Include every marker society has convinced you matters.
>
> On the right, beside each item, write what it supposedly guarantees—respect, security, happiness, freedom, love, significance. These promised outcomes fuel your pursuit of the corresponding markers.
>
> Now face these connections with brutal honesty. Has your experience confirmed or contradicted each pairing? Have prestigious titles actually delivered the respect you anticipated? Has financial status truly created the security it promised? Has ownership of certain

> possessions genuinely produced the happiness you expected?
>
> For each contradiction you identify, ask what actually delivers this outcome in your life. What authentic source has provided this benefit when the promised path failed?
>
> The answers will contain the seeds of your liberation.
>
> Now, draft a new definition of success based solely on what your lived experience has verified. This personal constitution, built from tested reality rather than inherited assumptions, will guide you with far greater accuracy than the maps others insist you follow.
>
> The most dangerous chains are those we never see. The most profound freedom comes not from gaining new things but from releasing beliefs that never served us. Our revised understanding will create a life defined not by external validation but by the wisdom of our own verified experience.

Here's a remarkable story that embodies this principle in action:

Bryan Stevenson's journey from humble beginnings to becoming one of America's most influential advocates for justice demonstrates how apparent limitations can become the foundation for extraordinary impact. Born in a poor, segregated community in Delaware, Stevenson faced racial discrimination and witnessed systemic injustice from an early age.

After graduation from Harvard Law School, Stevenson turned down lucrative corporate positions to work with death row

Hidden Powers

inmates in Alabama for a salary so low he couldn't afford to pay off his student loans. His early legal efforts met with resistance, threats, and even bombs at his office. The Equal Justice Initiative he founded operated out of a small office with unreliable funding and overwhelming caseloads.

In 1989, Stevenson took on the case of Walter McMillian, a black man wrongfully sentenced to death for the murder of a white woman despite dozens of witnesses who confirmed he was at a church fish fry during the crime. The local legal system refused to acknowledge the obvious evidence of innocence. Judges, prosecutors, and law enforcement worked against Stevenson at every turn.

"There is a strength, a power even, in understanding brokenness," Stevenson later wrote in his memoir *Just Mercy*.[5] What appeared to be insurmountable obstacles—limited resources, institutional racism, and a justice system resistant to change—actually shaped Stevenson's approach to advocacy in uniquely effective ways.

Through perseverance, Stevenson not only won McMillian's freedom but has since helped exonerate dozens of innocent prisoners, won Supreme Court cases prohibiting extreme sentencing for children, and created the National Memorial for Peace and Justice to acknowledge victims of racial terror lynchings. His EJI now employs over 150 people and has saved more than 140 innocent prisoners from execution.

"Hopelessness is the enemy of justice,"[6] Stevenson often says. His journey reveals how working within broken systems can spark their renewal, and how personal experience with injustice can fuel a lifetime of meaningful work.

Like the phoenix rising from apparent limitation, Stevenson reshaped societal obstacles into the foundation for far-reaching social change.

His example illuminates a universal principle that applies not just to systemic challenges but to our individual lives as well. His ability to find purpose in adversity offers a template for how we might approach our own setbacks, regardless of their scale. While few of us will confront the systemic injustices Stevenson battles, we all face moments that test our resilience and challenge our sense of identity.

When was the last time you experienced a significant setback? Not just a minor disappointment, but a genuine collapse of something you'd built your identity around?

Perhaps it was a career derailment—the promotion that went to someone else, the startup that failed despite your best efforts, or the industry that suddenly deemed your skills obsolete. Maybe it was a financial reversal that forced you to downsize your life and reimagine your future. Or possibly a relationship that ended and left you to question your understanding of yourself and what you thought you knew.

I've noticed that we often measure our worth by the distance between where we are and where we believe we should be. The mortgage broker who once closed million-dollar deals now sells insurance. The executive who now manages a small team after corporate downsizing. The parent whose carefully crafted life plan upended by unexpected challenges.

Society tells us these are failures to hide, embarrassments to explain away. But what if these apparent descents actually invite you to discover parts of yourself that success had kept hidden? What if your current struggle—the one that makes you feel diminished in the eyes of others—actually opens the door to your most genuine self?

> "Sometimes it's the very people who no one imagines anything of who do the things no one can imagine."— Alan Turing (Benedict Cumberbatch) in the film, *The Imitation Game*[7]

This striking observation from the movie reminds us that our greatest potential often emerges when we step outside society's predefined roles and expectations. Just as Turing's brilliance flourished despite—and perhaps because of—his outsider status, our own moments of apparent setback may be precisely when our unique gifts find their true purpose.

Next time you find yourself wincing at the question from a new acquaintance, "So, what do you do?" or avoiding the high school reunion because your life doesn't match what you'd planned, consider this: What if the measure of your life isn't the height you've reached, but the depth you've discovered in falling?

Sometimes, we must lose our old answers before we can ask better questions.

This dialogue creates what Makiguchi called "value creation"[8]—the ability to extract growth and meaning from any circumstance, including those we would never consciously choose.

Amelia Earhart reflected, "The most difficult thing is the decision to act, the rest is merely tenacity,"[9] Her words took on new meaning during my weeks of pizza delivery back in 1990. The initial decision to accept my circumstances, to embrace this radical change rather than fight it, proved far harder than the daily tasks that followed. Each delivery, each interaction, each moment of self-reflection built upon that fundamental choice to remain engaged with life, regardless of its current form.

My Buddhist practice, which had always been a vital force in my life's journey, now truly became an even deeper foundation. The daily rhythm of chanting and meditation established a stability that no external circumstance could shake, not to mention the inner strength it unleashed.

In the quiet hours inside my van before dawn, when the city still slept, I accessed deeper wells of wisdom and energy than I had known existed but now flowed freely.

The lesson of this period wasn't just about survival through adversity—it revealed the regenerative benefit of complete acceptance of change. The very circumstances that seemed to represent my greatest failure actually laid the groundwork for a vital evolution. Each pizza delivered, each humble interaction, each moment spent to acknowledge what existed rather than what had been or what might be, slowly enabled me to forge a new version of myself.

This process begins with a moment of honest recognition. When you find yourself caught in regret or anxiety about your future, pause and acknowledge your current reality with the simple statement: "This is where I am now." Each time you redirect your attention to the present moment without judgment or evasion, you strengthen your capacity to accept what is. Once this reality establishes itself in your mind, then you can begin to make the causes that will lift you up right from where you stand.

> ACTION: Start with just three deliberate moments of clear-eyed awareness each day, perhaps during routine activities like vacuuming the house or waiting in line at the supermarket. Then deepen your perspective and ask, "Am I really 100% present in this current reality?"

As I look back now, I can see how this period of apparent descent was actually an ascent in disguise. The ashes of my former life weren't just an ending—they were the fertile soil from which something new and much more authentic would eventually emerge. It was a magnificent feeling. The real phoenix didn't represent my career or my circumstances, but my understanding of what truly matters in a life well-lived.

Sometimes, we must lose everything we think defines us to discover who we really are.

The deepest fall can birth the greatest rise.

Glen Allison

The Wisdom of Failure

What defines success? I wondered, as I navigated the familiar streets of Los Angeles from this new vantage point. *Surely, true accomplishment must possess a more dynamic dimension.*

Years later, I would discover that my journey through bankruptcy and renewal illustrated what psychologists call "psychological capital"—a concept developed by Fred Luthans, Carolyn Youssef, and Bruce Avolio in their book, *Psychological Capital: Developing the Human Competitive Edge*. Their research identified four key psychological resources that determine our ability to thrive amid adversity: Hope, Efficacy, Resilience, and Optimism—HERO.[10] As I read their findings, memories of those challenging days acquired new meaning, like photographs that slowly develop in a darkroom, patterns were revealed that I couldn't perceive while I lived through them.

Hope, I learned, wasn't just about maintaining a positive outlook—it encompassed both the willpower to pursue goals and the waypower to find alternative paths when obstacles arise. The same determination that once drove me to capture the perfect architectural shot now fueled my resolve to rebuild—to rebirth myself and my career from nothing.

Efficacy—the confidence in one's ability to succeed—manifested in unexpected ways during this period.

You can chart your growth in a new direction using this "flipped-mind" approach:

Hidden Powers

Blastoff

What you perceive as a setback may actually be the universe's way of unveiling capabilities you've been blind to. Your current challenges don't just test you—they reveal you.

The discomfort you feel during major life transitions isn't evidence of failure but of accelerated growth. A turtle encounters no wind resistance whatsoever. Massive rockets shake the earth in their fiery ascent. The journey to great height generates tremendous heat. Abject failure perfectly sets the stage for magnificent rebirth.

What feels like regression when you hit obstacles, or rock bottom, isn't constriction—it's preparation for your quantum leap. Your perceived losses create vacuums that nature rushes to fill with unexpected gifts. The universe abhors empty spaces; where one door closes, three windows always crack open.

The laws of the Universe reveal hidden powers with absolute certainty and consistency.

Our most valuable assets often remain invisible until traditional strengths no longer serve. Like desert seeds that wait decades for fire before they can germinate then burst into explosive bloom, our greatest capabilities require the heat of adversity to emerge. The qualities that surface during extreme hardship—resourcefulness, adaptability, visionary insight—can outshine everything you thought you lost.

Extreme conditions don't just permit growth—they activate capabilities impossible in mild climates.

> When you face obstinate obstacles, ask: "What if these barricades are godsends in disguise?" Treasure these discoveries in their raw, often painful but ultimately splendid detail. This inverted perspective reveals not just who you were under crushing crisis but your true identity revealed only by walking through fire—a version of yourself impossible to even imagine from safer ground.
>
> Your current harsh circumstances didn't arrive to limit you but to expand you beyond dimensions your comfortable life never permitted. This expansion hurts—as all meaningful growth does—but it creates space for capabilities that lie dormant in easier times, eagerly waiting for necessity to awaken them.
>
> Bravery begets revelation.
>
> The seasoned navigator doesn't curse the storm but learns to read its patterns. Your difficulties contain coded messages crucial for your flight. The wisdom you extract today becomes the foundation upon which tomorrow's success will sprout—not despite your struggles but precisely because of them.
>
> Enjoy the exhilarating thrill of the launch. The shakiest liftoffs can lead to the most remarkable flights.

This mindset illustrates aspects of what philosopher Daisaku Ikeda called "human revolution"[11]—a capacity that can activate and foster genuine advancement often measured not in external achievements but in the continuous expansion of our inner capabilities and character.

The skills that had enabled me to become a successful photographer—attention to detail, timing, understanding of light and shadow and color—found new expression and new pathways. Buddhism had taught me to exert maximum effort toward whatever task lay before me. Each small victory built a new kind of confidence, different from the swagger of my previous success but somehow far more substantial.

An internal revolution gradually took hold deep within my life.

Each financial misstep, each overconfident decision that had led to my bankruptcy, ultimately evolved into not just a failure but a lesson, a data point in the grand experiment of living. The true measure of optimism, I discovered, existed not in denial of failure but in its perception as feedback, as vital information for the next attempt.

J.K. Rowling's journey from destitution to literary phenomenon exemplifies this revolutionary relationship with failure. In 1993, her life had collapsed into what she later described as "spectacular failure on an epic scale."[12] Recently divorced, unemployed, and raising her daughter alone, she subsisted on welfare in an unheated Edinburgh apartment and typed her manuscript on an old manual typewriter while her baby slept beside her. Depression enveloped her, so severe that she contemplated suicide.

"Rock bottom became the solid foundation on which I rebuilt my life," Rowling later reflected in her 2008 Harvard commencement address. Rather than view her circumstances as evidence of personal inadequacy, she recognized the clarifying effect of having nothing left to lose. "Failure meant a stripping away of the inessential," she explained. "I stopped pretending to myself that I was anything other than what I was, and began to direct all my energy into finishing the only work that mattered to me."[13]

The manuscript she completed during this period—"Harry Potter and the Philosopher's Stone"—faced rejection from twelve publishing houses before it found a home. The series went on to sell over 500 million copies worldwide and revolutionized not just children's literature but Rowling's understanding of resilience itself. "Failure gave me an inner security that I had never attained by passing examinations," she noted. "The knowledge that I had survived failure—not just failure, but very public failure—gave me the confidence to survive anything."[14]

Rowling's example stands as incredible, undeniable proof not merely for her rags-to-riches narrative, but for her recognition that failure wasn't something that happened to her—it was something that revealed her.

Your defeats don't diminish you—they decode you.

External success, once stripped away, creates space for sincere creative expression and marvelous self-discovery. Though my story is not comparable to the recognized global scale of Rowling's rebirth, it carries the same essential insight: beneath the surface of our perceived failures lies a more essential self that yearns to emerge.

There's a dignified story deep within all of us, that waits for the moment when life's challenges strip away our pretenses, when the doors finally open to reveal what truly matters.

Hidden Powers

The van that had become my home provided a perfect metaphor for fortitude. Its interior, once confining, evolved into a sanctuary of rebirth. At night, as I reviewed that day's effort and inner growth, I began to understand perseverance not as an ability to resist change, but as a capacity to flow with it. Like the willow metaphor in Robert Jordan's book *The Fires of Heaven*: "The oak fought the wind and was broken, the willow bent when it must and survived."[15]

In retrospect, I can see how my string of successes in photography had created a kind of psychological armor, a false sense of invulnerability that actually made me more vulnerable. Success, I realized, can act like a bright light that casts deep shadows and obscures the very things we most need to see.

> "It ain't about how hard you hit. It's about how hard you can get hit and keep moving forward ... That's how winning is done!"—Rocky Balboa in the movie, *Rocky Balboa*[16]

This raw wisdom cuts to the heart of true resilience. Throughout the Rocky films, the titular character never defines victory by flawless performance or even by winning every match. Instead, his greatness emerges from his capacity to absorb devastating blows and still rise for the next round.

In our achievement-focused world, we often measure ourselves by our ability to deliver success, to "hit hard" in life's arena. But the deeper measure of character isn't found in perfect execution—it's revealed in those moments when we're knocked down, disoriented, and face what looks like total defeat. The champions of life aren't those who never fall, but those who develop the extraordinary capacity to rise again and again as they learn from each setback and refuse to let it define them.

My own shadow inventory revealed specific blind spots in my professional life. The lavish staff meals, the casual disregard for fiscal prudence—these weren't just financial mistakes but symptoms of a deeper misunderstanding about the nature of success itself. *How strange,* I thought, *that I had to lose everything to gain everything.*

But intelligence, I learned, involves more than smarter financial decisions. It requires development of a deeper understanding of myself, of the patterns that had led to both my rise and fall. The Buddhist concept of the Middle Way[17] took on new meaning—not as a compromise between extremes, but as a path of sustainable growth and natural development.

The descent from successful photographer to pizza delivery boy traced not a straight line from success to failure—it carved a spiral path that led to deeper understanding. My daily rhythm of self-reflection established a stability that no external circumstance could shake. The bankruptcy that seemed like an ending was actually a beginning, a chance to rebuild not just my life but a more truthful way to exist in the world.

Martin Luther King Jr. observed, "The ultimate measure of a man is not where he stands in moments of comfort and convenience, but where he stands at times of challenge."[18]

We stand tallest not when life spares us its harshest blows, but precisely when it doesn't.

Chapter 14 - The Silent Ascent

A Decade of Nonstop Global Travel, 1990-2000

Armed with a single camera body and a few lenses rescued from my bankruptcy, I reassessed my life.

At forty-five, I stood at the precipice of reinvention as I contemplated an uncharted future. Travel photography beckoned—not merely as a vocational pivot, but as an epochal shift in my life. Its promise of odyssey and artistic fulfillment sang to my soul. Yet between me and that alluring future loomed a gauntlet of challenges that would plumb the depths of my determination. While seemingly daunting obstacles stood in my path, I grasped a fundamental principle—life's impediments must serve as cornerstones that enable us to forge ultimate triumph.

The Mystic Law had revealed to me that what appears as adversity often masks unlimited opportunity. Like a lotus rising from muddy waters, the very circumstances that seemed to constrain me could become the fertile soil from which my expansion could bloom. Even within my humble station as a pizza delivery boy, my inner flame refused to diminish. Complaint would have plunged me deep into a dark abyss. Armed with hard-won wisdom, I refused to fall prey.

Though I had yet to manifest my full potential, every second held infinite possibility for elevation. Joy springs not from circumstance but from the life force we bring to each moment.

Glen Allison

This period marked the first step of an ambitious ascent. My aspirations soared toward lofty heights—to capture the world's magnificence through my lens. The universe, responsive to my fervent resolve, started to unveil an auspicious path. In an unexpected turn, my nascent travel portfolio attracted the discriminating attention of Tony Stone Worldwide, a prestigious London stock photo agency. This glimpse of possibility sparked hope—but to convert that spark into flame would require a depth of determination I resolved to unleash.

Buddhist wisdom had taught me that external circumstances can change in direct proportion to the development of our internal strength. This principle now resonated with crystalline clarity—my current situation was neither punishment nor misfortune, but rather the perfect staging ground to manifest deeper dimensions of courage and conviction.

Bankruptcy proceedings cast their grim realities over my emerging dream, but where once I might have yielded, now, I stood firm and refused to let circumstance dictate my future life.

My hillside home above Los Angeles would remain mine for nine precious months before legal proceedings claimed it. Acting decisively, I secured a small group of British rock musicians as short term tenants—they needed a recording space for nine months; I needed operating capital. Since I didn't need to make mortgage payments during the nine-month bankruptcy period, the rock group's rental payment became my seed money; it financed hundreds of rolls of film. The very next morning, I quit my pizza delivery job and pointed my van toward the horizon, armed with only my camera and iron-clad resolve to forge a new path. I set out to photograph the country's iconic travel sights.

Hidden Powers

My prepaid nationwide gym affiliation became a lifeline that would provide morning workouts and essential showers. My van offered sanctuary through the nights; at dawn's light I documented America's majestic landmarks. From Liberty's luminous torch to Rushmore's stoic faces, each frame immortalized not merely national monuments, but the embodiment of unyielding perseverance.

Yet success proved elusive in those early days. Without today's instant digital connectivity, image licensing advanced at a glacial pace. That inaugural year yielded a paltry $700 in licensing royalties—far insufficient even for fuel costs. But each modest remittance fortified my resolve; it did not weaken it. In those days, stock photo agencies worked on the basis that the photography would cover the cost of image production while the agency would handle the marketing and sales, then the proceeds for licensed images would be split 50/50.

When bankruptcy seized my van and my home nine months later and thrust me toward homelessness, I made a pivotal decision; I sold my cherished Canon 600mm telephoto lens for $5000. This currency of hope purchased a ticket to Europe and a Eurail pass for the months ahead. That lens was gigantic; I couldn't have easily taken it with me anyway. Night trains would serve as my mobile abodes and reduce hotel expense. It was an audacious gambit that eliminated all paths of retreat.

Through Amsterdam's lacework of canals and along the grande boulevards of Paris, I hunted images that would craft an exemplary portfolio for my new photo agency. When my funds depleted, ravenous necessity compelled me to seek the kindness of strangers on the street for meals. Yet even as I balanced on

Glen Allison

this razor's edge between artist and vagrant, my lens remained fixed on the sublime beauty that surrounded me.

The universe operates in intricate rhythms that often appear as chaos to the untrained eye. What others might dismiss as lucky breaks, I recognized as synchronicities; these were cosmic echoes that responded to the vibrational quality of my own contributions. After decades of Buddhist endeavors and study, I had become attuned to these deeper patterns. Every seeming setback was actually a setup for breakthrough; every loss became an invitation to discover greater treasures within. I was more than ready for any battle that lay ahead. The Universe would soon test this resolve.

In Barcelona, a surprise $5,000 royalty disbursement from my photo agency offered renewed promise—until my Los Angeles bank imposed a five-day moratorium due to my insolvency status. This financial limbo launched me into an absurd odyssey across Europe, one that would test every ounce of my resourcefulness.

Yet deep within, I knew this was no mere test of survival, but a sacred threshold I was meant to cross. It was an opportunity to manifest the core revelation that had been cultivating within me for a quarter century of Buddhist practice: that our greatest power emerges precisely when all external supports fall away, revealing the infinite reservoir of wisdom and strength that resides in every human heart.

The Red Windmill's Promise

Fifty dollars from a Barcelona ATM. That was my last lifeline to solvency before I departed the city later that evening on a night train to Paris. For context, fifty dollars in the early 1990s held substantially more purchasing power than today—enough to cover a few days of modest expenses for a disciplined traveler, especially since I often slept on night trains using my fully-paid-upfront Eurail Pass.

With all credit cards surrendered to bankruptcy and only a mere hundred dollars accessible in my L.A. bank account with my debit card, I had decided to withdraw just half to cover my final expenses in Barcelona and then obtain the other half from an ATM in France to minimize exchange rates. Back then, the euro had not yet been introduced, and each European country still operated with its own national currency.

Somehow, I was determined to stretch those funds until my bank hold was released during which time I would photograph iconic landmarks of Paris: the Eiffel Tower, the Moulin Rouge, the Arc de Triomphe.

The prospect of those sequestered funds tantalized me with visions of proper meals and basic comforts, still temporally distant from reality.

A few hours earlier before my night train to Paris, I had captured the soaring spires of La Sagrada Familia as they pierced the Catalan sky, each frame a prayer cast into an uncertain future. Gaudi's organic masterpiece seemed to whisper ancient wisdom about faith and perseverance, its undulating forms and biomorphic structure a reminder that even with divine grace, man's psyche, behavior, and life remain vulnerable without protection, nourishment, and attention.

The remaining fifty dollars in Paris beckoned like a mirage—a shimmer of hope on the horizon of the next day that would soon vanish from reach.

Paris proved less than welcoming.

Usually radiant with promise, the city turned a cold shoulder. The era's primitive banking networks betrayed me. Each rejected ATM transaction resounded like a door slammed shut, until only the ten remaining dollars in my pocket stood between me and destitution. Later that evening, the City of Light, now draped in twilight's uncertainties, seemed to mock my dreams with its distant gleaming lights. Yet even as my resources diminished, an inner light burned steady—the same flame that had guided countless seekers through their darkest nights.

I battled surging trepidation and boarded a night train to Munich, where my German friend, Annelie, had extended an open invitation.

The refuge of a night train had become my monastery on wheels, each rhythmic click of rail joints a meditation on impermanence.

Through the countryside shrouded in darkness, I rolled eastward toward Germany as I watched my few remaining dollars evaporate like frost under first light. The sleeping passengers around me, wrapped in their cocoons of comfort, had no idea that among them sat a photographer whose entire world had compressed into a camera bag and five dollars' worth of hope.

Munich's ATMs proved equally hostile—no Deutschmarks for me.

Pride compelled me to conceal my financial limbo from my friend. After scarcely a day, I departed for Milan via overnight rail, with a desperate hope that Italian ATMs might prove more merciful. But Milan offered no salvation. Down to my last two dollars, I rationed them for water and a meager baguette before I boarded yet another night train back to Barcelona—the only city where I'd successfully withdrawn ATM funds.

At the French-Italian border, reality delivered another cruel blow—a last minute French railway strike had severed all routes to Spain. My path to Barcelona, and financial relief, vanished in an instant. The train reversed course toward Milan carrying me further from shattered hopes.

But an empty stomach and depleted resources hadn't loosened a single complaint from my lips. Instead, with steadfast resolve, I pulled out my trusty Eurail Pass and pointed myself back toward Munich on the next night train as I acknowledged that pride must yield to necessity.

You can imagine Annelie's perplexed expression at my precipitous return to Munich.

As I stood before her, pride finally crumbled at my feet, though I felt an unexpected lightness. The truth of my circumstance, once spoken aloud, converted from burden to bridge that opened a path forward. Annelie's gracious offer of a thousand-dollar loan wasn't merely currency—it represented a reminder that the universe often channels its energy through human hearts.

I had divulged the truth—$5,000 tantalizingly sequestered in L.A.

That evening, without pause, I boarded yet another train back to Milan, driven to capture images I'd missed in my desperate passage the day before. Annelie likely saw me as either mad or magnificently obsessed. The reality was that it was probably both.

Throughout these ordeals, verbalized discontent never breached my resolve; each reversal kindled renewed determination. Every impediment transformed into bedrock for growth. My Buddhist practice had enabled me to temper this steel within me—fortitude that defied my previous limits.

The remaining $4000 evaporated swiftly into film and essential travel costs over the next several weeks.

Hidden Powers

Parisian Billboards: The Turning Point

One frost-bitten evening back in Paris remains crystal clear in my memory: destitute once again, I had claimed a cold, unyielding bench for the night at Gare du Nord station. I curled around my camera bag, masquerading as a traveler who awaited the next train to nirvana.

Only hours earlier, I had photographed the Moulin Rouge. In that twilight hour, as its crimson windmill vanes split the gathering darkness, time seemed to halt its relentless march. Through my viewfinder, I framed a view of the Moulin Rouge's sinuous silhouette through the Art Nouveau ironwork of a Métro station across the street. My image transcended mere composition—it marked a moment of perfect alignment between artist, subject, and the infinite.

Even as my body shivered on that station bench later that evening, my spirits soared with the certainty that I had captured something timeless.

That solitary frame would emerge as my inaugural triumph during what would ultimately become a ten-year nonstop sojourn around the globe—one photo, an emblem of tenacity that marked the instant when indomitable resolve began to yield rewards.

In an extraordinary turn of events, over the next few years my Moulin Rouge photograph yielded an astonishing harvest—tens of thousands of dollars in stock photo royalties through Getty Images, the world's premier photo library that had acquired

Tony Stone Worldwide, my first stock photo agency. Almost overnight my financial fortunes reversed dramatically. When I returned to Paris years later, I discovered my Moulin Rouge photograph commanding attention from kiosks and Métro billboards throughout the city; it had been licensed from Getty by the popular weekly entertainment magazine, *Le Spectateur*.

By an extraordinary alignment of timing, I had arrived in Paris during the single week my image adorned the city at hundreds of public venues. In my mind, there was no doubt whatsoever that this synchronicity resulted from my rhythmical connection to the vibrations of the Mystic Law. As I stood before those displays and recalled that cold night at Gare du Nord, a torrent of emotion engulfed me. That shivering photographer on the station's hard bench could never have envisioned at the time that his work would one day appear so resplendently across the boulevards of Paris—the City of Light had fulfilled its promise.

This moment of validation guided me to Montmartre, where I secured an apartment for a year's duration mere moments from the Moulin Rouge and but a stone's throw from Picasso's erstwhile atelier. I began to study the French language—the fulfillment of another lifelong dream.

My imagery had caught the attention of prestigious publications like *National Geographic* and *Condé Nast Traveler*. Through Getty's extensive network, my photographs were disseminated for publication over a hundred thousand times through the ensuing years, which elevated me to be among the pantheon of the world's most celebrated travel photographers of that epoch.

The former pizza delivery boy had transformed into an artist whose work generated a few million dollars in royalties over the next decade. I spent the first ten years as a perpetual nonstop wanderer by choice, chasing light across more than a hundred countries. From secluded archipelagos to the venerable passages of the Silk Road between Istanbul and Islamabad my lens captured worlds I had heretofore only envisioned.

Beyond the monetary triumph and recognition lay deeper riches—the hearts of those I encountered, the ancient customs I witnessed, the inner evolution that occurred within me. From Parisian boulevards to Timbuktu's stark horizons, I sought to capture not just images, but the essential wisdom embedded in each culture's soul.

A decade later as I stood on Montmartre's summit once again, I gazed over the city that had once witnessed my deepest struggles. At that moment, I understood my truest achievement.

It wasn't measured in photographs or publications or the large sums of money I had earned, but in who I had become. When I met each challenge without complaint and pursued my vision without compromise, I began to experience something far more elusive than light—the very pulse of human experience.

The evolution from vagrant to celebrated travel photographer reflected more than financial rebirth—it demonstrated an immutable law: that steadfast determination, when paired with no complaint and an absolute refusal to surrender to circumstance, can bend reality itself toward one's vision. Each published image stood as a potent statement of unshakeable faith in one's chosen path.

Glen Allison

From Montmartre's summit, Paris unfurled below like a map of my ever-expanding self-created destiny. The Eiffel Tower rose triumphantly through the evening haze; it stood as an iron exclamation point to a decade's relentless journey.

Yet even now, with success firmly in hand, I recognized that each achievement was merely a path to greater accomplishment.

The odyssey would continue and evolve as times changed, and I with them. A true seeker never reaches a final destination, only higher vantage points from which to view the next horizon—and the next challenge.

Chapter 15 - Fortune's Adversary

Complaint devours good fortune like Darkness consumes Light.

Over the decades, I've trained myself away from complaint. No one wants to be near a complainer—except maybe another complainer. Misery loves company.

Like malevolent vampires, chronic grumblers cast a pall over every gathering they enter. They siphon vitality from the room; their words extinguish initiative and wither aspiration. A complainer's presence degrades vibrant sanctuaries into desolate wastelands of malcontent, leaving others struggling to breathe in an atmosphere heavy with cynicism.

Vast galaxies spiral through space without protest, stars burn fierce and bright without lament, planets trace their ancient orbits in perfect silence. Only humans have developed the peculiar habit of arguing with reality itself and resisting what IS.

Each whisper of discontent amplifies the gloom in our life. Like a treacherous riptide that pulls us seaward, perpetual grievance lures us into darker waters, where every struggle toward illumination leaves us more depleted and increasingly adrift.

Have you ever noticed how quickly your mood shifts after a simple comment about something that bothers you? Think about the last time you voiced frustration about traffic, weather, or a colleague's habits. Did it make the situation better—or did it pull you deeper into a fog of dissatisfaction? We often don't realize we slide down this slope until we reach the bottom.

The space between feeling bothered and speaking that feeling aloud holds significant potential, either positive or negative—a moment where you can either fuel what you don't want or redirect that same energy toward what you do.

Our complaints build actual grooves in our mental landscape. Each murmur of discontent cuts another line in the map that guides future thoughts. What begins as a casual negative remark can harden into our default route—the path our mind automatically travels when confronted with any new situation.

The invisible contours of our consciousness respond to repetition with religious devotion. If we criticize enough times, our mind becomes an elegant machine engineered to detect flaws with laser precision while remaining blind to possibilities. Time invested in complaint subtracts directly from time available to resolve what disturbs us. Calculate the minutes you spend voicing what's wrong—then visualize those same precious moments redirected toward creation. This isn't abstract theory: it's practical psychology. Our mind fortifies what we rehearse until it becomes automatic.

> **Silent Rebellion**
>
> You can rewrite this code today.
>
> When you substitute decisive action for incessant complaint, your consciousness must forge new unfamiliar connections. These fresh pathways strengthen with each

use, while the old complaint channels weaken from disuse. The neglected routes don't vanish overnight—they fade incrementally, like trails reclaimed by wilderness when footsteps no longer maintain them.

When irritation or difficulty arrives, begin with a ten-second pause—just one conscious deep breath. Note the impulse to complain, then consciously pivot toward a response that honors your highest values. In that infinitesimal interval lies the seed of your freedom and the foundation for monumental shifts in your character.

Next, direct your observation into one small, concrete positive action. This reroutes the energy that would have fueled complaint into constructive forward movement. Your action need not be dramatic—draft one paragraph, make one call, solve one tiny fragment of the larger puzzle. These modest redirections renovate our thinking more effectively than grand plans without execution.

Watch how your dispersed energy consolidates into focused intensity and how differently the world responds when your words invite abundance rather than lack. The same challenges will still exist, but your relationship to them fundamentally shifts.

Your words construct the channels your thoughts must follow. Will you create conduits to wastelands of criticism or to fertile valleys of creation? The template exists in your daily speech: reinforce the patterns of complaint or build an entirely different mental blueprint that will lead you out of misery. Initial redirections may feel awkward, even counterfeit—like writing with your non-dominant hand. Yet with consistent practice, these new pathways

> expand into boulevards, while former highways of perpetual complaint narrow to forgotten footpaths.
>
> Your future flows through avenues carved by your words. Choose them as if your destiny depends on them. It does.

The nature of complaint resembles a black hole in the vast firmament of human potential—a gravitational well of negativity so intense that not even light can escape its pull. Once caught in its orbit, even our most radiant dreams dim. They stretch and distort until they vanish beyond an event horizon of perpetual unhappiness.

My friend Michael in Los Angeles, a mid-level office worker, was trapped in a cubicle under a micromanaging boss. For years, his daily routine consisted of complaints about his two-hour commute, his stagnant salary, and his supervisor's unreasonable demands. His colleagues came to expect his litany of grievances at every lunch break. Yet this habitual complaining only deepened his rut.

Everything changed when he finally decided to redirect that wasted energy. Instead of steadily lamenting his circumstances, he invested those hours to develop specialized skills in data analytics. Within six months, he leveraged these new capabilities to negotiate a remote work arrangement three days a week which cut his commute time by more than half. Within a year, he positioned himself as an indispensable "linchpin" whose expertise made him more valuable than his difficult boss. His breakthrough began not with a job change, but with a complaint change.

With each complaint we utter, we unknowingly construct our own prison until our world of infinite possibility contracts to a singularity of discontent.

In his article, "The Psychology of Complaining," published in *Psychology Today*, William Berry, a psychotherapist and teacher at Florida International University, reports, "Another reason people may complain is that the brain is negative-biased." He goes on to explain that the brain perceives negatives at an approximated ratio of five to one, which makes complainers simply feel they have more to protest than to appreciate. This invariably leads to diminished happiness and increased suffering.[1]

Each grievance you utter fortifies a pessimistic predisposition, until you find yourself ensnared in an inexorable spiral of unhappiness. In stark contrast, those who rise above life's challenges and maintain a dignified reticence will create more forward progress than those who waste their energy cataloging grievances.

> **Verbal Destiny**
>
> Your words build the reality you inhabit tomorrow.
>
> Each syllable you speak doesn't merely describe your world—it constructs it. Complaints aren't observations; they're blueprints for future experiences. Every utterance of discontent etches deeper channels in our mind through which pessimistic thoughts flow with increasing ease.
>
> Masters of their destiny guard their speech like sacred treasure. They recognize that language isn't just

> expression but creation itself—each sentence shapes experiences yet to come.
>
> This isn't mystical fantasy: it's cognitive mechanics. The brain circuits we reinforce through habitual complaint become superhighways for spotting problems that leave roads of possibility to wither from disuse.
>
> Our mouth draws the maps our feet must later walk.
>
> Those who constantly speak of barriers find their paths blocked; those who articulate possibilities discover unexpected openings.
>
> Listen to yourself as if you are eavesdropping on a stranger. What future does this person invoke with each sentence? What universe do these words call into existence? The mirror of language reflects not just who you are but who you will transform into.
>
> We cannot speak of limitation daily and expect boundless outcomes. We cannot narrate scarcity and harvest plenty. The voice that constantly articulates problems cannot simultaneously invite solutions.

Daisaku Ikeda stated: "Sometimes we complain without thinking much of it, but the frightening thing about complaining is that every time we do, a dark cloud descends over our heart, and our hope, appreciation, and joy gradually wane."[2]

These three quintessential forces—hope, joy, and appreciation—constitute the cornerstones of an existence worth cherishing. Hope propels us forward through uncertainty. Joy illuminates our journey. Appreciation amplifies life's countless treasures.

Yet complaint acts as a corrosive force as it slowly erodes each of these pillars until our inner landscape lies barren.

Like water that wears away stone, complaint erodes the bedrock of our resilience. One drop might seem harmless—a casual criticism here, a moment of dissatisfaction there. But over time, these drops carve canyons of discontent in our character and redirect the very flow of our destiny toward something we most likely won't like.

The immutable laws of physics parallel the intricacies of human behavior. The world we perceive becomes a reflection of our inner dialogue.

This principle is corroborated by Anaïs Nin's insight: "We don't see things as they are, we see them as *we* are."[3]

Those endless European night trains could have become a litany of complaints—each uncomfortable seat, each failed ATM attempt, each empty stomach growl a reason for bitter lament. Instead, my silence in the face of adversity became a force more effective than gravity itself, one that bent the arc of my destiny toward triumph.

Sarah, a mother of three I met in San Francisco, had put her career on pause. She found herself trapped in a cycle of resentment. "I sacrificed everything for my family," became her daily refrain to friends, neighbors, and me. Her complaints about lost opportunities and financial dependence created an atmosphere of tension that affected everyone around her.

The transformation began when I shared insights about complaint's toxic impact. Although a bit resistant at first, she soon recognized how her negative words reinforced her perceived helplessness. With newfound determination, she allocated two hours each evening to launch an online consulting business based on her previous expertise. Instead of focusing on what she lacked, she built upon her assets—professional knowledge, industry connections, and discrete time blocks. Within half a year, her business generated a meaningful income stream that restored both her financial contribution to her family and her personal agency. Her breakthrough occurred not when her external situation changed, but when she changed her response to it.

This shift from expression of discontent to purposeful action represents a fundamental choice available to us daily. The imperative lies in our embrace of pragmatic methods—several of which this book explains later—that will enable you to access your boundless wellspring of wisdom and strength. When you tap your inner resources, you turn potential grievances into propellants toward meaningful progress.

> "You have a choice. You can either be angry for what you don't have or thankful for what you do have."—Coach Carter in the movie, *Coach Carter*[4]

This straightforward wisdom addresses the fundamental crossroads we face countless times each week. Throughout the film, Coach Ken Carter challenges his players to rise above their circumstances not by denying difficulties but by refusing to allow life's challenges to define them. The young men initially respond with resistance and complaint, seeing only limitations—

their troubled neighborhood, underfunded schools, and challenging home lives.

Yet Carter recognizes that their very perception of these circumstances determines whether they become barriers or simply conditions to navigate. This choice between complaint and gratitude isn't just about attitude: it's about agency. When we fixate on what's missing or unfair, we surrender our power to external conditions. When we acknowledge what remains available, we reclaim the ability to direct our own journey regardless of the terrain.

I'm absolutely certain my brief tenure as a pizza delivery boy shifted so swiftly because I adamantly refused to voice complaint about my circumstances. Rather than deepen my predicament through expressing discontent, my positive demeanor created space for possibility.

This absence of complaint ignited a cascade of good fortune—almost instantaneously. Unforeseen portals of opportunity appeared, newly opened doors that propelled me into a series of extraordinary global circumnavigations lasting nearly a decade.

Complaint infiltrates like an insidious toxin that gradually weakens our innate fortitude. It exposes a fundamental flaw in character that corrupts our perception and erodes our resolve to persevere. Rather than confront life's challenges directly, chronic complainers unconsciously amplify their own suffering, turning manageable obstacles into insurmountable walls.

A concept attributed to Carl Jung suggests, "What you resist not only persists, but will grow in size."[5] Jung's insight points to a counterintuitive reality: our resistance often strengthens what we oppose.

Our judgments act as prisms that refract all incoming light. Call an event "devastating," and watch as your mind assembles evidence to support this verdict. Label the identical scenario "instructive," and entirely different aspects suddenly become visible. The facts remain unchanged, but their impact reverses completely.

A mind focused on injustice will always find it; one attuned to possibility will perpetually discover openings where others see barricades. Your circumstances merely provide raw material. You decide whether to shape it into a prison or a launch pad to progress.

Nick Vujicic's extraordinary journey illustrates the regenerative benefit of a refusal to complain despite circumstances that would justify endless grievance. Born in 1982 with tetra-amelia syndrome—a rare disorder characterized by the absence of all four limbs—his entire body consisted of just a torso, a head, and a few toes on a partial foot. Vujicic's early life presented challenges most would consider overwhelming. Without arms, hands, and legs, even the simplest daily tasks like going to the bathroom required ingenious adaptation and extraordinary challenge.

As a child in Melbourne, Australia, Vujicic endured relentless bullying at school. At age ten, he attempted suicide by trying to drown himself in the bathtub. He later revealed, "I felt like giving up... I was wondering, 'What's the purpose? Why do I go to school? Why take up oxygen?'"[6] Depression and isolation threatened to define his existence.

The pivotal shift in Vujicic's life came when he made a conscious decision to redirect his focus from what he lacked to what he could offer. Rather than dwell on his physical limitations or complain about unfairness, he began to explore what remained possible. At seventeen, encouraged by his mother to read an article about a disabled man who had accomplished great things, Vujicic had an epiphany: "I realized I could use my life to encourage others."[7]

The journey that unfolded defied all expectations. Vujicic learned to write with the two toes on his partial left foot, to use a computer at 43 words per minute, to throw tennis balls, swim, play drum pedals, and even surf. Rather than lament his circumstances, he channeled his energy into the development of his talents as a speaker. He earned degrees in accounting and financial planning, but found his true calling in motivational speaking.

Today, Vujicic has addressed over 3,000 audiences in more than 57 countries, and reached hundreds of millions of people. As founder of Life Without Limbs and Attitude is Altitude, he has reshaped his unique perspective into a global message about purpose beyond limitations. "If I fail, I try again, and again, and again," he often says. "If you fail, will you try again? The human spirit can handle much worse than we realize."[8]

The dynamic influence of Vujicic's example lies not just in his achievements but in his absolute refusal to waste energy on complaint. "I'm ridiculously underprivileged,"[9] he quips with characteristic humor. This approach converts potential self-pity into self-awareness that disarms audiences. Rather than see himself as a victim, he recognized that complaint would only imprison him in circumstances he couldn't change, while redirection of that same energy toward possibility created a life of extraordinary impact.

In her article "How and Why You Should Stop Complaining," Elizabeth Scott, PhD, a wellness coach and health educator, stated, "Too much complaining can worsen your mood, make you feel helpless, and lead to a negative outlook on life. Perhaps not surprisingly, people who rate high on the trait called agreeableness are the least likely to complain." She suggests that when we justifiably need to express dissatisfaction, we should shape our concerns to advance our goals rather than protest without purpose.[10]

Ikeda also explained, "Complaints and evasions reflect a cowardly spirit; they corrupt and undermine life's natural creative thrust. When life is denuded of the will to struggle creatively, it sinks into a state of hellish destructiveness directed at all that lives.[11]

Sebastian, an American craftsman I met during my travels through Thailand, had built a fifty-year career in traditional manufacturing. When his industry pivoted toward automation and artificial intelligence, understandably, his first reaction included harsh criticism—about modern trends, younger competitors, and what he called "the death of craftsmanship." These verbal attacks provided momentary emotional relief but accelerated his business decline.

A complete reversal occurred when he confronted his discomfort and embraced the very technologies he had previously condemned. He combined his half-century of hands-on expertise with cutting-edge AI design tools to create a unique hybrid approach. Neither pure traditionalists nor tech-focused competitors could match his distinctive blend of old and new. Now, at seventy-three, he leads a prosperous enterprise that unites time-honored craftsmanship with state-of-the-art technology. This renaissance didn't start with external market changes—it began the moment he replaced his complaints with genuine curiosity about new possibilities.

The universe operates through immutable laws. Mountains rise through sheer persistence, flowers bloom by adherence to their essential nature, and the deepest evolutions occur through a resolute commitment to flourish.

The choice is yours: You can spend your precious life force in discontent only to watch your dreams dissolve like starlight at dawn, or you can direct that same energy to forge a marvelous destiny through the depth of your determination and your efforts to build emboldened dignity.

It has always been this way, and it will always be.

Seven hundred and fifty years ago, Nichiren Daishonin summed it up perfectly in his letter, "The Three Kinds of Treasure," written to his disciple Shijo Kingo on September 11, 1277. He declared: "Do not go around lamenting to others how hard it is for you to live in this world. To do so is an act utterly unbecoming to a worthy man."[12]

Glen Allison

Chapter 16 - Lessons in Flow and Fearlessness

"Saigon's Symphony"

Ho Chi Minh City, Vietnam, October 15, 1994

My early Sunday morning flight carried me over cerulean seas to Hong Kong, where I changed planes for Ho Chi Minh City—Saigon, as it persisted in my mind.

The city immediately assaulted my senses with its cacophony of organized chaos. Streets surged with a dizzying array of bicycles and motor scooters; their riders wove through traffic with a grace that defied conventional logic. Every movement embodied a flow state that seemed to arise from collective consciousness rather than traffic laws.

I had arrived in the country soon after it had been reopened to American tourists after more than three decades. So I expected to find barely concealed animosity that boiled beneath the harsh memories of the Vietnam War. But no one ever made mention of this haunting past. On the drive into town, my taxi driver asked where I was from. I was tempted to say Canada but told him I was American. To my surprise, his eyes lit up as he pointed out sights with the enthusiasm of someone revealing treasured secrets. He embodied the city's irrepressible will to move beyond past wounds.

He drove erratically, one hand on the steering wheel while the other fidgeted with an unlit cigarette. Despite his hurried manner, he gleefully pointed out landmarks—the sprawling Cholon market, ornate Buddhist temples, Chinese pagodas, and the imposing Reunification Hall. When we passed the old American embassy, I braced for tension—but he mentioned it as casually as any other landmark. I realized then how time and fortitude can alleviate even the deepest pain and recast it into merely another waypoint on humanity's journey forward.

The city's architectural layers told their own story of resilience and adaptation. Elegant neoclassical buildings whispered of French colonial influence. Their faded grandeur contrasted sharply with utilitarian structures that dominated other areas.

At street corners, fresh-baked croissants perfumed the air alongside the pungent aroma of durian fruit—an olfactory metaphor for Vietnam's remarkable ability to synthesize past and present, East and West, tradition and progress.

This Vietnam revealed the depth of human perseverance—far removed from the war-torn country that had haunted American consciousness for decades. Here, the weight of history coexisted with an irrepressible optimism for the future; everyone seemed to carry both burden and hope with equal grace.

As evening descended, I ventured into streets that had blossomed into rivers of humanity. Young couples on motorbikes, love in the air, crowded Dong Khoi Street. The laughter and the purr of engines created a vibrant urban chorus.

There were no traffic lights.

Glen Allison

I stood at a curb and confronted what appeared to be an impenetrable flow of traffic—a perfect metaphor for life's seemingly unending challenges. For a few seconds, I remained motionless as I contemplated this chaotic scene.

At that moment, I recalled a fundamental Buddhist principle: true power lies not in opposition to life's flow but in harmony with it. With deliberate calm, I stepped off the curb and into the stream of vehicles. What unfolded next illuminates an essential link between trust and natural order.

The sea of motorbikes parted around me like water flowing around a stone in a stream. As I moved slowly, drivers adjusted their course with fluid precision. They created a protective bubble that moved with me as I walked steadily forward into oncoming traffic. This wasn't chaos—it was a sophisticated synchronicity between mutual awareness and respect, a living demonstration of how individual actions can align in perfect harmony when each participant trusts in the fundamental goodness of the whole.

This simple act of crossing a street in Saigon embodied decades of my Buddhist studies about the interconnected nature of all things—each driver and pedestrian participated in an unspoken choreography, their movements guided by an intuitive understanding that surpassed formal rules. Here was the Middle Way in action—neither reckless abandon nor paralytic fear, but mindful engagement with present reality. And there I was, fully immersed in this living system. I adapted to its movements and flowed in perfect harmony with its rhythm. I reached the opposite curb unscathed and perhaps a touch more enlightened.

Hidden Powers

The Vietnam I witnessed had risen above its painful past not because it forgot the pain but because it changed the pain into wisdom. Every street vendor's smile, every graceful navigation through seemingly impossible traffic, reflected a people who had learned to dance with destiny rather than fight it. Their resilience seemed to spring not from hardened hearts but from lives that had learned to bend without breaking, to flow without losing their essential nature.

As night deepened over Saigon, the city's energy shifted but never dimmed, another city that never slept. Street vendors repurposed bare sidewalks into fragrant feast halls, while portable cafes materialized instantly like mushrooms after rain. In that evening's evolution, I observed another lesson: adaptability extends beyond mere survival—it unveils new ways to thrive.

The Vietnamese people appeared to have mastered an art few societies achieve by honoring their wounds without being defined by them. Obviously, they had chosen to move forward, not motivated by blame. Instead, they were recasting their history of occupation and conflict into a foundation for remarkable reinvention.

In Saigon's streets, I found confirmation of what my Buddhist practice had already taught me: true strength flows not from resistance but from integration, not from forgetting but from reshaping. The city itself became my teacher, and its every corner offered lessons in resilience, adaptation, and the formidable capacity unleashed when we choose to advance with honorable grace, even while carrying a haunted past.

Glen Allison

Confronting Humanity's Shadow

Dawn broke over Saigon with deceptive gentleness.

Golden light spilled across my hotel breakfast table where a dog-eared guidebook lay open, its pages already coffee-stained. The previous day's immersion in the city's vibrant energy had awakened my enthusiasm to capture its cultural treasures—the Emperor of Jade Pagoda, the bustling Cholon market, the vibrant city life. Yet something deeper tugged at my consciousness, an understanding that to truly know this place, I needed to confront its darkest chapters before I ventured deeper into the country.

It was about an hour later that I stood before the War Crimes Exhibition—a squat, unremarkable building set back from the street behind a manicured courtyard. A man in a khaki uniform cleared his throat and handed me a brochure. Its title alone—"U.S. Imperialists' Aggressive War Crimes in Vietnam"—seemed to sap the heat from the tropical air.

The pages contained descriptions that caused my insides to erupt: the 1968 My Lai Massacre, an entire village obliterated, its inhabitants slaughtered without mercy. I read about a GI who had rammed his assault rifle deep inside a young girl's vagina after raping her, and then blew her guts out from the inside. The details were so graphic, so horrifying, that each word ripped my heart out.

The courtyard offered a stark prelude—rusted wreckage of U.S. warplanes, army tanks, and broken artillery pieces spread across the ground like the discarded toys of some monstrous child.

Inside, the exhibition's photographs lined the walls like an endless procession of man's capacity for cruelty: A Viet Cong soldier, pushed from a helicopter when he refused to "cooperate." Piles of corpses unceremoniously dumped in ditches. But it was the image of three young children that shattered my composure. Their faces contorted in agony, clothes and hair aflame, skin peeled from their bones as they ran and screamed—victims of napalm, their innocence consumed in America's war.

The final images delivered a devastating blow: a mother cradled her dead child, the lower half of his body missing, entrails spattered grotesquely across her dress. The second photo showed the same woman crumpled to the ground, her own face obliterated. The juxtaposition of maternal love and unspeakable violence embodied the ultimate perversion of our shared humanity.

When I emerged from the exhibition, the Saigon sunshine felt surreal. The cheerful bustle of the streets—the honking horns, chattering vendors, the aromatic waft of street food—seemed to trivialize the atrocities I had just witnessed.

As I walked aimlessly through the city, I grappled with a whirlwind of emotions: shame, guilt, and a deep, aching sorrow. These atrocities were committed in my country's name. How could I reconcile the vibrant, welcoming Vietnam I saw before

Glen Allison

me with the war-torn hell depicted in those devastating photographs?

I turned onto Le Loi Boulevard; the sun beat down mercilessly, yet the sidewalks buzzed with life. Vendors lined the pavement, their wares displayed in a dazzling array of textures—vibrant fabrics, gleaming trinkets, aromatic spices that tickled the nose and awakened the senses. Then I saw her: an elderly woman seated on a threadbare blanket arranging bamboo spoons with meticulous care.

Her face was carved with deep lines—a life lived fully, if not easily, I imagined. One arm ended abruptly at the elbow, and where her legs should have been, there was only empty space beneath the folds of her faded skirt. Yet her eyes sparkled with an enthusiasm that defied her circumstances; her smile radiated with unconditional grace.

As she calmly negotiated with customers, her movements shaky but assured despite her limitations, I witnessed living proof of human resilience. This woman embodied what Buddhist principles reveal about the capacity to change pain into purpose —not as resignation, but as a foundation to move forward with dignity and purpose.

I raised my camera, seeking her permission with a respectful bow. Her response was immediate and touching—a gracious nod that reached beyond language. Through my lens, I captured not just her image, but an embodiment of the human capacity for endurance. Her smile conveyed not just acceptance of her circumstances, but a quiet triumph over them.

Hidden Powers

Overwhelmed by emotion, I lowered the camera.

The anguish I felt wasn't just for this woman, for the waste of her limbs and the hardships she must have endured. It encompassed all of it—the countless lives cut short, the dreams deferred, the love and hope and effort squandered in the senseless machinery of war. Yet her radiant presence offered living proof that even in our darkest hours, we can maintain the capacity for joy and dignity.

As I walked back toward my hotel, the woman's smile lingered in my mind's eye—a beacon of hope in a world that often seemed determined to extinguish it with devastating cruelty.

This encounter, more than any museum exhibit or historical site, had illuminated the true cost of war—and the remarkable capacity for renewal that lives within human life.

Sometimes, the seemingly smallest occurrences have the most profound impacts—like in Chaos Theory, where a butterfly's wingbeat in one place can trigger a storm elsewhere.[1] This woman's quiet dignity had created waves of insight in my understanding far beyond our brief encounter.

Glen Allison

The Language of the Soul

Hué, Vietnam, October 20, 1994

The Reunification Express carried me northward through Vietnam's heartland; each mile revealed the country's gradual evolution from past to present.

The landscape unfurled like an ageless scroll, each scene more enchanting than the last. Mirror-bright water-ladened rice paddies stretched toward the horizon. In these fields, tradition and progress coexisted in delicate balance—women in conical hats moved with ancestral grace, their wooden plows pulled by water buffaloes alongside modern harvesting machines, the old ways slowly giving way to the new. I traveled as an interested and curious observer through this tableau of time and space. My camera preserved the moments; my thoughts absorbed the deeper value.

Later that evening my train pulled into the station of my final destination Hué after a full day's journey. In shades of amber and violet, twilight draped the city, home of the ancient imperial capital. Hunger led me to a bustling sidewalk café where every table overflowed with local families. Through open doors, I glimpsed the controlled chaos of the kitchen—stacks of steaming bamboo baskets promised unknown delicacies, while copper pots caught and multiplied the warm light.

In this whirlwind of activity moved a remarkable figure—a small man in a vibrant red shirt whose boundless energy and radiant smile changed his inability to speak or hear into an extraordinary gift for communion. His name was Lac, as his daughter Lan Anh explained when she appeared at my table. Her oversized apron and impeccable English reflected aspirations beyond her youth.

Without words, Lac's movements embodied the artistry of hospitality. A complimentary beer appeared, followed by his recommended specialty—banh khoai, a sublime creation of crispy crêpe that cradled fresh bean sprouts and succulent shrimp smothered in spicy peanut sauce. Each dish that followed opened new horizons of flavor, but it was Lac's infectious joy that truly nourished the soul.

Sixteen-year-old Lan Anh shared her dreams as she served. She spoke of future studies in America with an optimism that could shatter borders. Her love for a country she knew only through books and media offered a striking reminder of how hope can flourish even in soil once poisoned by conflict.

The evening's most poignant moment arrived with small footsteps. A diminutive young boy approached my table, his eyes fixed on my remaining food. The boy's worn clothes and shy demeanor reflected a life of hardship, yet his gaze held an innocence that pierced my heart. When I gestured toward an uneaten spring roll, he produced, with practiced care, a small bowl from beneath his arm.

Lac, who had been gently deterring young beggars throughout the evening, witnessed this exchange and responded with quiet perception. He dashed off and soon returned with a fresh plate of rice and vegetables, which he placed at the edge of my table.

His positive nod conveyed volumes without a single word. I watched the boy meticulously transfer this unexpected bounty into a wrinkled plastic bag he'd pulled from his torn pocket; my thoughts turned to the unseen family who would share in this modest feast.

The evening encompassed more than mere dining to become a lesson in the universal language of compassion—a language I had once forgotten but was now learning anew as a humble student appreciating this gift of renewal.

Lac and his daughter refashioned potential barriers—physical limitations, cultural differences, historical wounds—into bridges of understanding. Their farewell handshakes vibrated with genuine warmth, while even other patrons joined to bid goodbye. Their waves dissolved the boundary between tourist and honored guest.

As I stepped into the Hué night, I carried with me more than memories of exceptional cuisine. The true flavor of Vietnam revealed itself not in grand monuments or historic sites, but in these intimate moments of human interaction—a smile that needed no translation, a gesture of kindness that crossed all borders, the simple sharing of food that spoke directly to the soul.

As I navigated the lantern-lit streets back to my lodging, the night air resonated with deep meaning. Lac's silent choreography of hospitality, his daughter's boundless dreams, a hungry child's grateful smile—all mirrored the human capacity for expansion even when harsh reality prevails.

The Gift of Innocence

Nha Trang, Vietnam, October 29, 1994

Among the many entrepreneurial children I encountered in Vietnam—their arms laden with trinkets and postcards, each never proffered for less than a dollar each—Nguyen Thanh stood apart.

From our first meeting outside a small Nha Trang restaurant, a disarming sincerity in his presence struck a deeper chord. His big brown eyes held both timeless wisdom and irrepressible hope, which reflected dimensions of human vitality I had nearly forgotten existed.

"My name is Nguyen Thanh," he proudly introduced himself in surprisingly fluent English. "Nguyen is my family name. You can call me Thanh." I told him my first name but he insisted on calling me, "Mr. Glen."

Unlike other children who pressed their wares with practiced persistence, Thanh seemed genuinely interested in conversation and learning, in how he could share his world. He carefully placed his bag of postcards next to his side and never offered to sell me anything.

Over steaming bowls of noodle soup, his story emerged. His knowledge of America both touched and humbled me. "I know America has fifty states," he declared with infectious enthusiasm. Then came the casual mention of his grandfather's death from Agent Orange—a stark reminder of how history's wounds ripple through generations. Yet here was this child, who bore the weight of a war he'd never known as he faced each day with undimmed optimism.

Our lunches became a daily ritual. Each encounter dissolved another layer of unnecessary cynicism I'd kept buried over the years. The apparent gap between our lives narrowed. This connection worked as a purifying force—it turned poison into medicine.

Through Thanh's young, enthusiastic eyes, Nha Trang revealed itself anew. His dream to become a doctor "to keep people from dying" resonated with long ago dreams from my younger days. In Thanh's ambition, I glimpsed a nation not defined by its war-torn past but propelled forward by the pure aspirations of its youth.

The morning of departure brought with it unexpected heartache.

As I waited before my hotel, bags already loaded onto a cyclo, Thanh's absence felt almost unbearable. He had promised to bid farewell, yet minutes ticked by without his appearance. If I didn't leave soon, I'd miss my flight. I chose to wait. But doubt soon crept in—had our bond meant as little to him as countless other tourist encounters? The thought felt like betrayal, yet I couldn't silence it.

Just as hope began to fade, Thanh's young voice cut through the morning air: "Mr. Glen! Mr. Glen!" The sight of him, as he pedaled furiously on a borrowed bicycle too large for his frame, awakened new hope within me. He'd raced across the city, determined not to miss our goodbye. In that moment, I understood how deeply we'd touched each other's lives.

Our farewell at the airport overflowed with raw emotion. As I embraced him, I felt his rapid heartbeat against my chest and realized this child, this stranger, had become so dear. The one hundred postcards I purchased from him at that last moment weren't mere souvenirs but tangible links to this awakening. The small camera I impulsively bought for him at the airport shop wasn't just a gift but a prayer that he might capture and share his unfiltered vision of the world.

As my plane taxied from the gate, I watched Thanh's diminishing figure through the window as he eagerly clutched his new camera with one hand and offered a fervent wave with the other.

Once airborne, Vietnam's landscape unfolded below—a patchwork of rice paddies stretched to the horizon, each plot a reminder of human perseverance inscribed upon the earth. As these visions blurred into an impressionist canvas of greens and golds, Thanh's face drifted through my mind—his yearning smile, those eyes full of insight beyond his years. This image burned itself deep into my consciousness, a shield against future cynicism.

As the last glimpses of Nha Trang disappeared beneath clouds, I understood the depth of my experiences in Vietnam. I was humbled by the country's lessons in resilience, inspired by its capacity for renewal, and irrevocably altered by the pure-hearted understanding of a child who had never learned to harbor bitterness.

Chapter 17 - The Infinite Power of Resilience

Escape does not heal pain.

My Vietnam encounters revealed how internal fortitude and adaptability springs not from avoiding wounds, but from rebuilding them into foundations of strength.

What invisible line separates the moments that break us from those that build us? Think about the last time you faced a challenge that seemed to have no purpose—a difficulty that appeared random, cruel, or simply too much to bear.

Perhaps we should stop the fight against our reality and instead ask a different question: Rather than "why," how about "what's next?" This shift often marks the boundary between entrapment by circumstances and the discovery of room to breathe within them.

I recently spoke with a musician who described how his faulty amplifier during a crucial performance—a technical glitch that initially seemed disastrous—led him to discover an entirely new sound that became his signature style. The Vietnamese resilience I witnessed didn't come from dramatic heroics but from a consistent reinterpretation of a painful past—they found notes to play when instruments seemed broken. What melody might emerge if you revisit a recent disruption not as interference but as a new arrangement waiting to be heard?

You can start this reconstruction of wounds into solid foundations through a simple daily practice:

> **Apertures: Pain Transformed**
>
> Each scar you carry holds wisdom waiting to be unlocked.
>
> Your deepest wounds aren't merely injuries to endure—they're unique vantage points that offer perspectives unavailable to those who haven't walked your agonizing path. What breaks us wide open can ultimately expand our vision if we learn to look through rather than at our pain.
>
> **The Revelation Ritual**
>
> Find a quiet space where interruption won't reach you. Take a blank page and write at its top the wound that echoes loudest in your life today. Not as judgment, but as acknowledgment.
>
> Divide your page into three revelatory columns:
>
> 1. **Illuminations:** What has this experience taught you that comfort never could?
> 2. **Recognitions:** How does this wound help you see others more clearly, more completely?
> 3. **Contributions:** What unique gifts can you now offer that were forged in this fire?
>
> Let truth flow unfiltered and unadulterated through your pen. The insights that make you pause—those that catch your breath with unexpected clarity—mark the moments your wound has become a window.

> Complete your ritual with this declaration: "This experience has equipped me to understand…" Then allow your pen to move freely with whatever emerges, however surprising or meaningful.
>
> Your wounds don't define your limitations—they mark your starting coordinates on a map with territories only you can chart. What once confined you now becomes the lens through which you can witness worlds invisible to others.

This approach uncovers what many wisdom traditions describe as "wounded wisdom"[1]—the distinct clarity that only painful experiences reveal.

The War Crimes Exhibition in Saigon might have functioned as a monument to bitterness. Instead, it showed truth without vengeance—a vital distinction psychology researchers Worthington and van Oyen Witvliet examined in their landmark 2014 study "Forgiveness and Reconciliation." Their research found that societies that acknowledge past wounds while they pursue reconciliation display notably higher rates of collective well-being than societies locked in cycles of blame and retribution.[2]

We need only look to conflicts in the Middle East today to verify this truism.

This insight came alive in Lac's wordless poetry of hospitality at his Hué restaurant. Despite the weight of historical trauma—American bombs obliterated his city and its historical treasure—he built bridges of understanding where barriers might have understandably stood. He demonstrated what Maya Angelou meant: "History, despite its wrenching pain, cannot be unlived, but if faced with courage, need not be lived again."[3]

The Vietnamese ability to honor wounds yet refuse definition by them expands our view of human potential. Their example shows how true resilience forms not by building impenetrable armor, but by keeping the heart soft even after brutal blows.

You can cultivate this balance between honoring wounds while you reject their attempt to control your life:

> **Twin Truths: Beyond Your Scars**
>
> What cuts us need not confine us.
>
> Your hardships might seem to have indelibly marked you, but they haven't molded you unless you let them do so.
>
> When pain arrives, most people take one of two flawed paths: they either drown in their wounds or deny them entirely. Both choices lead to diminished lives. The first surrenders our future to past injuries; the second buries crucial parts of our soul alongside our pain.
>
> There exists a third way—one that acknowledges every scar and allows us to refuse to be imprisoned by them.
>
> Stand before the mirror of your experience. Look directly at what has hurt you most painfully without turning away, but also without mistaking the reflection for your entirety. The complete truth always contains two realities: what happened to you and who you remain despite the devastation.

> Say aloud: "I acknowledge and honor that..." then name your wound with unflinching clarity. Feel its weight and reality. Honor its place in your history.
>
> Then speak the complementary truth: "I am more than..." and declare your expanded identity beyond this experience. This isn't denial—it's completion of the narrative your wound began but could not finish.
>
> These paired declarations form a practice more potent than either protection or revenge. They create a space where your injuries become information rather than identity.
>
> Notice how this dual acknowledgment reshapes your relationship with past pain. The wound remains real, but its borders no longer define your boundaries.
>
> Your pain deserves its proper place in your story—but only as a chapter, never as the title.

This practice cultivates what many philosophers call "expansive identity"[4]—the ability to include our wounds in our self-conceptualization without being confined or defined by them.

This approach matches recent findings from the *Journal of Positive Psychology*, where researchers found "post-traumatic growth occurs not through avoiding pain, but through conscious engagement with it while we maintain openness to new possibilities."[5]

Admiral James Stockdale's survival through nearly eight years in Vietnam's infamous "Hanoi Hilton" stands as a supreme testament to human resilience. Shot down over North Vietnam in 1965, Stockdale faced unimaginable torture—captors wrenched his shoulders from their sockets, broke his back, and repeatedly shattered his legs. He was left to heal without treatment. And he lived four years in solitary confinement with his wracked legs shackled in heavy irons each night. However, Stockdale elevated his ordeal from mere survival to deep insight through his deliberate engagement with suffering.

As the highest-ranking naval officer in captivity, he devised a sophisticated communication system of wall taps and coughs that united prisoners and preserved their mental health. When Vietnamese captors attempted to use him for propaganda, Stockdale beat his own face with a stool, slashed his scalp and bruised his body beyond recognition to make himself "unpresentable" to visiting journalists.

Stockdale later wrote, "In a situation where there was no opportunity for self-determination, I still made hundreds of choices each day—choices about attitude, choices about actions." [6] His insights formed the foundation of what psychologists now call the "Stockdale Paradox": He held inexorable faith that he would prevail despite difficulties, while he faced the most brutal facts of his current reality.

> "Life is pain, Highness. Anyone who says differently is selling something."—Westley to Buttercup in the movie, *The Princess Bride*[7]

Throughout the film, Westley endures impossible hardships—from capture by pirates to torture in the Pit of Despair where he becomes literally "mostly dead." Each ordeal serves not just as an obstacle but as a forge that tempers his resolve. Westley acknowledges a fundamental reality: our struggles aren't meaningless detours—they provide the very substance from which we build our capacity to love, persist, and find meaning. What seems like a ruthless interruption often prepares us for opportunities we cannot yet imagine.

True resilience, Stockdale discovered, exists not in escape from suffering or blind optimism, but in finding meaning within it. He didn't survive the Hanoi Hilton by imagining himself elsewhere. He survived by fully acknowledging his imprisonment while refusing to concede his essential selfhood to his captors.

This ability to recast suffering as purpose lives not only in extraordinary military figures like Stockdale but in countless realms of human endeavor. When physical limitations threaten to destroy our most essential connections to the world, true resilience emerges not from denial but from radical acceptance followed by extraordinary adaptation. Few examples illustrate this principle more powerfully than the story of a man whose very identity and livelihood depended on the sense he was destined to lose.

Ludwig van Beethoven faced perhaps the most devastating obstacle possible for a composer—complete hearing loss. By age 28 in 1798, his hearing began to deteriorate. By 1814, almost complete deafness enveloped him. Terror and despair threatened to consume his life. In his Heiligenstadt Testament to his brothers, he admitted he had contemplated suicide. Yet Beethoven chose courage over surrender.

Without the ability to hear physical sound, he composed symphonies from memory and imagination alone. His Ninth Symphony, his crowning achievement, emerged from complete silence. During its premiere, Beethoven stood on stage, unaware of the thunderous applause until someone turned him to face the audience. His victory showcases not just artistic genius but extraordinary perseverance against seemingly impossible odds.

Beethoven's deafness wasn't conquered—it became incorporated into a new reality where limitations became the exact parameters for unprecedented creation.

Your circumstances may imprison your body, limit your options, or constrain your resources—but they cannot claim your response without your consent. This astoundingly simple perspective builds what psychologists call "cognitive flexibility"– the mental agility to hold contradictory truths simultaneously.[8]

Stockdale credited his survival to Stoic philosophy, specifically Epictetus's principle that we cannot control circumstances, only our responses.[9] After his 1973 release, Stockdale received the Medal of Honor and later became a college president and vice-presidential candidate. He turned his suffering into wisdom that now guides generations of leaders.

This capacity to convert anguish into mission dwells not only in exceptional people like Stockdale but in unexpected places— even in a young boy inexorably affected by the same conflict that imprisoned Stockdale.

Young Thanh in Nha Trang demonstrates this universal capacity. Despite inheriting the Agent Orange legacy through his grandfather's suffering, Thanh directed his pain toward healing others—miraculous insight for such a young age. His aspiration to become a doctor shows how deep wounds can fuel engines of purpose.

The walls that seem to confine us will eventually crumble—as they invariably always do dependent only on our resolve. We need to step beyond our mental confinements not as an escaped prisoner, but as a being whose light grew too intense to be contained by circumstance.

My Vietnam encounters lit up this path like brilliant lanterns in an unlimited sky—they proved that real change happens not through dramatic leaps but through quiet, persistent steps that connect who we are now with who we might develop into.

In our deepest wounds hide our greatest gifts to humanity.

When you learn from past setbacks and failures, there's one crucial question you should ask: "Who needs this knowledge?" Then share this insight with one person, even in brief conversation. This simple act will expand your compassion and magnanimity. It will change your experience from private pain to vital wisdom—and the effects have the potential to shift humanity's course.

Never limit your impact. The universe connects everything. A shift in you creates magnificent ripples. When we reject this view, we as individuals lose. And the world suffers immensely.

Such grand perspectives might seem distant at first. Yet the universe contracts when we impose limits on what might happen and expands when we don't. This is ultimate profundity on a cosmic scale. Dream huge.

Glen Allison

Chapter 18 - The Sacred Ascent

"Journey to Lhasa, Tibet revealed."

Kathmandu, Nepal, into Tibet, April 15, 1996

Dawn broke over Kathmandu as I stepped from my hotel into the pristine morning air; my heart drummed an unfamiliar rhythm—part anticipation, part primal warning.

The promise of Tibet's sacred realms beckoned as an ancestral calling stirred within me. Far more than a photographer's journey, it was a summons I couldn't ignore, though its full meaning remained veiled in mountain mysteries and the daunting challenges that lay ahead.

A small band of fellow adventurers waited in the minibus; their faces mirrored my own mix of excitement and unvoiced concerns. We would soon reach the final Nepalese outpost before we crossed into Chinese territory. The word "territory" itself felt wrong—a political fiction imposed on these timeless peaks.

Beyond lay the formidable Himalayan passage—a route I knew would demand more than mere physical endurance.

Though China's 1959 occupation cast dark echoes across my thoughts, the invincible spirit of the Tibetan people irresistibly pulled me forward. I yearned to capture their unflagging resilience in my photographs, yet wondered: *Could my photographs truly reveal the essence of their struggle? Would my lens prove worthy of their truth?*

The path to the Roof of the World unfurled before us—a grueling 600-mile odyssey from Kathmandu to Lhasa. Each mile would test not just our bodies but would probably challenge the very boundaries of what we believed minds could endure—at least the minds of inexperienced adventurers like us.

The magnificent but merciless landscape ahead commanded respect, and I braced myself for its challenges. At 17,000 feet, where each breath becomes deliberate labor, the mountain passes loomed in my mind stirring equal measures of awe and apprehension. Yet an intuitive wisdom within me whispered that true revelation demands we venture beyond familiar terrain —beyond the comfortable boundaries of our perceived capabilities.

Crumbling roads traced precipitous edges where a single misstep meant disaster. Looming avalanche zones hung like Damocles's sword above our passage. In the mountain passes, savage winds howled timeless warnings, while each labored breath in the thin air served as a stark reminder—both of human vulnerability and the price of perseverance. In these moments, I began to understand: the mountain wasn't just a test of our bodies—it stripped away every pretense, every comfortable illusion about who we thought we were.

Then altitude sickness hit me hard—dizziness made the world spin wildly. Nausea rolled through my stomach and a desperate thirst took over, forcing me to face a challenge I hadn't seen coming. As my symptoms intensified, I questioned how much

Glen Allison

more my body could handle in this rarefied atmosphere; my confidence waned with each labored breath. Just as desperation began to set in, a fellow traveler noticed my deteriorating condition and offered altitude medication that allowed my body to gradually find its equilibrium again.

At these heights, where life or death seemed only moments apart, I felt my own mortality right beside me. Each step became a battle between pushing forward or relenting, between wanting to escape and a stubborn determination that grew inside me—a strength I couldn't name yet but would later recognize as something ancient waking up.

As darkness settled over the peaks that first night high in the Himalayas, I huddled in my sleeping bag, my breath forming ghostly clouds in the frigid air. The altitude's fierce grip had recast even this simple act of breathing into conscious labor. Yet in that raw communion with my own fragility, I deepened my understanding about conquering obstacles and the timeless wisdom to be learned in the process.

Every difficult breath, every step against the heavy pull of gravity, unleashed more resolve. Up here in the thin air, my old self—with all its comfortable boundaries—was about to grow into something more, like a chrysalis ready to yield to something greater. I had no idea this challenging climb into Tibet would show me inner paths that would change not just my journey, but my understanding of my own limits.

Through Snow and Spirit: The Path to Lhasa

Across the Himalayas, Tibet, April 17, 1996

Our greatest test emerged when a newly fallen avalanche barricaded our route and halted our vehicle in its tracks.

"There's no way around it," our Sherpa guide announced grimly. "The only path is over the snow and ice." His weathered face reflected years of hard-earned mountain wisdom.

"Over that?" Janine, a New Zealand photographer, voiced what we all thought. The wall of snow before us stretched skyward like nature's fortress.

A cold certainty settled within me as I huddled over steaming tea to warmed my hands, and started to gather my resolve. The avalanche wasn't just a physical barrier—it mirrored life's formidable challenges. Sometimes, the only path forward lies directly through the obstacle—a concept I had always grasped intellectually but now understood in my bones, written into my very flesh by this unforgiving landscape.

"We must move with absolute silence," our guide cautioned, his tone grave. "One wrong sound could trigger another slide." The weight of his words hung heavy in the thin air.

With the first step, the cold pierced my layers of protective clothing. David, who had limited mountaineering experience, took point. "Watch my footsteps," he called back softly. "The snow's unstable here."

Each step through deepening snow brought the Himalayas' stark lesson: true resilience demands we meet our trials without flinching. As bitter gusts assailed us, nature stripped away any pretense of comfort.

"Form a chain!" David's urgent whisper carried back to us. "Let's link our hands—we're stronger together."

We locked arms, our lives quite literally in each other's hands. The human chain we formed wasn't just for physical safety—it served as a lifeline of shared courage as we faced the mountain's challenge.

We climbed for what felt like endless hours; the trail diminished to a thread as we ascended. Snow fell in steady drifts, casting an otherworldly silence. Dark clouds pressed close, intensifying our isolation.

As we crossed one knife-edge section, I glimpsed into the abyss below.

"Don't look down!" Janine called out, but too late. Far below, the ice-clogged river raged against its frozen bonds—its fury created a stark counterpoint to the hushed snowscape above. Massive snow cornices hung like frozen waves along the mountainside, poised to break at nature's whim.

Hidden Powers

"Keep moving," our guide urged quietly. "The cornices—they're not stable." His eyes darted nervously to the precarious formations above.

The cold infiltrated every seam of my expedition gear, ridiculing its promised protection. My gloved fingers, buried deep in my pockets, surrendered to numbness. Warmth became a distant memory as mountain winds knifed through the pass and sought ruthlessly for any breach in our layers. When I paused to clear my frosted goggles, I spotted a solitary black hawk riding the currents above—its fluid grace offered a sharp rebuke to our labored battle with the elements, indifferent to our personal struggles, not by malice but by nature.

The hawk soared effortlessly while we fought for each step, a living reminder that the universe holds no opinion of our journey. Life, the world, the cosmos—none stand against us, but neither will they bend to accommodate our passage. That responsibility falls squarely on our shoulders alone. It remained for us to watch our steps on the potentially lethal snow, to find our own balance in spaces never meant for human comfort. The snow beneath our feet and the hawk above shared the same absolute indifference—neither ally nor enemy, simply present. The mountain demanded that we adapt or retreat.

As we carved a path through mounting snow and ice, my determination warred with bone-deep apprehension. "Stay close," David called back. "The snow's getting deeper." Our hands locked in desperate grips—each life tethered to the next. Every step drew us deeper into this realm where nature ruled with absolute authority.

Glen Allison

The Other Side: What the Mountain Revealed

Tingri, Tibet, April 19, 1996

Two hours later, the remote outpost of Tingri materialized through a veil of snow flurries. Our replacement vehicle sat serenely parked next to the Yak and Yeti hotel, which made our demanding traverse seem almost absurd.

We rushed toward the blazing hearth inside, where merciful warmth embraced us after nature's bitter onslaught. The staff extended traditional hospitality—hot yak butter tea. Yet this promised comfort presented its own trial. The pungent brew, crowned with floating globules of smelly yak fat, challenged our altitude-weakened stomachs.

"We conquered the mountain only to face this?" I murmured as a wry smile played across my face.

But there I was, and there it was, and that was it. So, I allowed my expectations about the tea to be as indifferent to the situation as the snow and hawk had been to our passage hours earlier. Perhaps, I realized, I should take nothing personally. Not as something happening to me, but as something that simply was. I needed to move with life's current rather than thrash against it.

Some time passed in contemplative silence as this understanding settled within me. The tea strange as it was, became less an affront and more simply another experience to be observed.

Later, I found a local guide and together we wandered Tingri's crooked alleyways.

Contrary to my expectations, the temples and ornate monasteries held less allure than the faces of highland nomads—each inscribed with years of wisdom and endurance. Their weathered features spoke of lives hewn from these fierce mountains, while the serene bearing of the locals revealed a staunch inner fortitude.

I photographed merchants wearing traditional brocade hats with massive fur-lined ear flaps, women with turquoise and coral stones swaying from their hair, and children darting through doorways—each frame revealed a vitality beyond mere appearance.

Among the merchants, one particular elderly woman caught my attention. Her small stall displayed hand-woven yak wool scarves; their intricate patterns told stories I couldn't yet read. What drew me wasn't the craftsmanship of her wares, but the deep serenity etched in every line of her wrinkled face.

"These patterns," my guide said in halting English as he gestured to a rather complex design, "show mountain's wisdom." The old woman's eyes, bright with intelligence, met mine. She never stopped weaving another pattern into existence.

When I raised my camera in question, she nodded, but then held up one finger in a gesture that meant wait. She reached beneath her stall and retrieved a sheath wrapped in faded silk. As she unwrapped it and began to unfurl its contents, I glimpsed an ancient tangka—a sacred painting on cloth—its colors still vibrant despite obvious age.

"Her father's," my guide translated. "When Chinese came, many burned such things. 'Keep this safe. It carries our story,' her father had told her. 'In darkness, we must become light.'" My guide explained her words. The old woman's face held no bitterness, only quiet determination.

I couldn't help but notice the parallel between her father's message and the reality before me. Here she sat as she created beauty in the aftermath of occupation as she changed simple wool into intricate art that preserved her culture's legacy. Like the snow lotus that blooms in harshest Himalayan conditions, her vitality had not just survived but flourished.

My mind traveled back to my Los Angeles life before my bankruptcy—the hillside home with its carefully curated designer furniture, each piece selected as much for status as function. I had once measured value by price tags and brand names. Yet here, this simple wool elevated by skilled hands held a worth no luxury showroom could match. *What truly costs more—the sofa that depletes a bank account, or the cultural heritage woven into each thread of this old woman's creation?* One represented fleeting status; the other, the endurance of an entire people's vigor.

"Many years, very difficult," my guide continued. "But difficulty teaches strength, yes?" Though shaped as a question, his words carried the weight of certainty—a fact stated, not asked. His smile revealed a timeless understanding I had only begun to grasp.

As I photographed the old lady, I realized she embodied everything I'd witnessed in Tibet—the resilient mindset that reshapes adversity into wisdom, the courage that finds beauty even in life's harshest seasons. Her simple stall had become a sanctuary for one of life's deepest lessons: authentic strength flows not from external circumstances but from inner conviction.

Before I left, she pressed one of her scarves into my outstretched hand. When I tried to pay, she shook her head.

As the waning sun began to bathe everything in amber light, I lost myself in this perfect fusion of radiance and humanity. Only the mountain wind's icy whisper finally broke my reverie and drove me back to warmth and shelter.

The parting words of my guide touched deeply within me, "Mountain teaches—path never easy. Strength grows in winter's heart."

Glen Allison

Sacred Resilience in Shadow and Light

Lhasa, Tibet, April 22, 1996

Three days later, our sturdy band of travelers reached Lhasa at nightfall; our bodies pleaded for rest. Before dawn, mountain winds beckoned me from sleep. From my balcony, the Tibetan capital revealed its brutal paradox—timeless devotion persisted under modern oppression. In the Jokhang temple's timeworn sanctuaries, the pilgrims' unswerving devotion moved me beyond words. Their quiet resistance against cultural obliteration and unyielding suppression awakened in me a soul-deep understanding of their struggle.

The sight of pilgrims in perpetual prayer throughout the city commanded my reverence. Temple courtyards bore witness to centuries of devotion—their stone paving polished to luminescence by countless prostrating bodies across generations and centuries. Through their steadfast faith under severe oppression, the Tibetan people embodied an indomitable courage. Their endurance reflected a timeless principle—authentic strength flows not from avoidance of life's trials, but from discovery of meaning within them.

As dusk gathered that day, I ascended a steep hill west of the Potala Palace, the traditional seat of the Dalai Lamas and Tibet's spiritual heart. This ethereal realm was once renowned as Shangri-La, the Land of the Snow Leopard. The palace dominates the landscape from its granite throne as it soars four hundred feet above Lhasa's sprawl. Within its formidable walls lay a thousand chambers now hushed—meditation halls with resplendent altars, ancient bronze censers, gilded sanctuaries, and the stately tombs of past Dalai Lamas.

This sacred citadel once embodied the soul and sovereignty of a venerable people. Now it stands as a mute sentinel, its grandeur preserved in museum stillness—a haunting reminder of all that history's cruel march can steal.

The setting sun painted the palace walls in gold and shadow. Below, endless streams of pilgrims traced their sacred path around the holy city.

A tremor ran through me, not from cold but from witness to such unyielding devotion. With each advance, the faithful offered their bodies to the earth as they inscribed their reverence one body-length at a time in prostration. A single circuit could consume days, yet they persisted in their circumambulation of their cherished city—a realm for which generations had surrendered their lives, and for which countless more stood ready to do the same.

In timeless rhythm, they spun their prayer wheels with one hand while they pressed cherished images of their exiled leader to their hearts. Their steadfast devotion erased the line between witness and understanding, a spectacle that stirred an elemental force within me.

Tibet's devastation defies measure. The Chinese invasion razed more than six thousand monasteries and left endless tons of sacred artifacts plundered or shattered. In 1959, after the Dalai Lama's flight to India, Chinese forces crushed a massive uprising, unleashing carnage that littered Lhasa's streets with the bodies of thousands who had dared to resist.

As I contemplate the Tibetan people's endurance and their unconquerable heart, I hover between sorrow and awe. The fortitude to preserve their faith against crushing oppression deepens my understanding of human perseverance.

This passage through Tibet illuminated a soul-stirring realization that authentic strength transcends physical trials—it dwells in how we face life's darkest injustices with steadfast resolve and dignity.

Chapter 19 - Lessons from the Roof of the World

When was the last time you celebrated your pain?

The Tibetan pilgrims' unwavering devotion amid suffering reveals this essential wisdom: our deepest wounds, when embraced rather than denied, become wellsprings of extraordinary strength. Like their sacred persistence through oppression, your journey through personal darkness contains hidden potential for transformation.

In the Japanese art of kintsugi, broken pottery isn't discarded but repaired with pure gold. These master craftsmen don't hide the cracks—they highlight them with precious metal, transforming damage into the most striking element of the piece. What was once shattered becomes more beautiful, more valuable, and more authentic than the unblemished original. The golden veins tell a story of resilience and rebirth that perfect porcelain never could. Your broken places aren't flaws to disguise—they are the fissures through which golden light can emerge. Honor this elegance. Without your fractures, from where would your glory emerge?

Flip your mind upside down.

Our deepest wounds aren't merely scars to carry—they're maps that reveal regions of strength. When pain arrives, most people instinctively flee, yet our hurts contain hidden coordinates to extraordinary capacities that remain dormant until summoned by necessity.

Adversity remains life's one certainty, as immutable as Himalayan peaks rising into the sky. Each of us faces different kinds of challenges—each as demanding and significant as any distant peak. Our hurts aren't random collisions with misfortune; they're precise instruments that calibrate our capacity for extraordinary living.

What hidden reservoir sustains you when all external supports fall away? This vital essence dwells within every human life, though few discover its depths.

> ACTION: Select one past injury that still resonates painfully within you. Rather than examine what it took from you, investigate what it brought forth. Did living an honest, dignified life emerge from betrayal? Did compassion bloom from rejection? Did clarity crystallize from confusion? The gifts may seem small at first—a whisper rather than a shout—but acknowledge them with the same intensity you've given to the hurt itself.

The path forward doesn't require you to forget your wounds but to read them differently—not as evidence of what harmed you, but as instructions for what you can build despite the hurt.

One need not circumambulate ancient temples to find strength within. It exists in the ordinary moments of our extraordinary life—in your decision to pause before responding in anger, in choosing courage over comfort when facing difficult truths, in the quiet determination that lifts you from bed on your hardest mornings.

Hidden Powers

Have you ever wondered why some days you feel capable of handling anything, while other days the smallest inconvenience overwhelms you? The difference lies not in what happens to you, but in your access to the inner reservoir you and all of us possess.

When did you last discover a capacity within yourself that you hadn't known was there? Not in moments of triumph, but in the quiet aftermath of what should have devastated you? Perhaps it was the clarity you found after losing something essential—when the absence itself revealed what remains unshaken at your core.

I spoke heart-to-heart with a surgeon who lost sensation in her dominant hand after an accident—her life's work seemingly ended. "In those first dark months," she confided, "I discovered that my medical insight had never resided in my fingers. My understanding of healing lived in a deeper place no injury could touch." She retrained herself completely, eventually performing procedures with her non-dominant hand with greater precision than before.

What essential quality have you discovered only after something valuable was taken? These self-revelations help you uncover your limits. They connect us to the Tibetan pilgrims who press foreheads to time-worn stones, not because their religion demands worship, but because their chosen discipline itself builds fortitude and faith.

> ### Intentional Questioning
>
> Life confronts us with deep questions long before we learn to ask them ourselves.

The ordinary mind accepts limitations as immovable boundaries. The awakened mind questions these boundaries until they collapse.

Consider the challenge that stands before you now. What if it's not a barricade but a signpost? What if your obstacles aren't blocking your path but actually revealing it?

The questions we direct toward our difficulties will either diminish or magnify our capacity to overcome them.

Ask not "How do I escape this situation?" but "How might I forge it into benefit?" Not "When will this end?" but "What must begin within me for this to change?" Our most limiting belief isn't that we can't succeed—it could be that we can't reinterpret what success means.

The narratives we construct around our circumstances exert more influence than the circumstances themselves. Five minutes of deliberate inquiry can create more possibility than hours of anxious thinking. Don't dissect your troubles; interrogate your perspective. The distance between stagnation and breakthrough exists in millimeters of perception, not miles.

When we maintain the same mind that formulated our current limitations, it's difficult, almost impossible, to envision our future freedoms. Instead, we must cultivate a new mind through new questions. This isn't merely a technique—it's a revolution in consciousness that begins with our willingness to wonder differently.

> Our questions are lanterns; where we point them determines what becomes illuminated and what remains in darkness.

Many conventional self-help approaches suggest initial steps—gratitude lists, morning silence, mindful breathing, dips into cold water to shock the senses awake—but these efforts create only temporary awareness. In Part Two of this book, we'll venture far beyond such ephemeral practices to explore dimensions of inner strength that fundamentally alter our relationship with suffering itself.

What awaits isn't just incremental improvement—it's the activation of innate capabilities that have always existed within you, ready for your summons.

These latent abilities, once fully awakened, will enable you to alter the very trajectory of your life's path, to bend what once seemed like immutable fate, and to reshape your destiny through conscious choice. You'll discover how to channel energies so dynamic that obstacles which once loomed insurmountable become resplendent accelerants to fuel extraordinary renewal.

Yet when we yield to inner frailty, suffering seeps in like bitter mountain winds that threaten to overwhelm us.

Theodore Roosevelt emerged from the cauldron of personal tragedy with extraordinary resolve. As a child, debilitating asthma confined him to his bed while his friends enjoyed robust health. In a single dark day of 1884, he watched helplessly as both his young wife and beloved mother drew their final breaths

—his wife just hours after childbirth, his mother from typhoid fever. Later, while campaigning for president, an assassin's bullet pierced his chest, yet he finished his speech with blood seeping through his shirt.

From these depths of suffering, Roosevelt didn't merely survive—he forged himself anew. He transformed physical frailty into legendary vigor, crushing grief into compassionate leadership, and mortal danger into unflinching courage. It was this intimate knowledge of life's harshest blows that led him to observe: "I have never in my life envied a human being who led an easy life. I *have* envied a great many people who led difficult lives and led them well."[1]

Directly facing obstacles activates inner abilities that remain hidden when we choose avoidance. Rather than withdraw from difficulty—embrace it.

> "Do not pray for an easy life. Pray for the strength to endure a difficult one."—Bruce Lee in the movie, *Dragon: The Bruce Lee Story*[2]

This illuminating insight encapsulates Lee's evolutionary approach to life's challenges. Throughout the film, he faces relentless obstacles: racial discrimination in Hollywood, resistance from traditional martial arts masters, and physical limitations that threatened his career. Yet, these became the very forces that forged his revolutionary mindset and distinctive fighting style.

His journey reminds us that our greatest achievements don't arise from comfortable circumstances but from our courageous response to adversity. The prayer for strength rather than comfort acknowledges a fundamental understanding: our capacity for growth exists in direct proportion to the challenges we willingly embrace, not those we manage to avoid.

When calamity strikes with avalanche force, courage requires concentrated will. I witnessed this in Tibet's devoted pilgrims; their steadfast faith exemplifies extraordinary human endurance. Their circumambulation of Lhasa through the prostration of their bodies—a journey that takes days to complete—exceeds mere physical stamina. In their steady progression, one body-length at a time, they prove authentic strength lives not in muscle and sinew, but in how we confront life's darkest injustices with unwavering dignity.

Like Tibet's mountain passes, our life journey reveals treacherous passages that test our courage. The weak succumb. The strong prevail.

Josei Toda, a Japanese educator whose principles hardened in the furnace of war, went to prison for refusing to abandon his Nichiren Buddhist practice when authorities demanded allegiance to state-mandated Shinto doctrine. He emerged from incarceration with resolve solid as the Himalayas. His words echo with wisdom: "Those who live out their lives courageously, lead the noblest and most sublime existences."[3]

Viktor Frankl's journey through one of human history's darkest chapters further reveals this extraordinary capacity for inner resilience. As a Jewish psychiatrist imprisoned in Nazi concentration camps, including Auschwitz, Frankl endured unspeakable horrors. He lost his pregnant wife, his parents, and his brother to the Holocaust. Amid systematic dehumanization designed to strip away every hint of dignity, Frankl discovered insights that would reshape not only his survival but our understanding of human potential.

In the harshest conditions—starvation, forced labor, constant death threats—he observed that prisoners who maintained meaning survived longer than those who abandoned hope. As Frankl wrote, "Everything can be taken from a man but one thing: the last of the human freedoms—to choose one's attitude in any given set of circumstances, to choose one's own way."[4] This insight became the foundation of his logotherapy approach, [5] centered on the belief that our primary motivational force exists not as pleasure or power, but as the search for meaning.

The importance of Frankl's example extends beyond mere survival—he turned his suffering into wisdom that has helped millions. His book *Man's Search for Meaning*, written in just nine days after his freedom, has sold over 16 million copies and continues to awaken readers to their ability to find purpose even in their most challenging circumstances. His life demonstrates that our inner resources reach deeper than our external challenges—that within each of us waits a fountain of renewal.

> **The Hidden Compass of Your Purpose**
>
> Our true purpose in life doesn't arrive like sudden lightning—it emerges gradually, revealed through patient observation during our darkest hours.
>
> Listen closely to the quiet voice that persists when the world's volume seems to pierce the quiet.

Hidden Powers

There's a whisper you can hear during your sleepless nights and unexpected tears, through moments when time dissolves and hours pass unnoticed. Your purpose hides in plain sight, disguised as obstacles, curiosities, and inexplicable fascinations. The questions that follow you through decades, the challenges you instinctively step toward challenge while others step away—these aren't distractions from your path. They ARE your path.

When you find yourself repeatedly drawn to certain problems, pay attention. The issues that kindle your outrage, the injustices that haunt your thoughts, the broken systems you can't stop trying to fix—these aren't random irritations. They're benchmarks that point toward your unique contribution.

When you stand at life's harshest junctions, ask not what choice brings comfort but what choice brings alignment.

Which option feels like coming home to yourself? Which feels like liberation rather than escape? The road that resonates with your deepest nature, even when it promises difficulty, reveals your true direction.

Your highest calling exists at the intersection of what breaks your heart and what makes it beat faster. This reverse polarity—finding joy through addressing pain—creates the axis upon which meaningful lives rotate. What wounds call for your specific healing touch? What void awaits your distinctive light?

The world doesn't need another replica; it needs your singular melody. Our purpose isn't found by following footprints—it's discovered by leaving our own.

Freedom from fear awaits your claim, even when money worries darken like storm clouds or sickness approaches like an oncoming tempest. Your display of unfailing resilience and warrior determination lights up possibility for all who observe your fight against life's fiercest storms.

A bold heart can redraft your story. With clear, courageous choices you can shape your path into a brilliant example of victory and potential. When you accept your position as author of your fate, you connect to boundless wells of wisdom, as deep as mountain lakes and equally pure.

Country singer Dolly Parton concentrated this idea into crystal clarity: "If you don't like the road you're walking, start paving another one."[6]

Her insight pairs perfectly with Maya Angelou's vivid description: "The need for change bulldozed a road down the center of my mind."[7]

> **Parallel Lives: The Unimagined Future**
>
> Every decision we make—and equally, those we avoid—creates invisible pathways. While we walk one path today, countless parallel versions of our future exist just beyond the veil of our current vision. Our ability to imagine and dream of better circumstances isn't mere fantasy—it's a navigation system for realities that haven't yet materialized. Your current limitations aren't walls but windows with the curtains drawn. Pull back these veils of assumption to reveal vistas you've never allowed yourself to see.

> Most lives aren't derailed by external forces but by the artificial boundaries we maintain around our own potential. The constraints that feel most solid often dissolve with nothing more than a shift in perspective—a deliberate step sideways into adjacent possibilities that have always existed, patiently awaiting our notice.
>
> Select one situation where you feel boxed in by inevitability. Now complete this thought: "What I haven't yet considered is..." Don't evaluate or judge what emerges—simply allow these alternative futures to unfold in your mind's eye. These aren't idle daydreams but reconnaissance missions into territories of possibility.
>
> We become blind to options that lie just outside our habitual thinking. The mind calcifies around familiar pathways until we mistake our mental maps for the territory itself. Yet the map is never the journey—it's merely one interpretation of infinite possible routes.
>
> The futures you haven't yet considered aren't distant shores—they're parallel universes separated from you by nothing more than the thickness of a thought.

Even amid life's violent storms, when we choose to shine hope's light, we brighten the darkest places. Escape offers no bravery, creates no satisfaction, and builds no lasting legacy.

Fear demands our surrender and snuffs out our ability to launch significant change. But champions face their fears directly and push forward until bravery becomes instinct, much like Tibetans maintaining their faith through long years of oppression.

Hidden Inheritance: What Defeat Bequeaths

Every collapse contains a message. Every failure offers a fortune. Every rejection reveals a route forward that remains invisible until the very moment we fall.

Our defeats speak a language that our victories never could. When you stumble, listen closely to what the ground has to teach you. The earth against your face whispers secrets about balance, timing, and preparation that success would never have revealed.

Maya Angelou's wisdom guides us like an expert sherpa on this path: "You may encounter many defeats, but you must not be defeated. In fact, it may be necessary to encounter the defeats, so you can know who you are, what you can rise from, how you can still come out of it." [8]

Consider your most recent failure—not with resignation but with archaeological precision. Excavate it layer by layer. What discoveries lie buried beneath your disappointment? What muscles must you build to rise again? What illusions needed shattering for clarity to emerge?

The world reveres those who succeed but learns from those who fail with dignity.

Your setbacks aren't mere obstacles to overcome—they're laboratories where you can discover the exact composition of your character. The heat of disappointment burns away what's superficial and leaves only what is essential.

> Your losses aren't evidence of your limitations but diagrams for your reconstruction. They don't define your story's end but rather its most pivotal turning point. The question isn't whether you will fall, but what kind of person who will manifest in the rising.

Each challenge you face forms another step on your own sacred circumambulation, just like the enduring resolve of Tibet's pilgrims.

The 13th-century Persian poet Rumi illuminated this insight with elegant simplicity: "The wound is the place where the Light enters you."[9]

From the deepest valley rises the mountain we must climb—and it is precisely through these ascents that we discover our magnificent capacity to soar.

Glen Allison

Chapter 20 - Paradise Lost and Found

Bunaken Island, Sulawesi, Indonesia, June 13, 2009

One moment of abandon. That's all it took.

Five hundred irreplaceable images—each a perfect convergence of light, timing, and serendipity—dissolved into digital oblivion between one heartbeat and the next.

As the magnitude of my carelessness crystallized, my stomach twisted into a knot of surreal dread. These weren't mere photographs; they were unrepeatable moments that even a lifetime of return journeys couldn't recreate: a sea turtle emerging from a perfect shaft of sunlight, a school of barracuda forming a living tornado, and the kind of water clarity photographers spend careers waiting to encounter.

Just hours earlier, what seemed like a photographer's perfect convergence unfolded. A local boatman approached me with an offer that spoke to both my professional instincts and my ever-battled travel budget: a discounted day trip to the legendary coral reefs of Bunaken Island, a shared boat with two other tourists.

What he hadn't mentioned and I couldn't have known—and what would ultimately elevate this shoot beyond my wildest imagination—was that my companions would be two captivating Norwegian marine biology students. Their slim physiques and natural grace in the water later converted my envisioned images

Hidden Powers

into a storm of human interaction, a perfect fusion with the ocean's wonders.

Bunaken Island emerged from the Sulawesi Sea like an ancient stronghold, its coral reefs a living archive of calcium and color that had taken millennia to compile.

Through my viewfinder, I watched azure waters shift to sapphire as clouds played across the sun. Each change in light revealed new dimensions of underwater marvels.

The island itself was a masterpiece of contrasts: pristine beaches gave way to lush vegetation, while beneath the surface, delicate coral formations created an alien architecture where metallic fish darted through purple-fanned corridors.

Along the shore, mangroves stood like ancient guardians. Their tangled roots offered sanctuary to juvenile fish sparkling like living gems in the filtered sunlight.

My two Norwegian companions proved far more than just serendipitous additions to the scene. As marine biologists, they moved through water with practiced ease—instinctive displays of exotic rhythms that lent elegant scale and counterpoint to the reef's grandeur. Their fluid movements offered unexpected visual delight.

An intuitive impulse must have led them to bring two sets of bikini swimwear, a fortuitous addition of visual variety that enhanced my imagery.

Glen Allison

With each frame, I captured a rare phenomenon in environmental photography—the perfect synthesis of human wonder and natural splendor.

The girls' sleek silhouettes traced the delicate reef's contours. Their eager, innocent gestures of discovery added vital emotional resonance to what would have otherwise been purely documentary images. These weren't just photographs anymore; they were storytelling gold, the kind of shots that magazine editors covet.

Then came the moment of hubris that would shatter my professional composure.

"Omigod, photographer man! Drop that camera and get in here—now!" one of the girls called out from the sea. Her Nordic accent thickened with excitement as she treaded the water with ease. "This coral is absolutely unreal!" She splashed teasingly in my direction, her eyes gleaming with discovery. "Don't you want to see what we found? You're totally missing out!"

Her invitation proved impossible to resist, a perfect alignment with my growing confidence, or perhaps overconfidence. After all, I'd just captured what I already knew were some of my finest images: split-shots showed both above and below water perspectives, dramatic panoramas of the pristine coastline meeting turquoise waters, and striking compositions of the sleek diver-girls silhouetted against the glittering sea surface. Their lithe bodies moved with natural grace against the azure backdrop.

Hidden Powers

My unexpectedly fruitful images of the day had rendered me reckless. My senses were heightened by an intoxicating combination: the thrill of perfect images, my companions' infectious joy, and—if I'm honest—the undeniable allure of these two blond-haired Scandinavian beauties moving lissomely through the pristine water. Their laughter and fun, and graceful moves in the sea had clouded my typically cautious judgment.

Whatever the reason, I forgot the cardinal rule of photography: protect your equipment at all costs. I was caught up in some misguided fantasy of being an Olympic swimmer. I envisioned myself as Mark Spitz incarnate with his unrelenting stamina, swimming prowess, and chiseled physique.

My euphoria—and libido—collapsed ruthlessly after several minutes of play in the water with these wannabe mermaids, when the harsh reality of what I'd done hit me with stunning force.

The memory cards, safely dry in my pocket only moments ago, now rested submerged in nature's most efficient conductor. In that instant, I felt the weight of my foolishness crash over me. These weren't just vacation snapshots at risk—they were unique captures that could define a photographer's portfolio, moments impossible to recreate even with unlimited time and budget.

The salt water, life-giving to the marine world around us, proved to be kryptonite to my memory cards—a degradation of my precious images from vessels of creativity into waterlogged casualties.

As the implications sank in, my heart plummeted.

Glen Allison

Each passing second felt like another nail in my photo's electronic coffin. I couldn't escape the cruel irony: the very element that made this underwater paradise possible now destroyed my attempts to document it.

I rocketed back to the boat carving a panicked slipstream of desperation and self-reproach in my wake. Every photographer knows that moment of dread when technology fails—that instant when your livelihood hangs by a digital thread.

But this was worse.

As I jammed each card into my camera, the LCD screen delivered its merciless verdict: CARD NOT READABLE.

The entire day's images vanished into the ether as surely as salt relentlessly fuses into these tropical waters.

One memory card remained safe, still dry in my camera body left on the boat. When my nubile companions climbed back aboard and learned of the disaster, their expressions shifted from dripping bodies and sun-soaked glee to genuine concern.

They weren't just tourists who mourned lost vacation snapshots —as fellow scientists, they understood the gravity of lost research material. But in their eyes, I saw something that lifted my spirits: not pity, but determination. They weren't ready to accept defeat ... and neither was I.

The journey back to the mainland lent aspects of photographic perfection, brought by a sunset that seemed to taunt our predicament. Golden hour light painted the sea in impossible colors, the kind of natural splendor that normally would have my shutter firing in rapid succession.

But now, each passing moment of uncaptured beauty felt like a reminder of what we'd lost. Yet the otherworldly dynamics of that magnificent light display—nature's reminder of its endless capacity for renewal—strengthened my resolve to capture this one last exquisite moment. It triggered my determination to recover the day's lost images that seemed destroyed forever.

As the sun descended, I found bittersweet redemption as I framed one last shot. My companions, still clad in colorful swimwear, had moved to the bow for my final photo framed against an unreal crimson sky. Like suspended stars, the waning light caught droplets of sea spray cloaking their bodies in glistening luminescence.

Through my viewfinder, I witnessed more than just two students ending their day of adventure and tease—I glimpsed the human element that had elevated the experience from mere documentary work into a narrative of discovery and wonder.

My final frame, safely captured on my one remaining dry memory card, had to serve as both evidence and reminder of the day's ephemeral magic.

But somehow, I knew it wouldn't be our only surviving image.

I had already formulated a rescue plan.

Glen Allison

Euphoria

In my hotel room, desperation fostered innovation.

Fortified by several glasses of cabernet and armed with my eager companions' hair dryers, we improvised a digital triage station. While any professional data recovery service would have blanched at our improvised methods, we had no choice—in this remote corner of Indonesia, waiting meant certain loss.

The whirring of the hair dryers filled the room as we worked relentlessly with surgical precision, each memory card a patient on our makeshift operating table. The girl's scientific backgrounds lent unexpected validity to our desperate experiment.

We carefully extracted moisture with the hair dryers, aware that too much heat could warp the delicate components. With each small success, we struggled to resurrect the day's memories from their watery grave.

The next hour stretched like underwater time as we clustered fervently around my laptop with raised hopes for our digital recovery.

Then—impossibly—the first thumbnails appeared. Like deep-sea creatures emerging from darkness, reborn images began to populate my screen.

A sea turtle materialized from digital depths, followed by a barracuda tornado, then split-shots that showed two worlds simultaneously—marine wonders and merged bodies of two mesmerizing mermaids frolicking in the sea.

Five hundred photographs representing not just artistic vision but scientific documentation were resurrected from what might have been certain obliteration. Each recovered image felt like a small miracle, a victory against probability.

By sunrise, the memory cards themselves were casualties of war, their circuitry irreversibly corroded by salt. But their precious cargo—the previous day's convergence of science, art, and human connection—had been copied to a hard drive and preserved against all odds.

That long night's celebration carried with it the euphoria of unexpected results. The resurrection of hope spiraled beyond wild expectations creating a space where possibility materialized into reality.

That long night's celebration carried with it the euphoria of improbable redemption. The confluence of catastrophe and serendipity had yielded something extraordinary: a visceral lesson in impermanence and resilience, where recovery became not merely about salvaging what might have been lost, but embracing the unexpected gifts that materialize when we navigate life's turbulent waters with steadfast determination.

Chapter 21 - The Power of Unwavering Spirit

Victory hides at the threshold of surrender.

On that unforgettable day in Bunaken, surrounded by beauty both natural and human, the memory cards may have succumbed to the sea, but the battle to salvage the images reflects that our greatest triumphs often emerge from the depths of apparent defeats. Victory frequently arrives in the moment just after we consider giving up, but our limits extend far beyond where logic suggests we should stop.

> "Just keep swimming."—Dory in the movie, *Finding Nemo*[1]

This simple mantra captures the essence of indefatigable resolve. When Dory faced the vastness of the ocean and seemingly insurmountable challenges to find Nemo, her childlike persistence—"just keep swimming"—became not just a catchphrase but an enduring life philosophy.

Like my efforts to recover those memory cards, the difference between triumph and defeat rarely hinges on circumstances but on that crucial moment when we decide to persist rather than surrender. When we continue forward despite seemingly impossible odds, we often discover solutions invisible to those who quit. Our persistent courage illuminates hidden paths that logical thinking alone could never uncover.

Hidden Powers

This principle of unwavering commitment reveals itself not just in everyday challenges but in feats that redefine the boundaries of human possibility. When we meticulous prepare with absolute focus, what appears impossible to others becomes a summit waiting to be conquered. No modern achievement better exemplifies this unsurpassed determination than a climber who literally staked his life on each handhold during one of history's most daring ascents.

On June 3, 2017, Alex Honnold became the first person to free solo climb—without ropes or safety equipment—the 3,000-foot near vertical face of El Capitan in Yosemite National Park. For nearly four hours, he climbed using only his fingers and feet, aware that a single mistake, a moment's lapse in concentration, or an unexpected cramp meant certain death.

Honnold's feat astonishes not merely as physical prowess but through his extraordinary relationship with fear. He invested years in meticulous preparation—he plotted each move in detail, committed every handhold, inch by precarious inch, to memory, and mentally rehearsed the entire route. Brain scans show his amygdala—the area responsible for fear responses—remains inactive in situations that terrify most people. This remarkable quality stems not from mere biological anomaly but from deliberate, systematic desensitization through repeated exposure to increasingly difficult climbs.

"I've always thought about El Cap as the holy grail of free soloing," Honnold said in the months prior to his ascent. "I wasn't feeling confident, I wasn't feeling like El Cap was within my abilities."[2] Rather than rush toward his goal, he built his technical skills and mental fortitude patiently until the impossible became merely difficult, and the difficult became possible.

Harriet Beecher Stowe declared: "Never give up, for that is just the place and time that the tide will turn."[3]

The distance between where you stand and where you long to be isn't crossed through blind leaps but through calculated steps, each one building upon the last—the same approach that led to Alex Honnold's successful ascent of El Capitan. Your courage doesn't require reckless abandon—it demands clarity, preparation, and unwavering honesty about what stands between you and your summit.

Daisaku Ikeda eloquently observed, "Courage is the force that makes our lives brilliant, like a great work of art."[4] This brilliance comes not from avoiding challenges, but from how we face them with unbeatable determination.

Sustained resilience actually reconfigures our brains and creates new mental connections that make future challenges more navigable, reshaping our brain's structure each time we choose to continue despite apparent futility. In an article, "How to Rewire Your Brian," published by the Colorado State University, Grace Weintrob states: "Neuroplasticity is the brain's ability to reorganize itself by forming new neural pathways throughout life and in response to experiences. While the brain usually does this itself in response to injury or disease, when humans focus their attention enough, they can slowly rewire these pathways themselves."[5]

Hidden Powers

This remarkable capacity for mental adaptation manifests most dramatically through extraordinary cases of human endurance. History offers us vivid examples of individuals who, when faced with overwhelming adversity, not only survived but emerged transformed by their trials.

Ernest Shackleton's legendary Antarctic expedition stands as one of the greatest examples of unyielding will against overwhelming circumstances. In December 1914, Shackleton and his crew of 27 men set sail on the Endurance, attempting to become the first to cross the Antarctic continent on foot. Instead, they found themselves trapped in what would become one of the most extraordinary survival stories ever recorded.

Just weeks into their journey, the Endurance became imprisoned in pack ice. For ten months, the ship drifted helplessly before the crushing pressure of the ice finally splintered her hull. As Shackleton watched his vessel sink beneath the ice in November 1915, he faced a devastating reality: his men were stranded on floating ice, 1,200 miles from the nearest outpost of humanity, with no hope of rescue.

Shackleton delivered a masterclass in leadership and stouthearted will. For five months, the crew camped on ice floes that constantly threatened to break apart beneath them. When the ice began to melt, they launched three small lifeboats into the treacherous Southern Ocean as they endured hurricane-force winds and waves the size of buildings during a harrowing voyage to reach uninhabited Elephant Island.

But Shackleton knew this desolate outpost offered no chance of salvation. In what many consider the most daring small boat journey ever attempted, he and five men set out in a 22-foot lifeboat modified by the ship's carpenter across 800 miles of the world's most dangerous waters to reach South Georgia Island. After 16 days of relentless storms and navigating by sextant with only four brief glimpses of the sun, they miraculously made landfall.

Even then, their ordeal wasn't over. The whaling stations lay on the opposite side of the island, forcing Shackleton and two companions to make the first-ever crossing of South Georgia's unmapped, glacier-covered mountains with no mountaineering equipment—just a carpenter's adze, some ship's rope, and screws from the lifeboat driven into their boots for traction.

Through it all, Shackleton never wavered in his absolute commitment to save every man. "Optimism," he wrote, "is true moral courage."[6] When he finally secured a rescue vessel and returned for his stranded men, it had been 634 days since they had last touched land. Against all probability, every single man survived.

Shackleton's story stands exceptional not just for physical endurance, but for his psychological mastery in maintaining morale. He understood that survival depended as much on mental state as physical resources.

We absolutely need to take full responsibility for our inner state before outer circumstances can change. Just as Shackleton refused to surrender his crew's fate to Antarctica's merciless terrain, we can establish command over our response to life's challenges.

Each time we push slightly beyond our breaking point, we redefine that threshold. Then the next impossible challenge finds us stronger, more adaptable, more capable. Our current limitations mark not our permanent boundaries but merely our present position. The distance between where we stand and what we can achieve narrows with each refusal to surrender.

Victory almost always arrives one step beyond where most people quit. But what shifts this endurance from mere stubborn persistence into meaningful resilience? The answer lies in clearly understanding your immediate goal, your long-range vision, your ultimate mission.

> **Relentless Purpose**
>
> What values make your difficulties worth facing? What dream justifies your struggle? What worthy accomplishment pulls you forward when momentum stalls? Without these anchors, your determination will crumble when difficult circumstances intensify.
>
> The most resilient people on earth don't simply outlast challenges—they advance meaningful aims despite formidable opposition. They understand exactly why they refuse to yield. This clarity changes exhausting endurance into purposeful progress.
>
> Imagine facing identical obstacles but with radically different awareness. In scenario one, you push forward without clear purpose, fueled only by stubborn refusal to quit. In scenario two, you advance with absolute clarity about how each step, however difficult, moves you toward what you value most. The external circumstances remain

> identical, but your internal experience differs dramatically.
>
> This connection between persistence and purpose creates sustainable motivation. Without it, our resolve becomes brittle, vulnerable to circumstances. With it, setbacks strengthen rather than diminish our commitment.

True grit demands we maintain resolve when logic suggests futility; when experience counsels retreat; when conventional wisdom commands us to stop. The drive to never yield forms the bedrock of human achievement. Our unyielding resolve can extract victory from the jaws of defeat.

Daisaku Ikeda offers this perspective: "When your determination changes, everything will begin to move in the direction you desire. The moment you resolve to be victorious, every nerve and fiber in your being will immediately orient itself toward your success. On the other hand, if you think, 'This is never going to work out,' then at that instant every cell in your being will be deflated and give up the fight. Then everything really will move in the direction of failure."[7]

Like physical strength, unflagging determination develops through progressive challenges—a process that necessarily involves considerable determination, sustained effort, and radical honesty.

"The real test is not whether you avoid failure, because you won't. It's whether you let it harden or shame you into inaction, or whether you learn from it."[8]—Barack Obama in *The Audacity of Hope*.

This insight cuts to the heart of our relationship with setbacks. Just as those memory cards that sank into the sea could have meant defeat but instead became a story of triumph, our greatest test isn't to escape failure—it's what we do in its aftermath to strengthen our fortitude when facing obstacles.

The choice to press forward doesn't guarantee success—but surrender most definitely ensures failure. When the world says "impossible," the unyielding spirit whispers "watch me."

Glen Allison

Chapter 22 - Endurance and Perseverance

"The Unexpected Resurgence of Financial Collapse"

Bali, Indonesia, 2005-2009

The goal of creating a substantial financial base of passive income led me to consider investing half my liquid assets in what seemed an extremely promising rental property venture on the resort island of Bali in Indonesia.

Yet beneath my expanding prosperity lurked an unseen vulnerability. In retrospect, as my financial resources grew, I should have sought guidance from a seasoned investment advisor and hired a business manager whose expertise far exceeded my own. My dedication to artistic pursuits, while rewarding, had left me blind to crucial business acumen—a gap that would soon prove costly. Another unforeseen financial storm caused by external circumstances beyond my control gathered on the horizon. Of course, I didn't see it coming.

Meanwhile, a close friend, Benny Raj, in Bali, Indonesia, presented a compelling opportunity for investment on the island. He owned a prestigious catering company there that served the Bali's elite. His company orchestrated lavish celebrity weddings and high-profile international events, from IMF summits to government conferences that drew world leaders. His operation flourished among Bali's constellation of exclusive resorts, each boasting world-class facilities that rivaled any global destination.

Hidden Powers

Benny revealed an intriguing business model: wedding planners he worked with frequently converted the island's most opulent private villas into exclusive wedding venues, commanding up to $25,000 for week-long rentals. His calculations painted an enticing picture—a lavish, custom-built villa could host four such events monthly, potentially generating six-figure ongoing revenues every month.

The economics proved even more persuasive when he shared that construction costs in Indonesia hovered at mere fractions of Western prices. With skilled laborers earning a mere $5 daily at the time, the prospect of building a luxurious Balinese villa seemed remarkably attainable. Benny offered to connect me with the island's premier architects, contractors, and landscape designers—a ready-made network of trusted professionals to bring this vision to life.

My deep connection to Bali—forged through countless photography expeditions—had given me intimate knowledge of the island's soul. After I evaluated nearly two hundred potential building sites over a year with meticulous care, I found myself drawn to Ubud—a cultural jewel nestled in Bali's heartland.

This unique village wasn't merely a tourist destination; it represented the beating heart of Balinese arts, where ancient dance traditions and Hindu ceremonies painted daily life in vibrant hues.

Ubud's allure, already magnetic for luxury travelers, had only intensified after the book and movie, *Eat, Pray, Love*, captured the town's essence for global audiences. During my extended stay, I formed bonds with local expats whose real-life stories had inspired characters in the film, deepening my conviction that Ubud—with its blend of timeless tradition and contemporary appeal—was the perfect canvas for my vision.

The discovery of a three-hectare sanctuary minutes from Ubud's center felt like destiny—such expansive land parcels near town were rare treasures.

Indonesian law limited non-citizens to a long-term lease instead of outright land ownership. But the property's position on a canyon's edge commanding endless views of pristine jungle justified the compromise of building on leased property. Here, surrounded by nature's magnificence, I envisioned my dream taking root.

My design called for subtle perimeter walls that blended into the tropical landscape. They created an intimate haven where privacy merged seamlessly with wild beauty. This wouldn't be just another luxury villa—it would become a sophisticated jungle retreat where elite celebrations could unfold in secluded splendor.

The project awakened the trained architect in me, dormant throughout my years of photographic pursuits. Those childhood dreams of bold design, first sketched by a twelve-year-old's hopeful hand, and my time spent earning a degree in architecture could finally materialize in glass, stone, and tropical wood.

With half my liquid assets at the ready, I prepared to convert a half million dollars into what would represent a five-million-dollar masterpiece by Western standards. Yet mindful of past financial storms, I committed to an all-cash approach—no mortgages, no debt, no risk of repeating history's harsh lessons.

The region's modest construction costs liberated my imagination beyond conventional limits, allowing me to craft a vision that united architectural audacity with spiritual harmony.

Six distinct pavilions would rise from the hillside. Each structure would wear a crown of traditional Balinese thatch that floated above walls of glass, free-hanging from exposed steel beams. The design flowed organically down the hillside—twin chambers for master and guest quarters would stand sentinel over three interconnected pavilions for living, dining, and kitchen.

At the heart of this composition stood the sixth pavilion, my Buddhist sanctuary—my tribute to fortune's gifts and the significant awakenings that led me to this paradise.

Below this ethereal world, I conceived an underground river that would serve as both passage and gallery, where art would line a path of stepping stones through the water. Above, the glass-enclosed overlapping pavilions would offer a unique perspective as they staggered down the hillside. The intricate beauty of exposed traditional thatch viewed from the inside, created a dialogue between ancient craft and modern vision.

The true magic emerged in the structures' form—six stylized inverted pyramids that appeared to levitate above twenty-one levels of infinity pools. These crystalline sheets of water would cascade down the steep slope, each pool reflecting sky and structure in an endless play of light and shadow.

Glen Allison

This wasn't just ambitious architecture; this was theater of the soul. Every element—from the floating, inverted structures to the cascading waters—was orchestrated to create an otherworldly experience that would attract couples seeking an extraordinary setting for their most sacred celebrations. The design created both visual harmony and a sense of awe.

The villa would function as both masterwork and investment that would generate income during my international photography pursuits. My catering mogul friend saw my audacious designs and affirmed their income-producing potential.

I was ready, willing and able, or so I thought—blind to the looming obstacles that would soon test the very foundations of this visionary dream.

Engineering Challenges and Financial Collapse

Beneath this creative concept lay formidable technical challenges. The site itself was precarious—perched between water-laden rice paddies looming above and a canyon that plunged below.

The steep hillside slope presented significant construction requirements that exceeded my earlier site investigations and sample bore holes to determine the depth of bedrock. As unexpected foundation costs soared into the stratosphere, the project's scope revealed itself like an iceberg—what lay beneath dwarfed what showed above.

I drew deeper into my cash reserves far exceeding my original planned maximum investment, buoyed by steady multiple six-figure annual stock photo royalties, and my unyielding faith in future wedding venue revenues. The mathematics of success seemed irrefutable, requiring only the fortitude to see it through —a strength I'd cultivated through decades of Buddhist practice.

This project didn't just represent mere determination; it embodied my life's philosophy manifested in concrete and steel.

Two years into construction with my photography career on hold and the project only halfway complete, the 2008 global economic tsunami struck without warning.

Overnight, my once-robust stock photo royalties withered to a ghost of their former glory—they now barely reached 5% of previous annual earnings. Yet I convinced myself this was merely a temporary storm to weather and began to withdraw massive sums from my cash reserve that I had promised myself I wouldn't touch.

By then, I had evolved into the project's general contractor. I personally orchestrated a symphony of 120 workers as an endless procession of concrete trucks arrived daily. The finish line seemed too close, the investment too deep, to even consider retreat. My determination burned white-hot, even as the world's markets crumbled.

It didn't take long for the half million dollars in reserve to get swallowed by the voracious appetite of monthly construction costs. Since my primary income had evaporated so quickly, desperation drove me to decisions I had sworn never to make again.

I watched my bluechip stock investment portfolio bleed out at fire-sale prices, then I crossed a line I had drawn in stone after my previous bankruptcy—I began to tap credit cards for huge cash advances in the tens of thousands of dollars to feed the project's overwhelming monthly expenditures. The global recession had backed me into a corner as I broke my most sacred financial vow: never again to be shackled by debt.

In a cruel twist of timing, I had sold my Los Angeles property at the market's peak just months before the crash, pouring those proceeds into Bali, as well. Now, with no American assets to leverage and my photo royalty income reduced to vapor, US banks recoiled from funding a foreign construction project in the midst of global economic chaos.

I initiated my Social Security pension but it offered little relief—exorbitant credit card interest devoured it like a ravenous beast, claiming two-thirds of each check before it could reach my hands.

As this financial abyss deepened, I faced the unthinkable: ultimately I had to halt construction entirely. Nature showed no mercy; in short order, relentless jungle vegetation crept over my half-finished dream converting steel and concrete into a modern ruin.

The property stood frozen in time—unsold, unchanged except for the wild wilderness that encroached upon it. Within a year, my architectural masterpiece had morphed into remnants resembling a lost civilization. Toppled trees and eroded earth created an unintended monument to ambition overwhelmed by circumstance.

Yet through it all, my Buddhist practice burned brighter and intensified with each new challenge. I had navigated treacherous waters before, so I drew deeply from the Mystic Law's wellspring of strength within my life and refused to let my spirit dim despite the gathering storm.

Eleanor Roosevelt's wisdom echoed through my experience: "If you can live through that [a difficult situation], you can live through anything. You gain strength, courage, and confidence by every experience in which you really stop to look fear in the face. You are able to say to yourself, 'I lived through this horror. I can take the next thing that comes along.'"[1]

Glen Allison

With my dream suspended in Bali's jungle, I left the project under the watchful care of round-the-clock security guards and a network of the island's premier real estate agents, all hoping to salvage something from the wreckage of the global economy.

Bangkok beckoned with its strategic position at the crossroads of Southeast Asia—a region I knew intimately, where low travel expenses still allowed for possibility.

But the digital revolution had unleashed a tsunami of images: smartphones and digital cameras flooded the internet with billions of photographs seemingly by the second, drowning the once-profitable stock photo market. The global recession also compelled large corporations to drastically downsize their advertising budgets. My previous livelihood wasn't just struggling; it was vanishing before my eyes.

At 65, when many seek the comfort of routine, I chose reinvention. I would roam Southeast Asia with nothing but my Social Security pension and an artist's dreams. I would forge a new path for my life. Yet even this pivot to fine art photography presented a cruel irony—decades of published images, distributed anonymously through stock photo agencies, had left me both widely seen and almost completely unknown, with no significant trail of credit lines to build a reputation upon.

I had earned the respect of my peers when I co-founded the Stock Artists Alliance in 2000 when we rallied 600 of the world's top photographers to defend our intellectual property rights against corporate giants. But my name remained largely unknown to the public. The very photographers who knew my work were already too successful to need the photo workshops I contemplated offering.

Nevertheless, this unforeseen financial collapse, though devastating, opened a door to fundamental revelations about life's true purpose. In the wreckage, I discovered wisdom I never knew I sought.

Glen Allison

When Dreams Surrender to Despair

When the global economy crumbled in 2008, some of society's wealthiest chose to end their lives, unable to face a future stripped of fortune. They saw their financial ruin as an inescapable black hole, a darkness too deep to navigate. Without a compass to guide them toward renewal, they surrendered to despair's final whisper.

Yet life itself always holds worth beyond measure. Within each of us lies dormant wisdom vast enough to comprehend the infinite mysteries of the universe. When awakened, this inner power reshapes every obstacle into a thrust-generating launch pad.

As economic chaos engulfed the world, my own financial foundation crumbled beneath me. But throughout the next decade of fierce financial struggle, a life state typically not expected emerged—a steel-forged resilience and a clarity of purpose that no market crash could ever shatter. Each hardship honed my spirit to a sharper edge, which prepared me to face whatever new challenges that might emerge.

After ten years of financial purgatory, the universe offered an unexpected gift. A buyer emerged with a vision to transform my long-abandoned dream project into a luxury yoga retreat. The sale closed mere weeks before COVID-19 swept across the globe. This razor's-edge timing proved miraculous. Deep within my soul, I knew that the precise timing of this sale was an extraordinary occurrence directly resulting from my half-century-long efforts to fuse with the universal rhythms of the

Mystic Law—undeniable actual proof. The impending expiration of my land lease would have soon rendered the property worthless in the pandemic-paralyzed global market.

Yet the path to closure twisted through a labyrinth of obstacles. A cunning fraudster attempted to wrest control of my property through legal deception, while simultaneously, a member of Bali's royal aristocracy materialized with ancient land records that claimed dominion over my access road. Their vast hereditary holdings had allowed this crucial strip of land to slip beneath notice for generations—until now, when my million-dollar investment lay half-finished in the jungle after two years of construction labor and a decade trying to sell the project. All my prior savings had been poured into Bali's unyielding earth.

The final blow came when I discovered the local farmer who had leased me the access parcel was merely a tenant himself; his family's decades of working the land had created an illusion of ownership. This critical detail had somehow eluded even my attorney's meticulous due diligence land ownership investigation, revealing how easily truth can hide in Bali's layers of tradition and time.

The royal family's demands were staggering—a ransom for the access road that exceeded the property's worth and mocked my empty coffers. Without this vital access artery, my entire investment would dissolve into a mangle of unsalvageable jungle destruction, leaving no possibility for a sale. Yet five decades of Buddhist practice had forged an unyielding strength within me stronger than circumstance—an adamant conviction that far surpassed mere hope.

Then, as if in response to this resolute spirit, the impossible yielded.

The royal family suddenly softened its stance and crafted an agreement that honored both my stake and the farmer's legacy. After a decade frozen in limbo, the gates finally opened, allowing me to salvage a portion of my buried fortune from Bali's verdant depths.

From this purifying fire emerged not just survival but wisdom.

The decade-long financial ordeal had stripped away illusions and revealed how my own desires had repeatedly drawn me to the precipice of ruin. Yet this revelation wasn't an ending—it was a gateway to rebirth.

Today, with hard-won clarity, I face the future not just to pursue opportunities but to keep challenging my innermost weaknesses. The path ahead still bristles with trials, but each one gleams with potential for an expanded life. My resolve has deepened beyond mere ambition; it has become an insatiable quest for renewal, where every obstacle serves as a teacher and every setback shapes a stronger soul. This conviction now resonates in the marrow of my bones—a whispered certainty that echoes louder than any doubt ever could.

Chapter 23 - When Wounds Become Wings

Perseverance exceeds mere optimism or dedication; it embodies an unconquerable will that refuses to yield. Far beyond dutiful persistence, true perseverance flows from passion and purpose. When joined with resolute conviction, it becomes an unstoppable force against life's trials.

At its core, perseverance is an unyielding pledge to endure, undaunted by the magnitude or duration of difficulties. We must anchor ourselves in the certainty of eventual triumph, whatever tempests we face. The key lies in awakening the latent wisdom and untapped strength within us all.

"Endurance is not just the ability to bear a hard thing, but to turn it into glory,"[1] observed the perceptive twentieth-century Scottish theologian William Barclay.

While endurance represents resilience to withstand hardship, perseverance manifests as the unbending commitment to continue despite barriers. Contemporary challenges require a more evolved inner strength—one emphasizing mental flexibility rather than just physical stamina. Successfully navigating today's complex landscape demands we approach uncertainty with both intellectual curiosity and creative problem-solving, meeting each obstacle with refreshed determination and adaptive thinking.

Glen Allison

When we summon our innate courage and build unyielding determination, we can emerge as steadfast warriors ready to overcome any obstacle, within ourselves or beyond.

Harriet Tubman's extraordinary journey from slavery to freedom fighter embodies this remarkable conversion of adversity like few stories in history. Born into slavery around 1822 in Maryland, Tubman endured unimaginable brutality from early childhood. At age thirteen, she suffered a traumatic brain injury when an overseer hurled a two-pound metal weight at another slave but struck her instead. The injury caused lifelong seizures, severe headaches, and hypersomnia—a condition that would cause her to fall asleep without warning.

Most would consider such a disability devastating under any circumstances, but for someone attempting to guide fugitive slaves through hostile territory at night, it represented an almost insurmountable barrier. Yet remarkably, Tubman reshaped this liability into an unexpected spiritual asset.

During her seizures, she experienced vivid dreams and visions that she interpreted as divine guidance. These "sleeping spells," as she called them, became integral to her navigation system as she led escaped slaves along the Underground Railroad. She recast her seizures into spiritual guidance that illuminated her path through darkness.

Similarly, when we face what appears to be an insurmountable obstacle, it actually signals the imminent arrival of new possibility. This perspective doesn't minimize suffering but reframes it as a necessary passage rather than a permanent state. When we maintain our resolve through our hardest times, we can discover that adversity isn't just something to endure but a vessel that shapes our character into something much stronger and more luminous than before, just as Tubman did through the many dark nights she spent trying to free slaves under near impossible circumstances. Her unrelenting bravery rallied the spirits of those she was trying to save.

> "The night is darkest just before the dawn. And I promise you, the dawn is coming."—Harvey Dent in the film, *The Dark Knight*[2]

This compelling line in the movie speaks directly to the evolutionary nature of perseverance through our most difficult moments.

After Tubman secured her own freedom in 1849, she made the extraordinary decision to return to slave territory—not once, but thirteen times—to rescue approximately seventy enslaved people, including family and friends. The journey required traveling nearly 90 miles each way, mostly on foot, through swamps and forests, in all weather conditions, while evading slave catchers who had posted a $40,000 reward for her capture (equivalent to over $1.3 million today).

Tubman's story stirs such awe not merely through her physical courage but through her remarkable mental fortitude. "I had reasoned this out in my mind," she later explained. "There was one of two things I had a right to: liberty or death. If I could not have one, I would have the other; for no man should take me alive."[3] This absolute commitment to freedom—for herself and others—recast her from a victim of circumstances into a creator of liberation.

During the Civil War, Tubman served as a scout, spy, and nurse for the Union Army, and later became the first woman to lead an armed expedition, guiding the Combahee River Raid that liberated more than 700 slaves. In each phase of her journey, she demonstrated an extraordinary ability to turn limitations into opportunities and to forge new paths through seemingly impenetrable barriers.

"I never ran my train off the track," Tubman proudly stated of her Underground Railroad journeys, "and I never lost a passenger."[4] This wasn't mere bravado but a reflection of how adversity had refined her instincts, sharpened her problem-solving skills, and deepened her spiritual resolve. The very system that sought to crush her determination instead forged her into one of history's most effective freedom fighters.

Have you ever questioned the link between your wounds and your wisdom? Ponder for a moment about the adversities you've faced that seemed most unfair, most senseless in their arrival. What unexpected capacities emerged precisely because of—not despite—these difficulties?

I've noticed something remarkable in conversations with people who've navigated impossible terrain: the exact circumstance that appeared most cruel often cultivated the exact capacity they later needed most. Like Tubman's seizures becoming her navigational system, our most significant limitations often conceal unusual gifts.

What current difficulty might be fashioning within you an essential capacity you don't yet recognize? This isn't about finding false comfort in platitudes or minimizing genuine pain, but about recognizing the peculiar intelligence within struggle itself. The obstacle before you may contain precisely the mineral composition required to forge the exact tool your future self will need. What if you examined your current challenge not merely as something to overcome but as something specifically designed to cultivate wisdom unavailable through any other means?

Similar to Tubman's physical disability that became the foundation for her spiritual strength, the hardships I encountered in Bali tested not just my financial stability but my fundamental values, recasting obstacles into opportunities for deeper awareness and resilience.

Yet with each challenge, my resolve deepened. Now I am a different person.

Each of us possesses the innate ability to stalwartly rise again, regardless of the battles we must face.

Starting with the first chapter in Part Two - The Revelation, I'll share several compelling concepts in detail. They aren't mere philosophical ideals but combat-tested understandings that serve as trustworthy tools for survival and triumph that showed me the way forward through my darkest times.

But first, I must relate pivotal lessons unveiled in Timbuktu.

Glen Allison

Chapter 24 - Wisdom Beyond the Horizon

"The Flash That Betrayed the Shooter"

Bamako, Mali, Africa, April 1999

The cacophony of Bamako assaulted my senses—oppressive noise pummeled my ears, acrid pollution burned my nostrils, relentless heat penetrated my skin.

The fierce Harmattan winds, nature's ancient messengers from the Sahara just hundreds of kilometers north, had changed the capital of Mali into a swirling cauldron of dust and chaos.

Visibility diminished by the minute as my taxi driver—a man whose English emerged through layers of French intonation—attempted to navigate the paralyzed traffic. Horns created a dissonant symphony around us. Walking might have proved faster, but in this North African, landlocked nation where thirty tribal languages intertwined beneath the official French, my solo navigation through streets with indecipherable signage would have resulted in beautiful futility.

Suddenly, through the haze and smog, a figure materialized—an elegant African woman adorned in vivid fabric that seemed to vibrate with color even in stillness. She moved with deliberate grace between immobile vehicles, most of which bore the scars of countless journeys, metal bodies that yearned for restoration. The woman's striking features—high cheekbones and sculpted contours—revealed a remarkable dignity that rose above the surrounding pandemonium.

The photographer in me stirred. I often shoot candid images of locals wearing traditional attire, though without formal permission or the model releases required by stock photo agencies for commercial licensing. I know certain cultures believe photographs capture fragments of the soul. This spiritual consideration weighs heavy upon me—I struggle enough to maintain my own soul's integrity without inadvertently disturbing another's.

My Nikon 28Ti—an unassuming yet sophisticated camera that many professional photographers used during the days of film, had extraordinary optics disguised in a compact body. This prized possession, costing a thousand bucks back then, rested securely in its pouch clipped to my belt. Its unimposing presence often allowed me to work without attention from potential thieves; it presented me as merely another tourist rather than a professional with valuable equipment.

As the woman approached, I discreetly retrieved this tiny Nikon, activated it with practiced movements, and positioned it casually at the edge of the window. I had perfected the art of shooting "from the hip," composing images without the viewfinder's guidance.

The shutter released with a subtle click—followed by an explosion of light.

In a single frame, shot without holding the camera to my eye, I had captured a fabulous image—the woman's face displayed both strength and serenity, a living embodiment of dignity amid chaos. But in my haste, I had neglected a critical detail. I had failed to disable the built-in flash, which betrayed my attempt at discretion. The woman screamed in alarm.

Trapped between vehicles at a traffic signal, our taxi became a momentary prison. A police officer materialized instantly. He wrenched open the door and tried to extract me and my prized piece of equipment, whose considerable value he seemed to clearly assess. But I braced my foot against the door frame and refused to surrender my body or my camera.

Fear registered in my driver's eyes while determination hardened in mine. The officer struggled to pry the camera from my grasp as I resisted with equal fervor. The beautiful woman's expression had quickly shifted into righteous indignation as she unleashed what could only be forceful protestations in one of Mali's many languages—Bambara, Kalongo, Masasi, Somono, Malinké, Songhay, or Tamasheg—the specific dialect escaped my recognition, lost amid the escalating tension.

My courage began to evaporate under the harsh African sun. No photograph, regardless of its potential artistic merit, justified such conflict. The chance to obtain a model release form had vanished completely. More importantly, the expensive Nikon wasn't worth a sacrifice to brute force.

In a decisive moment, I opened the camera back, extracted the film containing thirty-six exposures now ruined, and tossed it toward the cop. The traffic light changed. My driver seized the opportunity and accelerated away as I ducked instinctively, half-expecting gunfire to pursue us.

Sacred Mud and Childhood Innocence

Sometimes we witness the domino pieces begin their fatal cascade. In those critical moments before complete collapse, we face a choice—intervene or remain spectators to the unfolding disaster.

Days after my Bamako fiasco, I journeyed northward to Djenné. After securing accommodation, I wandered through labyrinthine alleys until I reached the central square dominated by the legendary Djenné Mosque—earth's largest mud structure and a masterpiece of Sudanese organic architecture.

Late in the day, the waning sunlight cast enchanted shadows across three towering minarets, their facades punctuated by the stubs of wooden beams that served dual purposes: distinctive aesthetic elements and practical scaffolding for repairs after rare but potentially devastating seasonal rains that could quickly dissolve the mud construction.

The mosque's entrance steps symbolized humanity's transition from mundane existence to divine connection. Within, ninety pillars reportedly supported a massive wooden ceiling—a sight no longer accessible to non-Muslims. Years prior, a European fashion photographer had desecrated the sacred space by using it as an exotic backdrop for scantily-clad models in provocative pose, which understandably prompted religious authorities to restrict entry to believers only.

The following morning, I sought to capture Djenné's quintessential image defined by this unique architectural edifice.

Glen Allison

For a substantial sum—exorbitant by local standards—I arranged for a dozen women in brilliant traditional attire to gather before the iconic mud structure, with their model releases secured in advance.

What should have unfolded as a straightforward shoot evolved into unexpected drama when several mischievous boys on bicycles repeatedly interrupted the composition. They rode through the background with the sole intent to have fun by ruining my photo. I threatened to withhold payment if my facilitator couldn't resolve the disruption.

His response chilled me.

He seized a nearby substantial branch and charged toward the children with unmistakable intent. I instantly abandoned photographic concerns and rushed to intercept him before violence erupted. No image, regardless of potential acclaim or profit, justified harm to innocent children. A paternal instinct awoke within me—a fierce protectiveness that rose above cultural and linguistic barriers.

The children, who sensed the intent of my intervention, quickly disappeared before they got clubbed. The facilitator retreated, and I resumed work, though the session remained tainted by what had nearly occurred.

When we concluded the shoot, my pulse had steadied enough to pay the agreed sum, though I silently vowed never to engage this man's services again, and to note cultural rules of ethics and behavior.

Later, as I sorted through the day's images, I found one frame—imperfect yet revealing. There, between smiling faces and ancient mud walls, the blurred ghost of a bicycle wheel. Some realities will always emerge in our stories, no matter how carefully we try to compose them away.

Glen Allison

Dogon Cliffs and Ancient Spirits

Mali cradles the legendary Timbuktu, but before I ventured there, I embarked on a five-day expedition across the African Sahel—that transitional zone where desert gradually yields to savanna—to photograph the remarkable Dogon villages that cling to the 500-foot Bandiagara Escarpment.

This journey fulfilled a decades-old promise. During my architectural studies at UC Berkeley in the mid-60s, I encountered the book *Architecture without Architects*[1] featuring extraordinary images of remote Dogon settlements—modular structures defying gravity as they clung to vertical cliff faces. I had pledged to witness them personally one day.

That day had finally arrived in the middle of nowhere.

At first light, I scaled the Bandiagara cliffs as I documented conical thatched-roof dwellings, women grinding millet, and men performing ancient funeral dances. Evenings brought me back to my tent on the desert floor, where I connected with local children through universal languages of play and laughter.

Spring in this region unleashes the often violent Harmattan winds, sand-laden tempests that carry Saharan heat across northern Africa. An estimated 300 million tons of dust and sand migrate annually, which cloaks clear skies in an impenetrable orange haze resembling photography shot through vaseline-smeared amber filters.

Hidden Powers

My first night camping required strategic preparation—four massive boulders anchored each corner of my tent against potential midnight flight. Throughout the impenetrable darkness, winds howled with primeval ferocity, amplifying the otherworldly presence of the cliff dwellings suspended above.

The Dogon practice animism. Their history passes through oral tradition, which reveals they weren't the escarpment's original inhabitants. A mysterious people called the Tellem—small in stature but reportedly mighty in magical ability—preceded them. They buried their dead in elevated caves above settlement areas.

Dogon belief holds that souls linger within their villages after death. Three separate ceremonies must occur before spirits join ancestral realms. Initial burial happens immediately after death, with bodies often hoisted by ropes to ancient Tellem burial caves. However, the soul remains within the family dwelling for up to a year—which allows proper mourning and accumulation of resources for elaborate celebrations that feature copious quantities of millet beer.

Following these festivities, the deceased's spirit leaves immediate family but remains somewhere within the village for another five years. Eventually, ornately masked dancers guide departed souls beyond village boundaries to rejoin ancestors.

Alone in my tent with Harmattan's fury surrounding me, I couldn't help but wonder whether ancient spirits might seek shelter within my canvas walls.

Dogon cosmology embraces fascinating duality.

They believe each soul manifests both masculine and feminine aspects until circumcision rituals. Physical alteration—removal of foreskin or clitoris—allows definitive gender expression. Yet the rejected aspect doesn't vanish; Dogons believe excised portions evolve into animals—clitoris becomes scorpion, foreskin becomes lizard—which allows spiritual twins to persist in natural forms.

Square-shaped granaries with thatched roofs characterize Dogon architecture. Each features intricately carved wooden doors that depict village life through bas-relief. Few original examples remain, as they have fallen prey to souvenir hunters and unscrupulous art dealers.

Perhaps more unusual are circular structures called "maison des femmes" or menstruation houses. Like many traditional societies, Dogons consider menstruating women ritually impure, so they temporarily relocate them to these peripheral buildings. Many such structures display elaborate mud carvings that depict exaggerated sexual characteristics, some even incorporate human pubic hair.

On my trek's final day, I encountered a craftsman selling wooden figures that embodied Dogon duality—sculptures that presented male attributes on one side, female on opposite faces, which symbolized perfect spiritual union.

With only American dollars that the seller declined, I stood at an impasse. Then, ancestral cultural values offered an unexpected solution: the craftsman simply asked when my guide would return—potentially months later—and insisted I take the sculpture immediately, as he trusted that payment would eventually find its way back to him.

This demonstration of trust touched me deeply. I later learned Dogons believe cheating brings certain death.

I contemplated how Western commerce might evolve under such a principle of integrity. When my journey concluded, I changed my money and happily provided my guide with payment for the wooden sculpture. I appreciated this lesson in honor-based exchange. And, yes, I wasn't ready to die.

Glen Allison

Arrival at the Edge of Everywhere

The next day, I boarded a small aircraft bound for Timbuktu—that legendary outpost whose name has become synonymous with the furthest reaches of civilization, the boundary where maps once ended.

When I stepped onto the deserted runway in Timbuktu, I faced an immediate sensory assault. An intense flurry of sand particles stung my exposed skin as Harmattan winds reached full fury.

Around me stretched endless sand waves punctuated occasionally by mud structures and modest mosques. No water, no vegetation—evidence of rainfall's absence that spanned geological timeframes and perhaps eons of drought.

Heat radiated with such intensity it seemed able to liquefy flesh. Nothing could flourish here. Every direction offered identical vistas—parched desolation that extended beyond vision's limit. Human presence appeared noticeably sparse.

This barren landscape shattered my preconceptions of the legendary Timbuktu, the crossroad where Trans-Saharan trade once flourished, where Tuareg nomads had guided camel caravans laden with gold and precious resins across millennia. Reality had not merely diverged from my expectations—it had dismantled them entirely.

Amadou's Desert Wisdom

That very day, I encountered one such Tuareg tribesman. Then a window opened.

He materialized from the swirling sand like an apparition, a man tall and regal in indigo robes that billowed around his slender frame. A tagelmoust—the traditional head covering—concealed all but his eyes, which held both weariness and wisdom.

"I am Amadou," he said in sparse English. "You American? You look very ... how to say ... out of place here."

His unexpected English startled me. When I mentioned this, Amadou explained that he'd spent four years studying agricultural science at a university in Michigan on an international NGO scholarship program. But, he'd returned to Mali, disillusioned by what he called the "too much rush, too much things" of American life.

"I learn much in America," he said, as he adjusted his indigo veil against the wind. "Good education, yes. But losing my ... soul? My people ways. I come back to find again what matter most."

I explained my journey through Mali, my passion for photography, my search for untouched heritage in this remote legendary place.

Amadou's eyes crinkled with amusement. "You take many photos, yes? But camera only see outside of things."

Glen Allison

This insight in his simple observation resonated profoundly. How many times had I hidden behind my viewfinder and captured surfaces while I missed deeper realities?

Amadou gestured toward sand dunes beyond town. "My family camp not far. You want visit? See real Tuareg life?" Against conventional wisdom—yet driven to follow some deeper intuition—I accepted his invitation.

We trudged through sand for nearly an hour as the humble structures of Timbuktu diminished behind us. Eventually, we reached several tents arranged in a semi-circle, where children played and women prepared evening meals over small fires.

Amadou's family welcomed me with unexpected warmth. His wife, Aisha, offered tea brewed in three separate pourings. When I asked about this custom, Amadou struggled slightly with the explanation.

"First tea bitter, like when life give problems," he said, as he poured the dark liquid. "Second tea sweet, like good friendship. Third tea gentle, soft—like going to sleep after long day work."

As I sipped the intensely bitter first brew, I reflected on how this simple ritual contained essential wisdom. Life's difficulties often come first, followed by sweetness that we can only appreciate through contrast, which ends with peaceful acceptance and potential rebirth.

The family shared a modest meal of millet and some kind of dried animal flesh I silently prayed wasn't desert snake.

Hidden Powers

As night settled around us, the temperature plummeted in typical desert fashion. My evening chants intrigued Amadou. He asked me to teach him the words. Light lifted his eyes; he seemed to innately grasp this universal rhythm as the embodiment of all he'd ever learned from the desert's mysterious rhythms and wisdom. Later, we gathered closer to the fire, and Amadou began to share stories of his people.

"My grandfather, his grandfather, all grandfathers before—they cross this sand ocean," he said, as he gestured toward endless dunes now silvered by moonlight. "No GPS, no map. Only stars and knowing the way in heart."

"How did they survive such harsh conditions?" I asked.

Amadou considered this as he struggled to find the right words. "Desert teach important lesson. Cannot carry many things here. Every thing must be ... necessary. Worth its heavy." He tapped his chest. "Man who want many things cannot survive desert. Water more important than gold here."

I thought about my equipment, my possessions, my constant pursuit of more—more experiences, more images, more validation. In the silence that followed, a deeper realization formed within: perhaps life's greatest wisdom comes through reduction, not accumulation.

I suddenly recalled a poignant quote: "Perfection is achieved, not when there is nothing more to add, but when there is nothing left to take away."[2]—-Antoine de Saint-Exupéry, *Airman's Odyssey*

As temperatures continued to drop, Amadou's teenage son added brush to the fire. The flames illuminated weathered faces that had adapted to this unforgiving environment for generations. In their relaxed demeanor amid such harshness, I glimpsed resilient contentment.

"Your cameras good for catching what eyes see," Amadou said suddenly. "But desert wisdom underneath." He scooped a handful of sand and then let it sift through his fingers. "Look at dune—always moving but always dune. When big wind come, dune just ... change shape. No fight, just become\ different, same thing."

His imperfect English somehow made the insight even more meaningful.

I contemplated the rigid structures we build—of identity, belief, expectation—and how they shatter under pressure. Meanwhile, the seemingly fragile sand endures precisely because it yields. True strength, I realized, flows not from rigidity but from adaptability.

"In Bamako, when police want your camera," Amadou continued after I had relayed my experience, "you afraid, yes? But this not bad thing. This learning thing."

Perhaps my unspoken tension had revealed confrontation to his desert-trained eyes.

"Harmattan wind that make you not see good—same wind bring rain to lands far away," he added. "Bad thing here, good thing there."

Hidden Powers

As he spoke, I reflected on my journey through Mali—and life—the confrontation in Bamako, protection of children in Djenné, discovery of Dogon trust. Each experience had stripped away something unnecessary to reveal essential lessons I couldn't have learned otherwise. A conformational realization formed: we don't grow despite adversity but because of it.

Amadou's youngest daughter approached, offering dates harvested from distant oases. As she retreated shyly, Amadou spoke with evident pride.

"Long time ago, Timbuktu have many books. More books than cities in Europe," he said. "My ancestors carry these books across desert, many hundred miles. Why? Because knowing things good, but understanding things better."

I contemplated how many travelers must come in search of Timbuktu's legendary status. They expect grand monuments and exotic treasures, only to depart disappointed. In their disillusionment, they likely missed the desert's most poignant lesson: magnificence exists in simplicity; abundance flourishes within apparent emptiness.

I slept in deep peace that night.

Before dawn, Amadou invited me to climb a nearby dune to witness sunrise. The ascent proved challenging; each step sank into soft sand and required twice the effort of normal walking. When we finally reached the crest, my legs burned with exertion.

As first light gradually illuminated endless sand in all directions, I experienced one of those rare moments of perfect clarity. The desert appeared lifeless, yet contained tremendous vitality—plants with roots that extended probably hundreds of feet beneath sand, animals adapted to extreme conditions, people who thrived where others couldn't survive.

"Desert seem empty," Amadou said, as he swept his arm across the horizon. "But is most full place. Like life—sometimes when have nothing, we see everything."

As sunlight gradually revealed Timbuktu in the distance—humble, unassuming, yet legendary—I understood why this journey concluded my decade-long, nonstop quest during the 90s as I circumambulated the globe numerous times.

Beyond photography, beyond adventure, I'd discovered that life's most meaningful teachings emerge not from accumulated experiences but from distilled essence.

The change didn't happen out there—it happened within me.

"Many people come Timbuktu thinking 'famous place,'" Amadou remarked as we descended. "They leave thinking 'nothing special.' But special thing not for eyes."

His simple words crystallized everything.

I realized that Timbuktu became legendary not because it was unreachable, but because what travelers found here—if they opened themselves to receive it—changed them. The journey's value lay not in reaching glorious destinations but in who we became along the way.

When I returned to Timbuktu proper, I viewed the modest settlement through remolded perception. I recognized that its true significance lay far beyond physical appearance. Here, where three ecological zones converged, where cultures and knowledge had mingled for millennia, where survival required resolute adaptation, lay wisdom more valuable than any treasure.

The internet access I discovered in town—that jarring juxtaposition of ancient and modern—suddenly seemed perfectly appropriate. Like humanity itself, Timbuktu existed at the intersection of seemingly contradictory realities.

Whether spelled Timbuktu, Timbuctoo, or Tombouctou, this place marked not geographic remoteness but spiritual frontier—the boundary between who we think we are and what might be revealed when stripped of pretense and confronted with the essential.

I had indeed reached the end of the earth ... and there discovered my beginning.

Glen Allison

PART TWO - THE REVELATION

Glen Allison

Chapter 25 - Absolute vs. Relative Happiness

Everyone craves enduring happiness.

Buddhism reveals two distinct states: relative and absolute. Relative happiness depends on external fulfillment—material gains and fulfilled immediate desires—but shatters when circumstances shift. Absolute happiness wells up from within and stands immutable against any challenge. It emanates from an invincible core that no external force can breach.

True happiness surpasses mere freedom from difficulties. It springs from our capacity to summon our innermost wisdom that allows us to confront obstacles directly and convert them into sources of strength. This deeper wisdom shapes our life into both a path of mastery and a force for positive change.

The world yearns for this depth of lived awareness.

Material possessions themselves don't create problems—they can enhance our lives and provide genuine joy. The issue emerges only when their acquisition becomes our defining purpose and when it eclipses deeper values and diminishes authentic relationships. True happiness flows from our essential sense of self rather than external circumstances. Our deepest fulfillment comes not from superficial achievements or appearances, but from the fundamental understanding of who we are at our core.

Many people see themselves chained by circumstance, certain that lasting happiness stands forever beyond reach, especially when they face formidable challenges. This mindset reflects what psychologists term "hedonic relativism"—a superficial view that chains happiness to external conditions.[1]

Eastern philosophies revere serenity and balance, while Western thought often glorifies achievement and external satisfaction. The "hedonic treadmill" describes how each external triumph elevates us briefly before we descend back to our baseline state. As Dan Pilat and Dr. Sekoul Krastev observe: "If you look around at what you already do have, there was likely a time when you thought that once you obtained those things, you'd be happier.... Eventually, your level of happiness returned to normal, and you began to desire new things."[2]

As Krastev explains, this insight illuminates why material success fails to deliver lasting joy: "Money can't buy happiness because with more money, your expectations and desires also change—your baseline level of happiness will have increased, meaning the experiences required to lead to an actual feeling of pleasure will have to be of a higher caliber than before."[3]

Like a drug, pleasure drives us toward stronger doses to maintain its peak effect and traps us in an emotional maze where we plummet between brief joys and deep lows but never stabilize.

Unhappiness reveals our separation from inner wisdom, not external misfortune. When we attempt to erase problems to secure happiness, we always stumble, as life perpetually presents new challenges. The Dalai Lama distills this reality:

"Happiness is not something ready-made. It comes from your own actions."[4]

Most suffering is rooted in our past choices. When we embrace this reality, the path to transformation begins. Often we reflexively blame external forces for our suffering, but such excuses only plunge us deeper into despair. This self-imposed prison separates us from absolute happiness, a state that soars above suffering and flourishes amid adversity.

The Buddhist concept of alignment with the Mystic Law reveals a dimension beyond fleeting pleasure. When we initiate this connection, we forge a path to absolute happiness—not as a transient state, but as our fundamental life essence. As our perspective expands and our life force intensifies, difficulties crystallize into fountains of strength.

A robust inner vitality, combined with deep wisdom, reshapes life's challenges from burdens into opportunities for expansion. When we tap into our fundamental life force and innate deeper wisdom, we gain the ability to redirect any situation toward positive outcomes. This contrasts with Stoic philosophical approaches to acceptance that can potentially constrain human flourishing.[5] As complete happiness fills us, anxiety, frustration, and fear lose their grip.

Inner strength thrives on adversity—we need not wait for perfect conditions like financial success, health, or harmonious relationships. From an unyielding life state, we unleash our innate potential and ignite our authentic selves to master life's turbulent waves. While earthly desires exist naturally, they often ensnare rather than free us. Our path forward unfolds not through denial of these desires, but through their redirection into vital purpose.

Daisaku Ikeda crystallizes the essence: "What, then, is absolute happiness? When we achieve such a state of life, this world, this strife-ridden saha world, will itself become a pure land. This is what we call attaining the state of Buddhahood.... Absolute happiness is something that doesn't change with time; it is eternal and unaffected by external factors."[6]

He implores us to expand our thinking and our world: "When we are open and engaged, we are experiencing the greater self. When closed off, we are putting forth our lesser self. The lesser self is a deluded condition, while the greater self is synonymous with the Buddha nature. To live for the greater self means to recognize the universal principle behind all things and, thus awakened, rise above suffering."[7]

This depth of happiness dwells not in fantasy but in fierce resilience. True lasting fulfillment doesn't exist in a life free from challenges—it emerges from our capacity to rise above whatever difficulties we encounter.

Our stalwart resilience, not the absence of struggles, defines our deepest happiness.

Chapter 26 - 3000 Realms of Existence

True empowerment springs from inner resolve.

There are essential life insights we recognize intuitively—felt in our core—even when they haven't fully surfaced to conscious awareness. This understanding about inner resolve stands as a fundamental principle, resonating with quantum theory's recognition that consciousness itself influences the manifestation of reality. In his book *Mind, Matter, and Quantum Mechanics*, Henry Stapp, a theoretical physicist who worked with Wolfgang Pauli and Werner Heisenberg, both Nobel Prize-winning pioneers of quantum physics, explores the relationship between quantum physics and consciousness. In this work, he discusses how observer consciousness influences quantum outcomes, providing scientific grounding for the connection between inner resolve and the manifestation of reality. The book examines how mental intention interacts with physical processes at the quantum level, which aligns with the concept that consciousness influences reality.[1]

We need to examine how we confront our limitations as we cultivate courage, empathy, insight, vitality, and imagination—qualities that emerge from disciplined inner work. Human experience weaves countless threads into complex patterns. Buddhist principles illuminate these diverse forces that shape our lives.

T'ien-t'ai, a 6th-century Chinese Buddhist scholar, articulated how three thousand realms of existence converge in each moment.[2] This number represents a comprehensive system for understanding reality, not a finite count. His principle illuminates the connection between our inner state and the external world, revealing the dynamic factors that shape our life's trajectory.

Global conflicts and self-serving leaders define our early twenty-first century. Yet Buddhist principles of dependent origination and the "three thousand realms in a single moment of life" expose how greed, anger, and foolishness created these crises. Our latent power, once awakened, can demonstrate how enlightened individuals can transform the world.

When we plant seeds of awakening now, we can unlock our highest potential and elevate those around us. As a more enlightened life becomes our natural state, infinite possibilities unfold, and our former sense of powerlessness dissolves.

Despite the reach of institutions and governments, each person has the potential to emerge as a formidable force that can initiate far-reaching change and wield influence through the web of universal interconnection.

The principle of three thousand realms in a single moment illuminates how personal evolution ripples through the world. This wisdom empowers us to access our deepest insights and to reshape our environment. When we unleash our capacity to create value and inspire others to do the same, we can ignite global change.

This ancient Buddhist understanding finds striking parallels in modern science. The quantum physics concept of particles existing in multiple states until observation (known as quantum superposition and wave function collapse) provides contemporary scholarly correlation with T'ien-t'ai's 3000 realm framework. Both systems recognize the profound interconnection between consciousness and physical reality, suggesting that our awareness itself plays a fundamental role in shaping existence. Theoretical physicist Brian Greene's widely respected work, *The Elegant Universe: Superstrings, Hidden Dimensions, and the Quest for the Ultimate Theory*, offers an accessible yet scientifically rigorous explanation of these quantum phenomena, describing how particles can exist in multiple states simultaneously until observation causes the wave function to collapse into a single definite state.[3]

Much like this quantum physics concept, T'ien-t'ai's structure shows how our conscious choices collapse infinite potential into our lived experience. Modern science thus echoes what Buddhist sages understood millennia ago—that the observer and the observed exist in profound interdependence, and that how we direct our consciousness determines which of countless possible worlds we ultimately manifest.

Glen Allison

The Ten Worlds: Navigating Our Inner States

T'ien-t'ai's 3000 realms concept originates from the Ten Worlds[4]—our fundamental states of life. Each world contains all the others, which multiplies their expressions tenfold. Ten distinct factors govern how these 100 states interact to create 1000 variations. These variations manifest across three realms of existence and thus yield 3000 realms of possibility present in every moment. However, we should view this concept as a conceptual framework without being bound by a finite number.

This paradigm, though complex in scope, reveals a vital focus: every human can evolve toward Buddhahood, the supreme state of enlightenment. Even those who embrace darkness possess this luminous potential.

The Ten Worlds map our daily spectrum of emotions and responses. These states ascend as they express increasing degrees of free will, compassion, and happiness: hell, hunger, animality, anger, tranquility, rapture, learning, realization, altruism, and enlightenment. They reflect our modes of engagement with life. While we carry the potential of all ten states within us, our environment triggers the first six, but personal effort unlocks the four "higher" realms.

Tranquility manifests as serenity and reason. This state reveals a harmonious world, ideal for relaxation and restoration. Yet its excess can breed lethargy. Like all Ten Worlds, tranquility harbors both light and shadow—its darker side appears as extreme inertia.

Hidden Powers

Picture a serene moment: birdsong floats on the wind, leaves whisper—until your neighbor's baby pierces the air with shrill screams. Your peace instantly shatters into irritation, perhaps even anguish. This descent mirrors the world of *Hell*. Unlike the mythic underworld of eternal torment, this hell manifests as acute imprisonment within our daily life circumstances.

Yet imagine at that moment you receive news you've won the lottery—euphoria floods in, launching you into *Rapture*. This elation might propel you toward the purchase of a new car or mansion, which reveals the state of *Hunger*. Such hunger extends far beyond mere food to encompass relationships and desires we believe will fulfill us. The dark face of hunger emerges when obsessive desire twists into torment if we cannot fulfill our wishes.

Our primal instincts govern a basic state of existence that Buddhism terms *Animality*. In this primitive realm, we react like animals to perceived threats and desires. Consider an encounter with that hot-tempered neighbor with the screaming child. If we look down on her with disdain, we slip into another base condition: the realm of *Anger*.

The state of anger extends beyond explosive outbursts. Instead, our inflated ego often manifests as quiet superiority and contempt for others and poisons our perspective with subtle arrogance.

Buddhism identifies six "lower" worlds: hell, hunger, anger, animality, rapture, and tranquility. External events serve as stimuli to spark these states within us, each represents a distinct reaction to our circumstances. Like a turbulent roller coaster, unexpected events can thrust us from one state to another in moments.

Four "higher" worlds await those who pursue them with deliberate effort. In the realms of *Learning* and *Realization*, we elevate our lives through both external study and internal discovery. A pianist who practices scales dwells in the world of learning; one who composes a masterful concerto has entered the sphere of realization.

The altruistic state, or the *Bodhisattva* realm, transcends self-interest, as one dedicates effort to ease the suffering of others and to nurture their development and joy.

The highest state of enlightenment, *Buddhahood*, radiates courage, compassion, wisdom, and vitality—a creative force of absolute positivity in our lives. When we strive to inspire hope in others from the ninth world of altruism, we initiate a catalytic stimulus that begins to unleash our own enlightenment, the tenth and highest realm. True altruism reaches beyond mere charity; rather than temporarily ease someone's burden, it empowers them to transform their fundamental life condition and their situations through their own efforts.

This noble path demands we ascend far beyond our baser instincts.

As Nichiren Daishonin wrote in the 13th century: "Worldly fame and profit are mere baubles of your present existence, and arrogance and prejudice are ties that will fetter you in the next one."[5]

Nichiren taught that the "lower" worlds remain an inescapable part of human nature. Unlike earlier forms of Buddhism, he asserted that the key lies not in eliminated these states but in the transformation of them into sources aimed toward creating value.

When anger rises, we face a choice: destructive action that harms ourselves and others—the hellish aspect; or we can channel that same force toward positive change—the enlightened aspect. Every basic emotion incorporated in each of our Ten Worlds contains seeds of enlightenment. Nichiren Buddhist principles illuminate this path and show us how to elevate our responses to benefit both ourselves and those around us.

I must add that just understanding the theory intellectually does not actually activate the innate power to refocus our baser instincts toward more enlightened outcomes. It's through tapping the Mystic Law innate in all things and beings, which we will discuss further very shortly, that we trigger the ability to fundamentally shift our lives toward the higher states.

This initial mental understanding of human nature extends far beyond the basic framework of ten states.

The Power of a Single Moment

T'ien-t'ai illuminated how each person's dominant life condition colors their entire worldview.

A naturally serene person views joy, lack, and conflict through peaceful eyes. An ego-oriented person, however, might interpret peace, suffering, and basic instincts through an anger-driven lens. Our elevated life states reshape not just our actions, but our entire perception of reality and ultimately, our reality itself.

T'ien-t'ai's principle of "mutual possession"[6] reveals how these Ten Worlds interweave. Rather than exist as separate realms, each state contains elements of all the others. This creates a conceptual framework of a tenfold set of distinct life conditions within us. Buddhism refers to this as "the mutual possession of the Ten Worlds."

This sophisticated framework illuminates the complexity of human psychology and explains why individuals respond so differently to similar circumstances.

Our quest for enlightenment elevates our perspective and allows us to navigate other realms from this heightened awareness. An enlightened person still experiences anger, desire, and joy, yet fundamentally reshapes these states into sources of value rather than use them as vehicles for self-absorption or harm.

T'ien-t'ai explained how these realms manifest in daily life through the Ten Factors,[7] a system he drew from the Lotus

Sutra's second chapter. This wisdom originated in Shakyamuni's final and highest teaching three millennia ago.

Life conditions reveal themselves through facial expressions, behavior, and demeanor. Our life state echoes in every word, action, and consequence. A desire-driven person acts far differently from one guided by altruism; a peaceful soul responds to challenges unlike someone consumed by suffering.

According to T'ien-t'ai's analysis, the hundred realms interact with ten facets of influence to create a thousand distinct elements. These Ten Factors flow through appearance, nature, entity, power, influence, internal cause, relation, latent effect, manifest effect, and their consistency from beginning to end.

Three of these core factors form our foundation of existence.

Appearance comprises our visible traits and characteristics. *Nature* embodies our intangible essence—our inherent qualities and dormant potential. *Entity* unites these as life's totality. If appearance and nature represent a door's two sides, entity is the door itself—these three remain forever unified and inseparable.

The next six elements reveal how cause and effect operate in our lives.

Power denotes our capacity to create change, while *influence* manifests when we activate this inherent force. *Internal cause* represents life's latent potential. *Relation* encompasses those internal and external conditions that awaken this potential, which creates deeper effects within life itself. The *manifest effect* emerges as visible outcomes. The tenth element, *consistency from beginning to end,* shows how these nine elements interweave—all reflect a unified state in each moment.

Five decades ago, this lesson about steadfast consistency radically altered my approach to professional photography.

Mediocrity lost its place in my world. This shift in mindset triggered my rapid success. Rather than chase talent, I tried to pursue absolute consistency in my craft. This dedication forged precise execution, resilient response, and a more masterful technique that exceeded my pursuit of photography itself.

Even bankruptcy became an opportunity to reshape my reality. The same stalwart resolve that elevated my photography sustained me through my time spent delivering pizzas, and illustrates how true consistency knows no hierarchy of work.

These Buddhist principles became my compass and unlocked extraordinary opportunities.

T'ien-t'ai revealed a continuous flow between individuals, their communities, and their environment. These three realms[8]—personal, social, and environmental—exist both separately and in unity. This structure illuminates how our life condition resonates with our surroundings. T'ien-t'ai called this dynamic principle "three thousand realms in a single moment of life."

The calculation of these three thousand realms might seem daunting, yet the concept rests on introspection: What emotional state defines us now—does suffering, desire, or anger color this moment?

T'ien-t'ai's philosophy posits that three thousand potential life conditions exist in each instant, with new possibilities born in the next. To which condition do we aspire? Do our deepest currents pull us toward enlightenment as our natural state? If not, how must we redirect our life's course?

Each singular moment awaits our determination to grasp it and take decisive action. As wisdom traditions remind us: reality unfolds exclusively in the Now. This essential insight stands at the core of Eckhart Tolle's transformative work, *The Power of Now*,[9] where he illuminates how our obsessive preoccupation with past and future disconnects us from the only point of genuine power—the present moment. Tolle explains that when we fully inhabit the Now, we access a dimension of consciousness beyond thought, where true liberation becomes possible. By bringing our complete attention to this present moment, we discover that most suffering exists only in our regrets about the past or anxieties about the future, while the present moment itself contains an inherent peace and creative potential waiting to be unleashed.

T'ien-t'ai illuminated these foundational principles twenty-six centuries ago, long before modern psychology and behavioral science took root.

The path to enlightenment unfolds through steady progress rather than sudden transformation. As Ikeda explained: "What does attaining Buddhahood mean for us? It does not mean that one day we suddenly turn into a Buddha or become magically enlightened. In a sense, attaining Buddhahood means that we have securely entered the path, or orbit, of Buddhahood inherent in the cosmos."[10]

This extraordinary opportunity defines our human potential.

Nichiren Daishonin recognized this truth nearly eight centuries ago: "It is a rare thing to be born as a human being. And if, having been born as such, you do not do your best to distinguish between the correct doctrine and the incorrect so that in the future you may attain Buddhahood, then you are certainly not fulfilling your true worth as a human being."[11]

Our actions alone can unlock this potential. The power to achieve victory lies in our determination and commitment to take action ourselves. This aligns perfectly with Buddhism's teaching that a single life-moment contains three thousand realms—our attitude and mindset possess the capacity to transform everything.

Here are four contemporary scientific references that support T'ien-t'ai's concepts:

1. The Ten Worlds

As reviewed earlier in this chapter, this concept describes ten fundamental states of life that humans experience: hell, hunger, animality, anger, tranquility, rapture, learning, realization, altruism, and enlightenment. Modern psychological studies and research about emotional states and consciousness align well with this framework.

Not only Nichiren Buddhism but other historic Buddhist traditions support T'ien-t'ai's revelations as relayed in *Visions of Compassion: Western Scientists and Tibetan Buddhists*

Examine Human Nature written by Richard Davidson and Anne Harrington. This book explores the neuroscience of various mental states and how they correspond to Buddhist conceptions of consciousness, offering scientific validation for the spectrum of experiential states similar to the Ten Worlds concept.[12]

2. The Mutual Possession of the Ten Worlds

This concept explains how each state contains elements of all others, creating complex psychological patterns. In Lisa Barrett's book, *How Emotions Are Made: The Secret Life of the Brain*, her constructionist theory of emotions proposes that emotional states aren't fixed categories but are constructed from more basic elements and influenced by context, supporting the Buddhist notion that different mental states contain and influence each other.[13]

3. The Ten Factors

These factors describe how life conditions manifest through various aspects: appearance, nature, entity, power, influence, internal cause, relation, latent effect, manifest effect, and their consistency from beginning to end. In *Mind: A Journey to the Heart of Being Human*, author Daniel Siegel's work on interpersonal neurobiology explores how the mind emerges from the interaction of brain, relationships, and consciousness, offering a scientific framework that parallels T'ien-t'ai's Ten Factors' description of how life conditions manifest through various aspects.[14]

4. The Three Realms of Existence

This concept describes how personal, social, and environmental realms exist both separately and in unison. The comprehensive work, *The Systems View of Life: A Unifying Vision*, written by Fritjof Capra presents systems theory and explains how individuals, societies, and environments form an interconnected whole with mutual influence patterns. This book scientifically supports T'ien-t'ai's Three Realms concept.[15]

These four contemporary scientific references represent just a starting point among numerous recent studies that corroborate ancient Buddhist wisdom. Together, they provide strong validation for T'ien-t'ai's two-and-a-half-millennia-old 3000 realms framework from modern neuroscience, psychology, and systems theory perspectives. Each explores aspects of consciousness, interconnection, and the nature of reality that align with the Buddhist concepts presented in this chapter. For readers interested in exploring the scientific foundations of these principles further, these sources offer valuable entry points into an expanding field of research.

Chapter 27 - The Nine Levels of Consciousness

Nichiren Buddhism identifies nine distinct levels of consciousness that operate within our lives, ranging from our basic sensory perceptions to the profound depths of our innate Buddha nature.[1] This theoretical framework explains how we can transcend our limited self-perception and tap into our highest potential for wisdom and compassion.

At birth, we begin to experience our environment through our first sensory encounters—touch, taste, sound, smell, and sight—forming our first five levels of consciousness. Through these five fundamental gateways, we ignite our awareness. An infant's cry emerges as a pure response to sensory stimuli, which marks our earliest dialogue with the world around us. From our first breath, we commence an intricate interplay with our surroundings.

Our expanded perception and deeper grasp of these sensory experiences leads us into the sixth level of consciousness—our conscious mind. This realm represents our active awareness, firmly anchored in the immediate reality of our perceptual inputs. Here, we connect multiple dimensions of lived experience to analyze our world and shape our responses. Through this process, we forge our initial sense of self and craft our identity through direct experience and conscious reflection.

Beyond the realm of immediate awareness lies the seventh level of consciousness—our subconscious mind, known in ancient Sanskrit as the "mano" level of consciousness. Here, we encounter an intangible landscape of abstract thought and insight that exceeds mere sensory perception. This domain reveals the subtle gradients between light and shadow, virtue and vice, and guides us through life's full range of emotions from the depths of suffering to the heights of extraordinary happiness.

Within this seventh sphere, we navigate the intricate balance between attachment and detachment. At this level, however, we can't fully access the deeper wisdom that lies within. Without access to this fundamental understanding, our choices often create new problems and difficulties for us. When we operate solely from this limited perspective—rooted in the seventh level of consciousness—we remain vulnerable to persistent self-doubt and difficult challenges.

Modern psychotherapy excels at illuminating the complex dynamics of our conscious and subconscious mind—the sixth and seventh levels of consciousness. While these therapeutic methods offer valuable insights and healing, they reach their limits at the seventh level, making it difficult to access or change the root causes of our inherent tendencies stored in the eighth level of consciousness. Fundamental change can occur only at this deeper stratum—the "alaya" consciousness—which forms the boundless repository of our past experiences and stores the effects of thoughts, words, and actions.

Death extinguishes the first seven levels of consciousness.

Modern quantum physics offers fascinating phenomena that many find conceptually resonant with Buddhist concepts of consciousness. While quantum mechanics describes physical systems rather than consciousness directly, quantum entanglement—where particles become correlated in ways that cannot be explained by classical physics, even when separated by vast distances[2]—provides a compelling scientific metaphor for interconnectedness.

Just as entangled particles demonstrate correlations that appear to transcend three-dimensional limitations of space, Buddhist philosophy proposes levels of consciousness that extend beyond individual experience toward universal interconnection. The Buddhist concept of the ninth level of consciousness suggests a fundamental unity underlying apparent separation.

Recent scientific research in consciousness studies has begun exploring theories of non-local aspects of awareness, though these remain hypothetical and distinct from quantum mechanics proper.

George Musser's book *Einstein's Spooky Action at a Distance: A Physicist's Exploration of the Deep Meaning of Quantum Entanglement*[3] explains this fascinating quantum phenomenon in terms accessible to non-physicists while maintaining scientific accuracy. He explores the philosophical implications of particles that remain connected across vast distances, including discussions of non-locality and interconnectedness. His book addresses historical debates about quantum mechanics (including Einstein's skepticism that gave rise to the "spooky action" phrase) that provide valuable context. Unlike purely technical references, Musser's work considers broader questions about reality and the nature of connection that offer interesting parallels to Buddhism's long-standing understanding that our deepest consciousness extends beyond conventional boundaries of individual existence.

These emerging scientific frameworks, while using different terminology, increasingly validate what Buddhist scholars articulated millennia ago: consciousness operates at levels far more profound and expansive than traditional understanding suggests.

Buddhist wisdom teaches that our karmic storehouse at the eighth level of consciousness endures beyond our mortal existence—a revelation that might seem either remarkable or unbelievable to many. This extraordinary understanding about karmic imprints that permeate throughout time exceeds standard thought and challenges our temporal grasp of consciousness and continuity.

From this illuminating Buddhist perspective, our actions—past and present—shape our existence. When dissatisfied with our current reality, this understanding kindles hope—through conscious choices made now, we can alter the flow of our personal karmic tendencies. Each present moment becomes a pivotal seed, not just influencing but actively sculpting our future, leading us toward choices made with deeper awareness and intention.

Such concepts naturally invite skepticism. How could they not? We have, after all, been conditioned to view our lives through a lens of external causation—believing that circumstances beyond our control dictate our fate.

And yet, consider the revolutionary implications: our destiny rests not in external forces but in our own choices, dissolving the illusion that other forces or people determine our suffering. This revelation unlocks our path to freedom—by embracing full responsibility for our present circumstances, we gain the capacity to shape our future with clarity and intention, reclaiming even our darkest moments as fuel for our awakening. This understanding prompts essential questions: Do we squander time's precious currency, or invest it wisely? Do we traverse life's sacred journey with casual indifference or sovereign intention? Do our actions enrich humanity's garden, or do we leave it untended?

Buddhism illuminates this eternal principle: our present perspective and trajectory chart the course of our future levels of happiness and suffering, and these effects resonate throughout eternity. Our full grasp and embodiment of this principle can trigger an extraordinary shift in our life experience.

As Winston Churchill observed, "The price of greatness is responsibility."[4]

Our accumulated karma, though weighted with past choices, remains fluid and capable of renewal when our conscious decisions create value that wisdom illuminates and positive intention infuses. This pattern of cause and effect extends into every dimension of our existence, from our outward appearance to our relationships, health, and the eternal imprint we forge upon the world

Past patterns—whether from abuse, addiction, or life's myriad traumas—reverberate from our accumulated karma stored at the eighth level of consciousness. Yet change is possible when we connect with our deepest nature—the ninth realm of enlightenment.

In this exalted state of consciousness, we embrace our full human potential beyond the bounds of time and space. This sublime reservoir of wisdom—the source of our essential nature—empowers us to reshape our past choices into avenues that lead us toward fulfillment and genuine expression. This deeper wisdom enables us to forge an unassailable foundation—one of crystalline self-awareness and invincible will.

Within the innermost depth of the ninth level of consciousness—the "amala" state—lies a realm of pristine authenticity where every cell in our body vibrates with insight and universal energy to orchestrate a life of supreme vitality.

This fundamental energy aligns with the natural patterns of enlightened awareness across all potential existences, allowing us to manifest our highest state of enlightenment—our individual expression of Buddhahood.

This constitutes a fundamental force—The Mystic Law—that once stirred, emerges from within us and connects with the greater wisdom and energy of the vast Universe. I'll delve much deeper into the dynamics of the Mystic Law and how to tap its natural rhythm in the last chapter of this book.

Chapter 28 - The Compassionate Revolution

Through compassion, we nurture courage in others, empowering them to uncover the source of their pain and master their personal challenges. This steadfast empathy reinvigorates our own life force, awakening innate strength and wisdom.

When we willfully choose to inspire others, despite our own present suffering, it becomes almost impossible to remain in misery ourselves. Just try it. As you exert effort to shine a bright light for others, your own journey mysteriously lightens.

This authentic compassion defines the ninth world of altruism—a state of life discussed in the chapter about the Ten Worlds. From this altruistic state, we expand beyond self-concern to embrace both our own growth and the collective well-being of humanity.

The British author Karen Armstrong, known for her books on comparative religions, declared: "In compassion, when we feel with the other, we dethrone ourselves from the center of our world and we put another person there."[1]

A genuine concern for others brings positive change to our society's most difficult problems. This awareness of our unique personal role in creating a more dignified world sparks deeper respect for all life.

Glen Allison

War, violence, environmental destruction, and systemic exploitation create deep divides between people. The drive to dominate others—to control and subdue them for selfish gain—ranks among humanity's most destructive impulses. This lust for dominance stems from unchecked ego and reduces others to mere tools for personal gain. However, at life's core lies the potential for true compassion—a natural counter to greed and dominance. This innate compassion opposes the drive to subjugate others for personal gain.

When we extend empathy to someone in pain, we create a divergent timeline—one where meaningful bonds replace isolation, where healing takes root instead of wounds festering.

The compassionate path requires more courage than indifference. Compassion drives our survival as a species. Empathy propels us toward generosity. When we engage this path, we ignite change that radiates from our lives into society.

This power of engagement resonates in Daisaku Ikeda's words: "When we dedicate our lives to a great vow ... the heart of a lion king rises up within us. If we remain focused on our limited personal desires and wishes, we cannot harness that power. We will be confined to a small, narrow self."[2]

Genuine compassion empowers others to find their inner strength. Rather than solving problems for them, this deeper level of compassion instills hope and fortitude and helps them face obstacles with confidence. At its core, compassion awakens the hidden strength within those who suffer and inspires them to embrace life with renewed vigor—the ability to change their own problems by themselves.

When we choose to be a light for others, darkness and despair lose their grip in our own lives, as well.

We author our experience more than we recognize. At each crossroads—whether to show compassion or indifference, courage or fear, responsibility or blame—we script different potential futures. Those who consistently choose connection, compassion, and responsibility create realities fundamentally different from those who don't, as these choices compound over time. While we cannot control every circumstance, we always command our response, and this internal locus of control builds resilience. When we claim full responsibility for our reactions to life's challenges, we often discover that our perceived limitations exist primarily in our minds rather than in reality.

This perspective is poignantly reflected in Takashi Tanemori's journey through the aftermath of Hiroshima. He was 8 years old when the atomic bomb devastated Hiroshima on August 6, 1945. The blast killed his father, mother, and two siblings, leaving him orphaned. He survived despite being less than a mile from the hypocenter, though he suffered radiation exposure that would eventually lead to blindness.

After years of intense suffering and hardship as an orphan in post-war Japan, Tanemori immigrated to the United States in 1956 in his late teens. Initially, he carried deep resentment toward Americans.

In his memoir, Tanemori describes how he lived with "bitter hatred in my heart" toward Americans after the bombing. He writes that his father's dying words to him were "Avenge my death. Avenge Japan," creating a burden he carried for decades. [3]

In his own words from his memoir *Hiroshima: Bridge to Forgiveness*, Tanemori writes: "For forty years I carried bitterness in my heart, like a tightly wound spring, wound up like a time bomb, a time bomb set to go off, to avenge my father's instructions."[4]

However, his life took a transformative turn. After decades of struggling with his trauma and hatred, Tanemori experienced what he described as a spiritual awakening in the 1980s. He came to understand that his anger was destroying him from within.

He explains this transformation: "Suddenly I realized the heavy burden I had borne all these forty years. I was carrying my father's bitterness, hatred, and desire for revenge. Now, I reasoned, if I wanted a world of peace, I must start with myself." [5]

Tanemori founded the Silkworm Peace Institute in Berkeley, California, and dedicated his life to sharing his message of reconciliation and healing. He traveled throughout the United States, speaking at schools, universities, churches, and community centers about his journey from hatred to compassion.

One of Tanemori's frequently cited insights appears in his writings: "Forgiveness is not something you do for someone else; rather it is a gift to yourself."[6]

Particularly moving was his practice of folding paper cranes as a symbol of peace—a tradition inspired by the story of Sadako Sasaki, another child survivor of Hiroshima who folded cranes while dying of leukemia caused by radiation exposure.

In a 2005 interview with the *San Francisco Chronicle*, Tanemori explained his philosophy: "The first requirement for peace is to have the courage to face the past honestly ... [We must] transform the destructiveness of the past through the power of forgiveness."[7]

Tanemori passed away in 2016, but his legacy continues through his writings, recorded testimonies, and the impact he had on thousands of people who heard his message of renewal. His story represents a dynamic example of how our deepest suffering can be converted into compassion and peace activism.

In the year 2000, Daisaku Ikeda compellingly addressed this theme in his annual Peace Proposal to the United Nations—one of 37 consecutive such proposals. He wrote: "Nothing is more barbarous than war. Nothing is more cruel.... Nothing is more pitiful than a nation being swept along by fools into the maelstrom of war." He further reflected that "the real struggle of the twenty-first century will not be between civilizations, nor between religions. It will be between violence and dialogue."[8]

Ikeda's vision echoes what Tanemori demonstrated through his actions—that true strength lies not in the ability to destroy but in the courage to heal. When faced with the aftermath of humanity's most destructive weapons, Tanemori chose the more difficult path of compassionate engagement rather than righteous anger. His example stands as a living embodiment of the dialogue Ikeda also championed throughout his life.

This doesn't mean we should ignore unjust external conditions or systemic challenges—rather, we recognize our authority over our internal response.

The limitless potential for human expansion reflects in Ikeda's observation: "In this age torn apart by anxiety and mistrust, fear and animosity, the world, more than ever, needs a philosophy that places absolute trust in the goodness inherent in human life and teaches the way of human revolution."[9]

When we choose compassion in our darkest hour, we forge the key that unlocks both prison and palace.

Chapter 29 - Awakening

True awakening begins when we recognize the path is not restricted, but waiting.

> "I can only show you the door. You're the one that has to walk through it."—Morpheus to Neo in the film, *The Matrix*[1]

This iconic line from the movie captures a fundamental understanding of about personal awakening: while guides can illuminate possibilities, the journey of growth requires our own decision and action.

Life offers diverse paths to wisdom and meaning. While some of us choose to embrace specific spiritual traditions, others prefer to carve their own unique path forward. Still, when we expand our perspectives, we ascend beyond individual concerns. A universal outlook anchors us firmly in our life's purpose and can empower us to cultivate a more enduring happiness—one that surmounts life's trials and better illuminates the path to overcome suffering.

In their illuminating book *Build the Life You Want: The Art and Science of Getting Happier*, Harvard professor Arthur C. Brooks and co-author Oprah Winfrey explore the scientific foundation of transcendent inner experiences. Brooks presents compelling evidence: "Here's the bottom line: spiritual, religious, and other metaphysical experiences are not an imaginary phenomenon. They affect your brain and give you access to insights and knowledge you can't get in other ways."[2] Brooks emphasizes that while each person's spiritual journey differs, research demonstrates that pursuing deeper dimensions of understanding correlates strongly with enhanced well-being and individual choices for personal fulfillment.

Building on Brooks' research about diverse spiritual paths, Oprah contributes her perspective in the book, affirming that each individual should connect to "the majesties of the universe through whatever form of spirituality is right for you."[3]

Ikeda explored diverse approaches to personal growth. He challenges us to examine the fundamental role of spiritual practices in human development: "Does religion make people stronger, or does it weaken them? Does it encourage what is good or what is evil in them? Are they made better and wiser—or less so—by religion? These are the questions we need to ask of all religions."[4]

At the core of Ikeda's inquiry exists a recognition that every individual harbors deeply felt aspirations, regardless of their spiritual orientation. He concludes: "Religion in the twenty-first century must provide people with the wisdom to be independent, to think and decide wisely for themselves how to live their lives."[5]

Beyond the particular path we choose, the quest to realize our highest potential remains a noble pursuit—one that requires us to overcome challenges until our final breath. Success requires that we discover and harness our innate capabilities while we build the vital energy and resolve to persevere through every obstacle.

This timeless insight resonates in Eleanor Roosevelt's observation: "The important thing is neither your nationality nor the religion you professed, but how your faith translated itself in your life."[6]

Another perspective on this regenerative journey comes from iconic singer Tina Turner in her book *Happiness Becomes You: A Guide for Changing Your Life for Good*. Turner reveals her path of self-discovery: "My awakening began five decades ago through my practice and study of Buddhist teachings." She extends her experience as a roadmap for others, offering insights and practical tools to help us surmount our personal challenges toward fulfilling our aspirations. She emphasizes that true happiness emerges through refreshing one's inner spirit. She concludes, "I want you to open up your heart and mind, refresh your spirit with new hope, courage, and compassion, and change the world by changing your life."[7]

Similar to many seekers of wisdom like Tina Turner, I too discovered Nichiren Buddhism five decades ago. These timeless teachings have illuminated essential truths and possibilities for me, much as they have for countless others.

The universal concepts shared in this book draw from both Buddhist principles and contemporary psychology, and offer practical approaches that can help reveal life's boundless potential.

Extending these insights about human potential and personal development, Ikeda addressed the growing complexity of our modern era. He observed: "People's hearts are growing more complex, more confused, and harder to understand. The same is true for human institutions. The darkness of this complicated and disturbed age may grow even deeper. This is why there is an even greater need for the brilliant inner light of culture, for education that polishes people's wisdom and character."[8]

In the gathering darkness of our convoluted world, our personal awakening can shine as a beacon that illuminates not just our own path, but the countless intersecting journeys of those whose lives we touch.

Personal Victory as Universal Medicine

The light of personal change often blazes brightest against the backdrop of our greatest challenges.

Life's journey through more than eight decades has presented me with countless challenges just as all human beings experience. Even now, I maintain vibrant energy and approach each obstacle with renewed purpose. My aspirations for future contributions remain exceedingly ambitious—perhaps improbable to some—despite significant health challenges that have surfaced and may still arise in my life.

During a medical check in Bangkok, tests exposed type-2 diabetes and coronary artery disease. The cardiologist's diagnosis ignited my immediate resolve to maintain vitality—a stark contrast to my younger years when difficulties often plunged me into despair. With this new challenge, an explosive will to survive erupted within me—fresher than at any time in my entire life. I was resolutely determined that my heart would grow younger, not older. My mission in life hasn't been finished yet.

The EKG results pointed to a need for exploratory surgery and likely placement of multiple stents to prevent cardiac complications. The doctor advised limiting physical exertion and stress. I decided to seek alternatives to surgery and inquired about metabolic treatment options. Undeterred by this potentially dire diagnosis, I continued my planned journey to India, fortified by my strengthened determination.

My friend Mark Harmel, MPH, a clinical research coordinator and diabetes educator, directed me to Dr. Dean Ornish's book, *Undo It!: How Simple Lifestyle Changes Can Reverse Most Chronic Diseases*.[9] Dr. Ornish's guidance addressed my arterial blockages and diabetes. I immediately adopted a vegan diet, eliminating meat, dairy, and excess sugar except for fresh fruit. My approach combined prescribed medications with moderate exercise and improved sleep patterns, though my continued frequent travel across multiple time zones present unique challenges at my age.

Dr. Ornish's emphasis on stress reduction complemented my five decades of Buddhist practice, where daily challenges serve as vehicles for advancement rather than burdens that induce stress. Years of spiritual practice have built a resilient foundation deep within my life that enables me to maintain equanimity even amid these serious health concerns.

I deepened my commitment to activate enhanced life force as I intensely engaged the Mystic Law with renewed enthusiasm. This strengthened my determination to prove tangibly the Mystic Law's effect in daily life. This renewed dedication unleashed vital energy that supported my undeniable full recovery within a year.

After six months, my blood sugar normalized, resolving the diabetes issue. After a year, the severe chest pains had subsided completely, eliminating the need and extensive cost for an invasive operation to insert stents.

Where once climbing a few steps triggered intense angina, I now navigate multiple flights with ease—two steps at a time.

Hidden Powers

Yesterday, I ran an hour on the treadmill at a gym in Bangkok. No heart pain whatsoever.

Much of this physical renewal occurred during my travels that landed me for several months in Udaipur, India—a magical city of shimmering lakes and resonating temple bells, where each night I visited rooftop restaurants several stories up in buildings without elevators. These climbs became effortless daily routines.

Recent EKG reports reveal no further cause for concern, signaling a positive outlook for my life.

Beyond Personal Victory: Inspiring Global Change

My approach to restore and reinvigorate my health combined modern medical science along with deepened Buddhist faith and practice. I recognized that complete recovery demands both practical action fortified by deep inner renewal. This spirit of absolute victory elevates personal triumph. When we conquer significant challenges, we reveal to others the unlimited potential that exists within their own lives. Each victory, whether over illness, adversity, or personal limitations, generates a ripple effect that can inspire countless others to persist in their own battles.

Marianne Williamson, bestselling author and spiritual teacher, eloquently captured this powerful dynamic: "We are all meant to shine, as children do.... And as we let our own light shine, we unconsciously give other people permission to do the same. As we are liberated from our own fear, our presence automatically liberates others."[10]

When we each shine brightly, we collectively create a network of change that reverberates across cultural boundaries and diverse fields of human endeavor.

Jazz legend Herbie Hancock articulates this perspective through the lens of global understanding and artistic innovation: "Globalization means we have to re-examine some of our ideas and look at ideas from other countries, from other cultures, and open ourselves to them." He continues, "And that's not comfortable for the average person.... I'm always interested in looking forward toward the future, carving out new ways of looking at things. It's people's hearts that move the age.... One thing that attracted me to Buddhism was the support for this larger vision of values."[11]

Hancock's philosophy has earned him recognition not just as a musical innovator but as a cultural bridge-builder whose influence extends far beyond the stage.

"Herbie Hancock embodies what it means to be a global citizen," said Soka University of America President Edward M. Feasel. "His peerless artistry and cultural leadership transcend borders, inspiring generations of musicians and youth through his groundbreaking music and unwavering commitment to peace, cultural exchange, and human dignity."[12]

Just as music transcends cultural boundaries to touch hearts worldwide, our individual actions possess the power to catalyze astronomical change far beyond our immediate sphere. When we embrace personal evolution and open ourselves to diverse perspectives, we ignite a cascading movement of transformation that recognizes no borders, no limitations.

Ikeda distills this boundless potential for renewal, observing: "The inner transformation resulting from even a single person's human revolution holds such hope. This is a revolution open to all, one that does not demand the sacrifice of a single life. When this process achieves a critical momentum—with waves of positive change spreading from one person to another—global society will be dramatically transformed."[13]

When one heart breaks its chains and rises, the echo awakens thousands, millions more—this is how galaxies begin.

Chapter 30 - The Mystic Law

All human beings yearn to transcend their suffering.

I am no exception. And in your quiet moments of honesty, I suspect you recognize this deep longing within yourself as well.

Within our struggles lies dormant energy waiting to be channeled. Many people move through life unaware of their capacity to reshape their destiny. When we discover how to access our hidden potential, we connect with a fountain of vitality that can remake our entire existence. This awakening occurs not through escape from difficulty, but through direct confrontation with it. The initial turning point comes when we realize our suffering contains the very seeds of our liberation. The strength to change already exists within us, waiting to be activated.

Though this book doesn't chronicle Buddhist history in depth, a pivotal breakthrough occurred in medieval Japan. The country witnessed a spiritual revolution when Nichiren Daishonin shattered orthodox Buddhist doctrine, unveiling humanity's hidden potential. While established religious schools preached escape from earthly struggles, Nichiren boldly proclaimed that enlightenment emerges only by directly confronting life's challenges, not fleeing them. This remarkable insight demolished barriers between common citizens and spiritual awakening, rejecting the prevailing wisdom that urged aspirants to subdue earthly passions to escape suffering.

Instead, Nichiren revealed that ordinary people could unearth their inherent ability to overcome life's torments, flinging open universal access to the transformative forces within. His vision blazed a new path that fully embraced human desires and daily struggles as catalysts for enlightenment.

He rejected external deities and the common practice during that era of venerating Buddha statues for comfort and favor. Instead, he illuminated how our innate potential already contains the qualities of an enlightened being—a revelation that echoed Shakyamuni's original teachings. This historical figure, who traveled India three millennia ago, never sought deification. Despite his royal birth, Shakyamuni renounced his princely status to share his awakened wisdom with common people, offering them a means to overcome their suffering. He was truly human just like those he taught.

In "The Three Kinds of Treasure," a letter to one of Nichiren's followers, he declared: "The purpose of the appearance in this world of Shakyamuni Buddha lies in his behavior as a human being."[1]

The tradition of venerating Buddha images began innocently; disciples created representative statues to honor their teacher's memory. Yet over time, this practice morphed into misguided worship, with followers revering these sculptural forms as distant celestial beings. Nichiren shattered this fundamental misconception. His teachings established that ordinary people could manifest Buddhahood while fully embracing their humanity and life's challenges, within the fabric of their everyday existence.

He illuminated both the path to awakening and the precise means to ignite this elevated life state. He stripped away centuries of misinterpretations that had obscured the historical Buddha's original intent—distortions that still persist in other forms of Buddhism practiced today. However, Nichiren's revolutionary principles reveal the fundamental laws governing human potential. These teachings unlock the inexhaustible wellspring of energy and wisdom within every life.

Traditional doctrine had deemed enlightenment virtually unattainable for mortal beings because it required countless lifetimes of spiritual struggle to overcome supposedly fixed karma. This view entrapped people in endless cycles of suffering, with liberation remaining far out of reach.

Nichiren obliterated these entrenched beliefs about immutable karma. He proclaimed that each person possesses the innate ability to reshape their own destiny and he clarified the exact method to achieve this.

While established teachings reserved such extensive capabilities only for Buddhas, sages, and the spiritual elite—excluding common people, wrongdoers, and women—Nichiren declared these abilities inherent in ALL people. He asserted that every person, regardless of past deeds or present station, could actualize this potential in their current life—a declaration that stunned medieval Japanese society.

His fearless proclamations nearly cost him his life. When he challenged Japan's towering religious institutions, whose influence penetrated the highest levels of government, he unleashed a lethal response.

Hidden Powers

Hei no Saemon, the deputy chief of military and police affairs, ordered Nichiren's death to be carried out at Tatsunokuchi's execution ground near Kamakura. As hundreds of armed samurai watched, the executioner's blade faltered when a brilliant orb blazed across the night sky. Unnerved by this synchronistic celestial omen, the government cancelled the execution and instead banished Nichiren to Sado Island—a desolate outpost of ruthlessly harsh winters from which few returned alive.[2]

Only a handful of Nichiren's staunchest followers defied restrictions, making treacherous journeys to bring him supplies. Even so, the savage winters and extreme deprivation tested his resolve. Yet amid these brutal conditions, he composed his most significantly influential treatises. When death failed to claim him, the authorities relented, pardoned him, and allowed his return to mainland Japan. He spent his remaining years in relative peace, advancing his teachings until his passing in 1282. He had accomplished his mission: establishing the validity of The Mystic Law of Life as humankind's birthright.

Nichiren taught that activating these dormant forces within life's depths would spark ever-expanding enlightenment, enabling all people to access deeper wisdom and energy. This awakened potential would empower them to make more value-creative choices in each moment, charting new paths for their lives. He understood that these insights would forever alter humanity's course—a vision that fueled his unyielding persistence.

In Nichiren Buddhism, "The Mystic Law" (Myoho) represents the fundamental principle underlying all existence—an eternal force residing at the core of every life. This universal law contains the complete wisdom and power of the cosmos, permeating all phenomena while transcending ordinary understanding. Though called "mystic," it isn't secret or exclusive, but rather reveals a profound truth: all beings inherently possess the capacity to overcome suffering and manifest their highest potential of enlightenment, or Buddhahood.

Centuries later, Mahatma Gandhi grasped this universal principle: "There is an indefinable mysterious power that pervades everything ... an orderliness in the universe ... an unalterable law governing everything and every being that exists or lives. It is no blind law, for no blind law can govern the conduct of living beings."[3]

Nichiren revealed how ordinary people could align with this cosmic rhythm, awakening the extraordinary potential that flows through all time and space. He taught that the essence of the Mystic Law is distilled in the phrase "Nam-myoho-renge-kyo," which practitioners intone as a primary daily practice.[4]

Unlike superficial guidelines for self-improvement, he proclaimed that this profound vibration empowers one to elevate any circumstance into fuel for growth.

Yet intellectual understanding alone falls short. The real challenge lies in how we cultivate the strength and perseverance to apply this principle consistently, as we create a life of innate prosperity and fulfillment, irrespective of life's often harsh circumstances. Nichiren taught that reciting this mantra unlocks access to absolute happiness—an indomitable state that eclipses the fleeting contentment dependent on external conditions.

Through this practice, he provided not mere philosophical concepts but the exact key to awaken wisdom within each person's life, which empowers one to surmount any challenge and to manifest infinite worth, enabling us to activate invincible fortitude to battle life's difficulties.

Daisaku Ikeda exclaimed: "What matters is living in accord with the Law and attaining an elevated state of life based on the Law. The state of life we attain, like the Law itself, is eternal.... The Mystic Law, the fundamental Law of the universe, enables us to reveal the nobility of our lives."[5]

Nichiren's teachings ignite more than personal change—they reveal a path to uplift all humanity. The practice he established lays the foundation for lasting peace in a reawakened world that honors the sanctity of life across all cultures and beliefs.

Ikeda also related: "The root cause of war is mutual mistrust and suspicion. Our movement encourages every individual to undertake the practice of what we call a human revolution to overcome such mistrust and create harmony with all people, not just in the abstract but in reality ... transcending ideological, ethnic, and national barriers."[6]

When we embrace the richness of human diversity, we forge avenues for meaningful dialogue and enduring solutions. When we recognize the inherent dignity in each person, we create a way of living that celebrates the full spectrum of human experience.

In the preface to Ikeda's multi-volume historical novel, *The Human Revolution,* published in sequence beginning in 1964 and completed in 2018, the opening lines embody visionary insight. Ikeda boldly declared: "A great inner revolution in just a single individual will help achieve a change in the destiny of an entire society and will cause a change in the destiny of humankind."[7]

Together, we can build a world that harmonizes our uniquely chosen individual paths toward enlightenment. Let us honor the diverse cultures, traditions, and beliefs that enrich our shared journey.

Let us herald a new dawn for humanity.

"Live with a dancing spirit. The stars in the heavens are dancing through space, the Earth never ceases to spin. All life is dancing: the trees with the wind, the waves on the sea, the birds, the fish, all are performing their own dance of life. Every living thing is dancing, and you must keep dancing too, for the rest of your life!"[8] ~ *Daisaku Ikeda*

Acknowledgements

Life's most treasured gifts often emerge through relationships that exceed conventional boundaries. Two extraordinary individuals have profoundly shaped both my personal journey and this book in ways that words barely capture.

Tina Rubin, author of the forthcoming memoir "Liftoff," has remained an irreplaceable presence in my life long after our marriage ended over four decades ago. What began as a romantic partnership evolved into a rare and most precious life experience—a fusion of mind and heart that defies simple explanation.

As a life-long professional book editor and an accomplished author, Tina's sharp editorial insight and deep wisdom have illuminated my path, and helped me navigate not just the intricacies of writing but the complexities of self-discovery.

Through her own journey of growth and renewal, documented so eloquently in her memoir, Tina has fully demonstrated how life's challenges can become driving forces for extraordinary expansion.

Her unfailing ability to recognize my potential, even when I couldn't see it myself, has over the decades repeatedly propelled me toward greater heights of self-awareness in my pursuit of life's marvels. Her influence extends far beyond the momentum she inspired in my literary expression. This book bears the subtle yet sublime imprint of her insightful wisdom on every page.

Glen Allison

Sometimes the natural rhythms in the universe orchestrate meetings that seem too perfect for coincidence.

Such was my first encounter with Giannis Angelou on a warm August evening in 1992; we both arrived at precisely the same moment to photograph Santorini's iconic white architecture. That serendipitous meeting on the Greek isle marked the beginning of one of life's most enriching friendships. Though we've met in person only six times since then, our near-daily correspondence over the past three decades has forged a brotherhood of the mind and heart and soul that spans continents, decades, and infinity.

Giannis infuses a unique combination of philosophical depth and practical wisdom into every conversation. His vast library of more than a thousand self-development and entrepreneurial works reflects not just a collector's passion but a seeker's dedication to understanding human potential.

When I shared my initial rather academic manuscript with Giannis, his impassioned response redirected the entire trajectory of this book.

With characteristic insight, he urged me to completely remake my book by weaving my personal experiences and cultural encounters across the globe throughout the text. He understands that universal principles resonate most powerfully when grounded in lived experience. His astute guidance and mentorship inspired in me the courage to share my own often painful story of personal change. This reshaped what might have been merely another self-help book into a more intimate exploration of human resilience and growth.

Through the influence of both Tina and Giannis, I've learned that true friendship and lifelong bonds aren't measured in years of physical proximity but in moments of genuine understanding that in our case, I am convinced, will extend throughout eternity. Their contributions to my writing pursuits—and my life—extend far beyond editorial suggestions or structural advice. They helped me shape the very soul of this book, and by extension, my own journey of awakening.

To both of you, I offer my deepest gratitude for relentlessly walking this path with me, and my profound appreciation for envisioning possibilities I couldn't yet see. Your inspiration enabled me to elevate personal insights into universal truths which might serve others on their journeys of discovery.

Glen Allison

About the Author

Glen Allison navigates the globe as an acclaimed novelist, travel photographer, and artist. He bases himself primarily in Southeast Asia and India where he roams with minimalist precision. His backpack contains little more than essential clothing, a laptop, and a camera as he collects firsthand experiences that fill his writings with authentic settings. He maintains no permanent residence.

As a Getty Images contributor, Allison built a distinguished photography career through his evocative travel imagery, licensed over 100,000 times by premier publications worldwide, including *National Geographic* and *Conde Nast Traveler*—which places him among the elite ranks of the world's most prolifically published travel photographers.

His extraordinary decade-long nonstop odyssey during the 90s spanned more than a hundred countries. That sojourn launched a subsequent three-decade commitment to nomadic living.

Allison graduated from the University of California, Berkeley, in 1968 with a Bachelor of Architecture degree. He co-founded the Stock Artists Alliance in 2000, a professional trade association that championed photographers' intellectual property rights.[1] For more than five decades, he has committed himself to the Soka Gakkai International, a Buddhist lay organization that champions peace, education, culture, and a steadfast dedication to human dignity.[2]

Glen Allison

His fictional love story novel, *The Journey from Kamakura*, mirrors his real-world experiences.[3] This book earned the silver medal for "Best First Book/Fiction" in the 2002 Benjamin Franklin literary awards. The new 2024 revised edition enhances the narrative with fresh compelling backstory, heightened sensory detail, and more illuminating insights.

Here's the Amazon blurb:

The Journey from Kamakura

"Readers are swept along on travel photographer Grey Matheson's quest to find the most dazzling sights and exotic experiences the world has to offer. In his drive to the peak of his profession, Matheson is sabotaged by self-destructive tendencies that not only shatter his marriage but send him on a roller coaster ride that challenges his will to survive. Roaming the globe in an ever-accelerating thirst for satisfaction, he discovers that great photographs come at a price, from nearly drowning in the riptides off Puerto Vallarta to being buried by a Tibetan avalanche. Despite a cycle that takes him from begging on the streets of Amsterdam to blowing through a million dollars in a matter of months, it's only when he comes face to face with a mysterious woman in Southeast Asia that his true journey begins, leading to perceptions no photograph could ever portray."

https://www.GlenAllison.com

His message: "Rise tall."

Bibliography

Essential Introduction

1. Yousafzai, Malala, and Christina Lamb. *I Am Malala: The Girl Who Stood Up for Education and Was Shot by the Taliban*. New York: Little, Brown and Company, 2013.

2. Yousafzai, Malala, and Christina Lamb. *I Am Malala: The Girl Who Stood Up for Education and Was Shot by the Taliban*. New York: Little, Brown and Company, 2013.

3. Obama, Michelle. *Becoming*. New York: Crown Publishing, 2018.

4. Yousafzai, Malala. "Nobel Lecture." Speech, Oslo, December 10, 2014. The Nobel Foundation. https://www.nobelprize.org/prizes/peace/2014/yousafzai/lecture/.

5. Seneca. "On the Shortness of Life." In *Dialogues and Essays*, translated by John Davie, 131-154. Oxford: Oxford University Press, 2007.

6. Gandhi, Mahatma. Quoted in *The Words of Gandhi*, compiled by Richard Attenborough, 71. New York: Newmarket Press, 2000.

7. Shaw, George Bernard. *Everybody's Political What's What?* New York: Dodd, Mead & Company, 1944.

8. Gibran, Kahlil. *The Prophet*. New York: Alfred A. Knopf, 1923.

9. Nin, Anaïs. *A Literate Passion: Letters of Anaïs Nin and Henry Miller, 1932-1953*. Edited by Gunther Stuhlmann. San Diego: Harcourt Brace Jovanovich, 1987.

10. Einstein, Albert. "Atomic Education Urged by Einstein; Scientists in Plea for $200,000 to Promote New Type of Essential Thinking." *The New York Times*, May 25, 1946.

11. Shaw, George Bernard. Quote in *The Independent*, October 29, 1996.

Chapter 1 - From Victim to Victor

1. Angelou, Maya. Interview by Dave Chappelle. Dave Chappelle's Block Party. Directed by Michel Gondry. Rogue Pictures, 2006. Film.

2. Isaac Newton, *Philosophiae Naturalis Principia Mathematica* [*Mathematical Principles of Natural Philosophy*], trans. I. Bernard Cohen and Anne Whitman (Berkeley: University of California Press, 1999), 417.

Chapter 2 - From Self-Sabotage to Inner Power

1. Campbell, Joseph. *The Hero with a Thousand Faces*, 3rd ed. (Novato, CA: New World Library, 2008), 89-100

2. Nichiren Daishonin. "The Entity of the Mystic Law." In *The Writings of Nichiren Daishonin*, Vol. 1, edited by The Gosho Translation Committee. Tokyo: Soka Gakkai, 1999.

3. Ikeda, Daisaku. *The New Human Revolution*. Vol. 30. Tokyo: Soka Gakkai, 2018.

Chapter 3 - Breaking Suffering's Code

1. Frankl, Viktor E. *Man's Search for Meaning*. Translated by Ilse Lasch. Boston: Beacon Press, 2006.

2. *Good Will Hunting*. Directed by Gus Van Sant. Miramax Films, 1997.

3. Mayo Clinic Staff. "Mental Illness." Mayo Clinic. Accessed April 14, 2025. https://www.mayoclinic.org/diseases-conditions/mental-illness/symptoms-causes/syc-20374968.

4. Dalai Lama, and Howard C. Cutler. *The Art of Happiness: A Handbook for Living*. New York: Riverhead Books, 1998.

5. Ikeda, Daisaku. *The New Human Revolution*. Vol. 18, "Dynamic Strides" chapter. Santa Monica, CA: World Tribune Press, 2018.

6. Kahlo, Frida. *The Letters of Frida Kahlo: Cartas Apasionadas*. Edited by Martha Zamora. San Francisco: Chronicle Books, 1995.

7. Herrera, Hayden. *Frida: A Biography of Frida Kahlo*. New York: Harper & Row, 1983.

8. Herrera, Hayden. *Frida: A Biography of Frida Kahlo*. New York: Harper & Row, 1983.

9. Dickens, Charles. *Great Expectations*. Edited by Charlotte Mitchell. London: Penguin Classics, 2003.

10. Ikeda, Daisaku. *Discussions on Youth*. Santa Monica, CA: World Tribune Press, 2010.

11. Ikeda, Daisaku. *The Human Revolution*. Vol. 1. Santa Monica, CA: World Tribune Press, 2004.

12. Nichiren Daishonin. *The Writings of Nichiren Daishonin*. Vol. 1. Edited and translated by The Gosho Translation Committee. Tokyo: Soka Gakkai, 1999.

Chapter 4 - The Flower Seller's Wisdom

1. Lean, David, dir. *Lawrence of Arabia*. Columbia Pictures, 1962.

2. Ikeda, Daisaku. *Buddhism Day by Day: Wisdom for Modern Life*. Santa Monica, CA: Middleway Press, 2006.

Chapter 5 - To Dream the Impossible Dream

1. Cervantes Saavedra, Miguel de. *Don Quixote*. Translated by Walter Starkie. New York: Signet Classics, 1957.

2. Lyons, Malcolm C., trans. *The Arabian Nights: Tales of 1001 Nights*. London: Penguin Classics, 2010.

Chapter 6 - The Science of Dreaming Big

1. Oettingen, Gabriele. "Strategies of Setting and Implementing Goals." In *Social Psychological Foundations of Clinical Psychology*, edited by James E. Maddux and June Price Tangney, 114-135. New York: Guilford Press, 2010.

2. Gaiman, Neil. *The Sandman, Vol. 6: Fables and Reflections*. New York: DC Comics, 1993.

3. Nin, Anaïs. *The Diary of Anaïs Nin, Volume 3: 1939-1944*. Edited by Gunther Stuhlmann. New York: Harcourt Brace Jovanovich, 1969.

4. Jarvis, Chase. *Never Play it Safe: A Practical Guide to Freedom, Creativity, and a Life You Love*. New York: Harper Collins, 2024.

5. Seligman, Martin E. P. *Learned Optimism: How to Change Your Mind and Your Life*. New York: Vintage Books, 2006.

6. "Changing Poison into Medicine." *Nichiren Buddhism Library*. Accessed September 12, 2024. https://www.nichirenlibrary.org/en/dic/Content/C/26.

7. Tedeschi, Richard G., and Lawrence G. Calhoun. "Posttraumatic Growth: Conceptual Foundations and Empirical Evidence." *Psychological Inquiry* 15, no. 1 (2004): 1-18.

8. Cervantes Saavedra, Miguel de. *Don Quixote*. Translated by Edith Grossman. New York: Ecco, 2003.

9. Bandura, Albert. *Self-efficacy: The Exercise of Control*. New York: W.H. Freeman, 1997.

10. Shapiro, Fred R. *The Yale Book of Quotations*. New Haven: Yale University Press, 2006.

11. Csikszentmihalyi, Mihaly. *Flow: The Psychology of Optimal Experience*. New York: Harper & Row, 1990.

12. Blakely, Sara. "Spanx Founder: Failure Is an Option." Interview by Poppy Harlow. CNN Money, October 29, 2013. https://money.cnn.com/2013/10/16/leadership/spanx-sara-blakely-failure/.

13. Schultz, Howard, and Dori Jones Yang. *Pour Your Heart Into It: How Starbucks Built a Company One Cup at a Time*. New York: Hyperion, 1997.

14. Schultz, Howard, and Joanne Gordon. *Onward: How Starbucks Fought for Its Life without Losing Its Soul.* New York: Rodale, 2011.

15. Schultz, Howard, and Dori Jones Yang. *Pour Your Heart Into It: How Starbucks Built a Company One Cup at a Time.* New York: Hyperion, 1997.

16. Schultz, Howard. Interview by Andrew Ross Sorkin. "Howard Schultz on a Potential Presidential Bid and the Rise of Big Business." *New York Times*, January 27, 2019. https://www.nytimes.com/2019/01/27/business/howard-schultz-president.html.

17. Frost, Robert. "The Road Not Taken." In *The Poetry of Robert Frost: The Collected Poems, Complete and Unabridged*, edited by Edward Connery Lathem, 105. New York: Henry Holt and Company, 1969.

18. Seneca, Lucius Annaeus. *Moral Letters to Lucilius (Epistulae Morales ad Lucilium).* Translated by Richard M. Gummere. Vol. 1, Letter 104.26. Cambridge: Harvard University Press, 1917.

Chapter 7 - Hope and Optimism

1. Ikeda, Daisaku. *Hope Is a Decision.* Santa Monica, CA: Middleway Press, 2017.

2. Tutu, Desmond, and Douglas Abrams. *The Book of Joy: Lasting Happiness in a Changing World.* New York: Avery, 2016.

3. King, Martin L. [attributed]. "Let your hopes, not your hurts, shape your future." Quotation of uncertain origin commonly attributed to Martin Luther King, Jr.

4. Ikeda, Daisaku. *The New Human Revolution.* Vol. 13, "Land of Happiness." Santa Monica: World Tribune Press, 2007, 341.

5. Mandela, Nelson. *Long Walk to Freedom: The Autobiography of Nelson Mandela.* Boston: Little, Brown and Company, 1994.

6. Mandela, Nelson. *Long Walk to Freedom: The Autobiography of Nelson Mandela.* Boston: Little, Brown and Company, 1994.

7. Mandela, Nelson. *Long Walk to Freedom: The Autobiography of Nelson Mandela.* Boston: Little, Brown and Company, 1994.

8. *The Shawshank Redemption.* Directed by Frank Darabont. Columbia Pictures, 1994.

9. Ikeda, Daisaku, Katsuji Saito, Takanori Endo, and Haruo Suda. *The Wisdom of the Lotus Sutra: A Discussion.* Vol. 1. Santa Monica, CA: World Tribune Press, 2000.

10. Long, Kara N.G., Sara J. Kim, Ying Chen, Matthew F. Wilson, Eric S. Kim, and Tyler J. VanderWeele. "The Associations of Hope with Health-Related Quality of Life and Mortality Among U.S. Adults." *Global Epidemiology* 2 (2020): 100018. https://doi.org/10.1016/j.gloepi.2020.100018.

11. Dalai Lama, Desmond Tutu, and Douglas Carlton Abrams. *The Book of Joy: Lasting Happiness in a Changing World.* New York: Avery, 2016. Chapter 9 - Diamonds in the Making.

Chapter - 9 - Diamonds in the Making

1. Nichiren. *The Writings of Nichiren Daishonin.* Edited and translated by The Gosho Translation Committee. Tokyo: Soka Gakkai, 1999.

2. Nichiren. "Hell Is the Land of Tranquil Light." In *The Writings of Nichiren Daishonin*, edited by The Gosho Translation Committee, 456. Tokyo: Soka Gakkai, 1999.

3. Ilibagiza, Immaculée, and Steve Erwin. *Left to Tell: Discovering God Amidst the Rwandan Holocaust.* Carlsbad, CA: Hay House, 2006.

4. Ikeda, Daisaku. "June 28, 2017 – Daily Encouragement by Daisaku Ikeda." *SGI-USA Buddhist Community Services* (blog). June 28, 2017. https://sgiusabcs.wordpress.com/2017/06/.

5. Parks, Rosa, and Gregory J. Reed. *Quiet Strength: The Faith, the Hope, and the Heart of a Woman Who Changed a Nation.* Grand Rapids: Zondervan, 1994.

6. Ikeda, Daisaku. "Rosa Parks." Daisaku Ikeda Website. Accessed April 18, 2025. https://www.daisakuikeda.org/main/peacebuild/friends/rosa-parks.html.

7. Winfrey, Oprah. "Oprah Winfrey Receives the Cecil B. DeMille Award - Golden Globes 2018." Speech, Beverly Hills, CA, January 7, 2018. NBC.

8. Oprah Winfrey, The Oprah Winfrey Show: Reflections on an American Legacy (New York: Abrams, 2007), 142.

9. Quote attributed to Indira Gandhi. n.d. Widely cited without verified original source.

10. Ikeda, Daisaku. "Strength - Quotations." *Daisaku Ikeda Website.* Accessed April 14, 2025. https://www.daisakuikeda.org/sub/quotations/theme/strength.html.

11. Gandhi, Mahatma. "Mahatma Gandhi Quotes." *BrainyQuote.* Accessed April 14, 2025. https://www.brainyquote.com/quotes/mahatma_gandhi_122084.

12. *Batman Begins.* Directed by Christopher Nolan. Warner Bros. Pictures, 2005.

13. Shakespeare, William. *King Henry VI, Part 3*. In *The Complete Works of William Shakespeare*. London: Oxford University Press, 1959.

14. Hariri, Ahmad R. *Looking Inside the Disordered Brain*. Sunderland, MA: Sinauer Associates, 2015.

15. Horace. *Odes and Epodes*. Translated by Niall Rudd. Loeb Classical Library 33. Cambridge, MA: Harvard University Press, 2004.

16. Keller, Helen. *The Story of My Life*. New York: Doubleday, Page & Company, 1903.

17. Dhabhar, Firdaus S. "Effects of Stress on Immune Function: The Good, the Bad, and the Beautiful." *Immunologic Research* 58, no. 2-3 (2014): 193-210.

18. Davidson, Richard J., and Sharon Begley. *The Emotional Life of Your Brain: How Its Unique Patterns Affect the Way You Think, Feel, and Live—and How You Can Change Them*. New York: Hudson Street Press, 2012.

19. Schweitzer, Albert. *Out of My Life and Thought: An Autobiography*. Translated by Antje Bultmann Lemke. Baltimore: Johns Hopkins University Press, 1998.

20. Wilcox, Ella Wheeler. *Poems of Power*. Chicago: W.B. Conkey Company, 1895.

21. Ikeda, Daisaku. "Speech at the Headquarters Leaders Meeting." Tokyo, Japan, August 29, 1996. https://

www.daisakuikeda.org/sub/quotations/theme/human-revolution.html. Accessed April 15, 2025.

Chapter 10 - The Prison of Pride

1. Hamilton, Edith. *Mythology: Timeless Tales of Gods and Heroes.* New York: Little, Brown and Company, 1942.

Chapter 11 - Breaking Free

1. "Sushma Swaraj Birth Anniversary: Top 20 Powerful and Inspirational Quotes About Leadership and Compassion by the 'Iron Lady' of India." Jagran English, February 14, 2023. https://english.jagran.com/lifestyle/sushma-swaraj-birth-anniversary-top-20-powerful-and-inspirational-quotes-about-leadership-and-compassion-by-the-iron-lady-of-india-10133730.

2. Bloom, Linda, and Charlie Bloom. *Secrets of Great Marriages: Real Truth from Real Couples about Lasting Love.* Novato, CA: New World Library, 2010.

3. Angelou, Maya. Commonly attributed and cited as coming from her public speeches or interviews rather than her written works. No verified original source.

4. Tolstoy, Leo. *A Calendar of Wisdom: Daily Thoughts to Nourish the Soul.* Translated by Peter Sekirin. New York: Scribner, 1997.

5. Isaacson, Walter. *Steve Jobs*. New York: Simon & Schuster, 2011.

6. Jobs, Steve. "Stanford Commencement Address." Speech, Stanford University, Palo Alto, CA, June 12, 2005. https://news.stanford.edu/2005/06/14/jobs-061505/.

7. Isaacson, Walter. *Steve Jobs*. New York: Simon & Schuster, 2011.

8. Jobs, Steve. "Stanford Commencement Address." Speech, Stanford University, Palo Alto, CA, June 12, 2005. https://news.stanford.edu/2005/06/14/jobs-061505/.

9. Yoda, *The Empire Strikes Back*, directed by Irvin Kershner (Los Angeles: Lucasfilm Ltd., 1980).

10. Dweck, Carol S. *Mindset: The New Psychology of Success*. New York: Random House, 2006.

Chapter 13 - Rising from the Ashes

1. Holiday, Ryan. *The Obstacle Is the Way: The Timeless Art of Turning Trials into Triumph*. New York: Portfolio/Penguin, 2014.

2. Makiguchi, Tsunesaburo. *The System of Value-Creating Pedagogy*. Translated by Dayle M. Bethel. Tokyo: Seikyo Press, 1989.

3. Bonanno, George A. "Loss, Trauma, and Human Resilience: Have We Underestimated the Human Capacity to Thrive After Extremely Aversive Events?" *American Psychologist* 59, no. 1 (2004): 20-28.

4. Darwin, Charles. *On the Origin of Species by Means of Natural Selection, or the Preservation of Favoured Races in the Struggle for Life*. London: John Murray, 1859.

5. Stevenson, Bryan. *Just Mercy: A Story of Justice and Redemption*. New York: Spiegel & Grau, 2014.

6. Stevenson, Bryan. *Just Mercy: A Story of Justice and Redemption*. New York: Spiegel & Grau, 2014

7. Moore, Graham. *The Imitation Game*. Directed by Morten Tyldum, performances by Benedict Cumberbatch and Keira Knightley, The Weinstein Company, 2014.

8. Makiguchi, Tsunesaburo. *The System of Value-Creating Pedagogy*. Translated by Dayle Bethel. Tokyo: Sōka Gakkai, 1972.

9. Earhart, Amelia. *The Fun of It: Random Records of My Own Flying and of Women in Aviation*. Chicago: Academy Chicago Publishers, 1977.

10. Luthans, Fred, Carolyn M. Youssef, and Bruce J. Avolio. *Psychological Capital: Developing the Human Competitive Edge*. Oxford: Oxford University Press, 2007.

11. Ikeda, Daisaku. *The Human Revolution*. Santa Monica, CA: World Tribune Press, 2004.

12. Rowling, J.K. *Very Good Lives: The Fringe Benefits of Failure and the Importance of Imagination*. New York: Little, Brown and Company, 2015.

13. Rowling, J.K. *Very Good Lives: The Fringe Benefits of Failure and the Importance of Imagination*. New York: Little, Brown and Company, 2015.

14. Rowling, J.K. *Very Good Lives: The Fringe Benefits of Failure and the Importance of Imagination*. New York: Little, Brown and Company, 2015.

15. Jordan, Robert. *The Fires of Heaven*. New York: Tor Fantasy, 1994.

16. Stallone, Sylvester. *Rocky Balboa*. Directed by Sylvester Stallone, performances by Sylvester Stallone and Burt Young, Metro-Goldwyn-Mayer, 2006.

17. Soka Gakkai. *The Soka Gakkai Dictionary of Buddhism*. Tokyo: Soka Gakkai, 2002.

18. King, Martin Luther, Jr. *Strength to Love*. New York: Harper & Row, 1963.

Chapter 15 - Fortune's Adversary

1. Berry, William. "The Psychology of Complaining." *Psychology Today*, June 12, 2013. https://www.psychologytoday.com/us/blog/the-second-noble-truth/201306/the-psychology-complaining.

2. Ikeda, Daisaku. *Discussions on Youth*. Santa Monica, CA: World Tribune Press, 2010.

3. Nin, Anaïs. *Seduction of the Minotaur*. Chicago: Swallow Press, 1961.

4. Schwahn, Mark, and John Gatins. *Coach Carter*. Directed by Thomas Carter, performance by Samuel L. Jackson, Paramount Pictures, 2005.

5. Jung, Carl G. *Aion: Researches into the Phenomenology of the Self*. Translated by R.F.C. Hull. Princeton: Princeton University Press, 1959.

6. Vujicic, Nick. *Life Without Limits: Inspiration for a Ridiculously Good Life*. New York: Doubleday Religion, 2010.

7. Vujicic, Nick. *Life Without Limits: Inspiration for a Ridiculously Good Life*. New York: Doubleday Religion, 2010.

8. Vujicic, Nick. *Unstoppable: The Incredible Power of Faith in Action*. Colorado Springs: WaterBrook Press, 2012.

9. Vujicic, Nick. *Unstoppable: The Incredible Power of Faith in Action*. Colorado Springs: WaterBrook Press, 2012.

10. Elizabeth Scott, "How and Why You Should Stop Complaining," *Verywell Mind*, last accessed September 6, 2021, https://www.verywellmind.com/.

11. Ikeda, Daisaku, Katsuji Saito, Takanori Endo, and Haruo Suda. *The Wisdom of the Lotus Sutra: A Discussion*. Vol. 1. Santa Monica, CA: World Tribune Press, 2000.

12. Nichiren. "The Three Kinds of Treasure." In *The Writings of Nichiren Daishonin*, edited and translated by The Gosho Translation Committee, Vol. 1, 851-52. Tokyo: Soka Gakkai, 1999.

Chapter 16 - Lessons in Flow and Fearlessness

1. "Chaos Theory," *Wikipedia*, last accessed April 15, 2025, https://en.wikipedia.org/wiki/Chaos_theory.

Chapter 17 - The Infinite Power of Resilience

1. Henri J. M. Nouwen, *The Wounded Healer: Ministry in Contemporary Society* (New York: Doubleday, 1979), 87.

2. Worthington, Everett L., Jr., and Charlotte van Oyen Witvliet. *Forgiveness and Reconciliation: Theory and Application*. New York: Routledge, 2014.

3. Angelou, Maya. "On the Pulse of Morning." In *The Complete Poetry*. New York: Random House, 2015.

4. MacIntyre, Alasdair. *After Virtue: A Study in Moral Theory*. 3rd ed. Notre Dame, IN: University of Notre Dame Press, 2007.

5. Tedeschi, Richard G., and Lawrence G. Calhoun. "The Posttraumatic Growth Inventory: Measuring the Positive Legacy of Trauma." *Journal of Positive Psychology* 11, no. 3 (2016): 291-302.

6. Stockdale, James B. *Courage Under Fire: Testing Epictetus's Doctrines in a Laboratory of Human Behavior*. Stanford: Hoover Institution Press, 1993.

7. Goldman, William. *The Princess Bride*. Directed by Rob Reiner, performances by Cary Elwes and Robin Wright, 20th Century Fox, 1987.

8. Ionescu, Thea. "Exploring the Nature of Cognitive Flexibility." *New Ideas in Psychology* 30, no. 2 (2012): 190-200.

9. Epictetus. *Enchiridion*. Translated by Robin Hard. Oxford: Oxford University Press, 2014.

Chapter 19 - Lessons from the Roof of the World

1. Theodore Roosevelt, "The Strenuous Life: Essays and Addresses" in *The Works of Theodore Roosevelt*, Memorial

Edition, vol. 13 (New York: Charles Scribner's Sons, 1926), 332.

2. Khmara, Edward, John Raffo, and Rob Cohen. *Dragon: The Bruce Lee Story*. Directed by Rob Cohen, performance by Jason Scott Lee, Universal Pictures, 1993.

3. Toda, Josei. "Song of Comrades." In *The Human Revolution*, translated by Burton Watson. Tokyo: Soka Gakkai, 1972.

4. Frankl, Viktor E. *Man's Search for Meaning*. Translated by Ilse Lasch. Boston: Beacon Press, 2006.

5. Frankl, Viktor E. *The Doctor and the Soul: From Psychotherapy to Logotherapy*. Translated by Richard and Clara Winston. New York: Vintage Books, 1986.

6. Parton, Dolly. *Dolly on Dolly: Interviews and Encounters with Dolly Parton*. Edited by Randy L. Schmidt. Chicago: Chicago Review Press, 2017.

7. Angelou, Maya. *I Know Why the Caged Bird Sings*. New York: Random House, 1969.

8. Angelou, Maya. *Wouldn't Take Nothing for My Journey Now*. New York: Random House, 1993.

9. Rumi, Jalal al-Din. *The Essential Rumi*. Translated by Coleman Barks. New York: HarperOne, 2004.

Chapter 21 - The Power of Unwavering Spirit

1. Stanton, Andrew, Bob Peterson, and David Reynolds. *Finding Nemo*. Directed by Andrew Stanton, performance by Ellen DeGeneres, Pixar Animation Studios, 2003.

2. *Free Solo*. Directed by Elizabeth Chai Vasarhelyi and Jimmy Chin. National Geographic Documentary Films, 2018.

3. Stowe, Harriet Beecher. *Old Town Folks*. Boston: Fields, Osgood, & Co., 1872.

4. Ikeda, Daisaku. *Discussions on Youth*. Santa Monica, CA: World Tribune Press, 2010.

5. Weintrob, Grace. "How to Rewire Your Brain." Columbine Health Systems Center for Healthy Aging, Colorado State University, May 31, 2022. https://www.research.colostate.edu/healthyagingcenter/2022/05/31/how-to-rewire-your-brain/.

6. Shackleton, Ernest. *South: The Story of Shackleton's Last Expedition 1914-1917*. London: William Heinemann, 1919.

7. Ikeda, Daisaku. *The Wisdom of the Lotus Sutra, Volume 1*. Santa Monica, CA: World Tribune Press, 2000.

8. Obama, Barack. *The Audacity of Hope: Thoughts on Reclaiming the American Dream*. New York: Crown Publishers, 2006.

Chapter 22 - Endurance and Perseverance

1. Roosevelt, Eleanor. *You Learn by Living: Eleven Keys for a More Fulfilling Life.* New York: Harper & Brothers, 1960.

Chapter 23 - When Wounds Become Wings

1. Barclay, William. *New Testament Words.* London: SCM Press, 1964.

2. Nolan, Jonathan, and Christopher Nolan. *The Dark Knight.* Directed by Christopher Nolan, performance by Aaron Eckhart, Warner Bros. Pictures, 2008.

3. Bradford, Sarah H. *Scenes in the Life of Harriet Tubman.* Auburn, NY: W.J. Moses, 1869.

4. Bradford, Sarah H. *Harriet, the Moses of Her People.* New York: Geo. R. Lockwood & Son, 1886.

Chapter 24 - Wisdom Beyond the Horizon

1. Rudofsky, Bernard. *Architecture without Architects: A Short Introduction to Non-Pedigreed Architecture.* New York: Museum of Modern Art, 1964.

2. Saint-Exupéry, Antoine de. *Wind, Sand and Stars.* In *Airman's Odyssey.* Translated by Lewis Galantière. New York: Harcourt Brace & Company, 1942.

Chapter 25 - Absolute vs. Relative Happiness

1. Brickman, Philip, and Donald T. Campbell. "Hedonic Relativism and Planning the Good Society." In *Adaptation-Level Theory: A Symposium*, edited by M. H. Appley, 287-305. New York: Academic Press, 1971.

2. Pilat, Dan, and Sekoul Krastev. "How to Get Off the Hedonic Treadmill." *The Decision Lab*, November 1, 2021. https://thedecisionlab.com/articles/how-to-get-off-the-hedonic-treadmill.

3. Pilat, Dan, and Sekoul Krastev. "How to Get Off the Hedonic Treadmill." The Decision Lab, November 1, 2021. https://thedecisionlab.com/articles/how-to-get-off-the-hedonic-treadmill.

4. Dalai Lama, and Howard C. Cutler. *The Art of Happiness: A Handbook for Living*. New York: Riverhead Books, 1998.

5. Nussbaum, Martha C. *The Therapy of Desire: Theory and Practice in Hellenistic Ethics*. Princeton: Princeton University Press, 1994.

6. Ikeda, Daisaku. *Unlocking the Mysteries of Birth and Death: Buddhism in the Contemporary World*. 2nd ed. Santa Monica, CA: Middleway Press, 2003.

7. Ikeda, Daisaku, Katsuji Saito, Takanori Endo, and Haruo Suda. *The Wisdom of the Lotus Sutra: A Discussion*. Vol. 2. Santa Monica, CA: World Tribune Press, 2000.

Chapter 26 - 3000 Realms of Existence

1. Stapp, Henry P. *Mind, Matter, and Quantum Mechanics*. 3rd ed. Berlin: Springer, 2009.

2. "Three Thousand Realms in a Single Moment of Life," *Dictionary of Buddhism*, Nichiren Buddhism Library, accessed May 1, 2025, https://www.nichirenlibrary.org/en/dic/Content/T/176.

3. Greene, Brian. *The Elegant Universe: Superstrings, Hidden Dimensions, and the Quest for the Ultimate Theory*. New York: W.W. Norton & Company, 2003.

4. "Ten Worlds," *Dictionary of Buddhism*, Nichiren Buddhism Library, accessed May 1, 2025, https://www.nichirenlibrary.org/en/dic/Content/T/82.

5. Nichiren Daishonin. *The Writings of Nichiren Daishonin*. Vol. 1. Edited and translated by The Gosho Translation Committee. Tokyo: Soka Gakkai, 1999.

6. "Mutual Possession of the Ten Worlds." *Dictionary of Buddhism*. Nichiren Buddhism Library. Accessed May 1, 2025. https://www.nichirenlibrary.org/en/dic/Content/M/143.

7. "Ten Factors of Life." *Dictionary of Buddhism*. Nichiren Buddhism Library. Accessed May 1, 2025. https://www.nichirenlibrary.org/en/dic/Content/T/49.

8. "Three Realms of Existence." *Dictionary of Buddhism*. Nichiren Buddhism Library. Accessed May 1, 2025. https://www.nichirenlibrary.org/en/dic/Content/T/165.

9. Tolle, Eckhart. *The Power of Now: A Guide to Spiritual Enlightenment*. Novato, CA: New World Library, 1999.

10. Ikeda, Daisaku. *The Wisdom for Creating Happiness and Peace: Selections from the Works of Daisaku Ikeda*. Part 1. Santa Monica, CA: Middleway Press, 2014.

11. Nichiren Daishonin. *The Writings of Nichiren Daishonin*. Vol. 1. Edited and translated by The Gosho Translation Committee. Tokyo: Soka Gakkai, 1999, 622.

12. Davidson, Richard J., and Anne Harrington, eds. *Visions of Compassion: Western Scientists and Tibetan Buddhists Examine Human Nature*. New York: Oxford University Press, 2002.

13. Barrett, Lisa Feldman. *How Emotions Are Made: The Secret Life of the Brain*. Boston: Houghton Mifflin Harcourt, 2017.

14. Siegel, Daniel J. *Mind: A Journey to the Heart of Being Human*. New York: W.W. Norton & Company, 2016.

15. Capra, Fritjof, and Pier Luigi Luisi. *The Systems View of Life: A Unifying Vision*. Cambridge: Cambridge University Press, 2014.

Chapter 27 - The Nine Levels of Consciousness

1. "Nine Consciousnesses," *Dictionary of Buddhism*, Nichiren Buddhism Library, accessed May 1, 2025, https://www.nichirenlibrary.org/en/dic/Content/N/62.

2. Musser, George. *Einstein's Spooky Action at a Distance: A Physicist's Exploration of the Deep Meaning of Quantum Entanglement*. New York: Scientific American/Farrar, Straus and Giroux, 2015.

3. Musser, George. *Einstein's Spooky Action at a Distance: A Physicist's Exploration of the Deep Meaning of Quantum Entanglement*. New York: Scientific American/Farrar, Straus and Giroux, 2015.

4. Churchill, Winston. "The Price of Greatness Is Responsibility." Speech delivered at Harvard University, Cambridge, MA, September 6, 1943.

Chapter 28 - The Compassionate Revolution

1. Armstrong, Karen. *Twelve Steps to a Compassionate Life*. New York: Alfred A. Knopf, 2010.

2. Ikeda, Daisaku. *Buddhism Day by Day: Wisdom for Modern Life*. Santa Monica: Middleway Press, 2006.

3. Tanemori, Takashi. *Hiroshima: Bridge to Forgiveness: Hiroshima Witness, Hiroshima Victim*. San Francisco: Ten Speed Press, 2007.

4. Tanemori, Takashi. *Hiroshima: Bridge to Forgiveness: Hiroshima Witness, Hiroshima Victim.* San Francisco: Ten Speed Press, 2007. 169.

5. Tanemori, Takashi. *Hiroshima: Bridge to Forgiveness: Hiroshima Witness, Hiroshima Victim.* San Francisco: Ten Speed Press, 2007. 170.

6. Tanemori, Takashi. *Hiroshima: Bridge to Forgiveness: Hiroshima Witness, Hiroshima Victim.* San Francisco: Ten Speed Press, 2007. 174.

7. Tanemori, Takashi. Interview by Cicero A. Estrella. "Hiroshima Survivor on Mission of Peace / He's Spreading the Word that Forgiveness is Healthier than Hate." *San Francisco Chronicle,* August 5, 2005. https://www.sfgate.com/bayarea/article/Hiroshima-survivor-on-mission-of-peace-He-s-2649235.php.

8. Ikeda, Daisaku. "Peace through Dialogue: A Time to Talk." 18th Peace Proposal to the United Nations. Tokyo: Soka Gakkai International, 2000.

9. Ikeda, Daisaku. *The Human Revolution.* Tokyo: Seikyo Press, 1965-1993.

Chapter 29 - Awakening

10. Wachowski, Lana, and Lilly Wachowski. *The Matrix.* Directed by Lana and Lilly Wachowski, performances by

Laurence Fishburne and Keanu Reeves, Warner Bros. Pictures, 1999.

11. Brooks, Arthur C., and Oprah Winfrey. *Build the Life You Want: The Art and Science of Getting Happier.* New York: Portfolio/Penguin, 2023.

12. Brooks, Arthur C., and Oprah Winfrey. *Build the Life You Want: The Art and Science of Getting Happier.* New York: Portfolio/Penguin, 2023.

13. Ikeda, Daisaku. *Soka Education: A Buddhist Vision for Teachers, Students and Parents.* Santa Monica, CA: Middleway Press, 2001.

14. Ikeda, Daisaku. *A New Humanism: The University Addresses of Daisaku Ikeda.* London: I.B. Tauris, 2010.

15. Roosevelt, Eleanor. *You Learn by Living.* New York: Harper & Brothers, 1960.

16. Turner, Tina. *Happiness Becomes You: A Guide for Changing Your Life for Good.* New York: Atria Books, 2020.

17. Ikeda, Daisaku. *Soka Education: A Buddhist Vision for Teachers, Students and Parents.* Santa Monica, CA: Middleway Press, 2001.

18. Ornish, Dean, and Anne Ornish. *Undo It!: How Simple Lifestyle Changes Can Reverse Most Chronic Diseases.* New York: Ballantine Books, 2019.

19. Williamson, Marianne. *A Return to Love: Reflections on the Principles of A Course in Miracles*. New York: HarperCollins, 1992.

20. Hancock, Herbie, with Lisa Dickey. *Possibilities*. New York: Viking, 2014.

21. Soka University of America. "Jazz Legend Herbie Hancock to Receive 2025 Soka Global Citizen Award." Accessed April 15, 2025. https://www.soka.edu/news-events/news/jazz-legend-herbie-hancock-receive-2025-soka-global-citizen-award.

22. Ikeda, Daisaku. *The New Human Revolution*. Santa Monica, CA: World Tribune Press, 1995-2018.

Chapter 30 - The Mystic Law

1. Nichiren. "The Three Kinds of Treasure." In *The Writings of Nichiren Daishonin*, vol. 1, edited and translated by The Gosho Translation Committee, 851-52. Tokyo: Soka Gakkai, 1999.

2. Soka Gakkai International. "The Tatsunokuchi Persecution." In *The Nichiren Buddhism Library*. Tokyo: Soka Gakkai, 2008.

3. Gandhi, Mohandas K. *Young India*. Ahmedabad: Navajivan Publishing House, 1924.

4. Nichiren Daishonin. "The Entity of the Mystic Law." *In The Writings of Nichiren Daishonin, Vol. 1*. Tokyo: Soka Gakkai. Accessed May 1, 2025. https://www.nichirenlibrary.org/en/wnd-1/Content/47.

5. Ikeda, Daisaku. *The Wisdom of the Lotus Sutra: A Discussion*, vol. 3. Santa Monica, CA: World Tribune Press, 2000.

6. Ikeda, Daisaku. *The New Human Revolution*. Vol. 21. Tokyo: Soka Gakkai, 2008, 336-38.

7. Ikeda, Daisaku. Preface to *The Human Revolution*, vol. 1. Santa Monica, CA: World Tribune Press, 2004.

8. Ikeda, Daisaku. *Life: An Enigma, a Precious Jewel*. Tokyo: Kodansha International, 1982.

About the Author

1. "Stock Artists Alliance." Wikipedia. Accessed April 15, 2025. https://en.wikipedia.org/wiki/Stock_Artists_Alliance.

2. Soka Gakkai International. "About SGI." Accessed April 16, 2025. https://www.sokaglobal.org.

3. Allison, Glen. *The Journey from Kamakura*. Revised edition. Los Angeles: Ten World Press, 2024. https://www.amazon.com/Journey-Kamakura-REVISED-Glen-Allison/dp/B0DKFDTZ92/.

Glen Allison

www.ingramcontent.com/pod-product-compliance
Lightning Source LLC
Chambersburg PA
CBHW070324010526
44107CB00004B/400